"ARISE, MY LOVE..."

Books by William Johnston

The Mysticism of "The Cloud of Unknowing"
The Still Point
Christian Zen
Silent Music
The Inner Eye of Love
The Mirror Mind
The Wounded Stag
Being in Love
Letters to Contemplatives
Mystical Theology

Translations

Silence by Shūsaku Endō
The Bells of Nagasaki by Takashi Nagai

"ARISE, MY LOVE..."

Mysticism for a New Era

William Johnston

Maryknoll, New York 10545

Sixth Printing, October 2005

The Catholic Foreign Mission Society of America (Maryknoll) recruits and trains people for overseas missionary service. Through Orbis Books, Maryknoll aims to foster the international dialogue that is essential to mission. The books published, however, reflect the opinions of their authors and are not meant to represent the official position of the society.

To obtain more information about Maryknoll and Orbis Books, please visit our website at www.maryknoll.org.

Manufactured in the United States of America
Manuscript editing and typesetting by Joan Weber Laflamme

Library of Congress Catologing-in-Publication Data

Johnston, William, 1925–
    Arise my love—: mysticism for a new era / William Johnston.
       p.   cm.
    Includes bibliographical references and index.
    ISBN 1-57075-312-1 (pbk.)
      1. Mysticism—Catholic Church—History. 2. Mysticism—Comparative studies. I. Title.

BV5031 .J64 2000
248.2'2—dc21
                                             99-086520

For
A.L.

Arise, my love, my dove, my beautiful one
   and come away;
for now the winter is past,
   the rain is over and gone.
The flowers appear on the earth;
   the time of singing has come,
and the voice of the turtledove
   is heard in our land.

                —The Song of Songs

Contents

PART III

The Great Conversion

Introduction

———— ▓ ————

One of the great prophetic events of the twentieth century took place at Assisi on October 27, 1986, when religious leaders came together to pray for peace. On that day history was made. A page was turned. The world would never again be the same.

The host was John Paul II. Before issuing the invitation he had consulted the Dalai Lama, the chief rabbi of Rome, and the archbishop of Canterbury, who was secretary general of the World Council of Churches. All agreed that the time had come for the religions to pray together for world peace, for international justice and for the preservation of our Mother Earth. The patron was to be St. Francis of Assisi, the humble and joyful *poverello,* whose love for friends and enemies, together with his rapturous song to the sun and the moon, has captivated the hearts of men and women everywhere.

The most moving sight, eyewitnesses tell us, was that of the Dalai Lama with representatives of all the religions (Mother Teresa of Calcutta was there) humbly entering the basilica to be welcomed by the bishop of Rome. After singing Psalm 148 in Greek—"Let everything that lives praise the Lord"—all paused for some moments of silent, wordless prayer. Then they made their way to twelve different places in Assisi where they prayed separately according to their own traditions.[1]

Throughout Assisi prayer was offered with the Vedas, the Sutras, the Qur'an, the Avesta, the Psalms and the Gospel. People prayed with incense, flowers, water, fire, with song and dance, with drum and peace pipe. In five churches Christians knelt silently before the blessed sacrament, closely united with innumerable people throughout the world, all praying for peace. What unity in diversity! What diversity in unity! "The challenge of peace transcends all religions," said John Paul in a statement that remains bafflingly enigmatic.

The Assisi meeting was quite different from interreligious dialogue, where learned academics, sitting around a table, engage in theological discussion about what the religions have in common and where they differ. At Assisi there was no rationalistic theology and no attempt to find agreement through compromise. Each group prayed according to its own convictions, using the words of its own religious tradition. Yet there was no clash, because the words rose from the silent and spiritual core where human beings find the deepest union.

John Paul was clear about the aim of the gathering. The participants "had not come for an interreligious conference on peace, but rather to invite the world to realize that there exists another dimension of peace and another way to promote it."

Another way to promote peace?

Yes, the way of prayer. Well did the poet Tennyson say that "more things are wrought by prayer than this world dreams of." If only the religions could pray, promote prayer, and proclaim to the world with one voice that prayer is a powerful way to promote peace!

The message of Assisi then is prayer. "Pray, pray, pray," said Teresa of Avila to her sisters; and now the Assisi event reiterates the same call, not just to Carmelites but to all religions and to the whole world. Assisi tells people to pray in their own religion and in their own way. Prayer, far from being an escape, is the answer to our problems, particularly to the problems of war and violence and destruction of the earth.

And as we enter the third millennium, mystical prayer or mysticism assumes an importance it has never had before. This is because the culture of Asia, which is fast spreading to the whole world, is preeminently mystical; and there are indications that the Western world also is searching for mysticism.

Here it is necessary to say what I mean by mysticism.

By mysticism I mean wisdom. I mean the wisdom that goes beyond words and letters, beyond reasoning and thinking, beyond imaging and fantasy, beyond before and after into the timeless reality. There are flashes of mysticism in the life of anyone who prays; quite certainly the spirit of wisdom pervaded Assisi. But some people reach a *state of mysticism*; that is to say, they reach a state where this formless wisdom is always in their consciousness. This is the mystical state.

Mysticism, then, is quite different from the knowledge that comes from understanding and judging. Mystics of all religions will say that the wisdom I call mystical is not acquired by human effort. It is a gift that may come suddenly and unpredictably. Yet it can coexist with ordinary knowledge, and it does so after a new level of consciousness has been awakened in the human mind. Mystics assure us that to compare scientific knowledge with mystical wisdom is like comparing a tiny candle with the noonday sun.

Though wisdom is a gratuitous gift, the religions paradoxically teach a way to its attainment. Buddhism has its practice or training (in Japanese, *shugyō*) and Christianity has its asceticism. But more important than any training or asceticism is *compassion* in Buddhism, and *love* in Christianity.

The Buddhist path to transcendental wisdom *(prajñāpāramitā)* is outlined in the *Heart Sutra,* which depicts the bodhisattva Kannon looking with compassion on the suffering world, having vowed not to enter nirvana until all sentient beings are saved. The path of the compassionate Kannon is one of total emptiness. She has renounced clinging to anything whatsoever, material or spiritual. She becomes nothing. Yet this emptiness or "nothingness" is the highest wisdom, for Kannon is fully enlightened.

The highest wisdom of the Hindu mystics (*saccidananda*: being-consciousness-bliss) is rather similar to the transcendental wisdom *(prajñāpāramitā)* of Buddhism. Both can be called mysticism.[2]

This book, however, is concerned principally with Christian mysticism. Here also the path is one of emptiness in imitation of Jesus who "emptied himself, taking the form of a slave." "Nada, nada, nada," cries St. John of the Cross, telling us that *nada* will lead to *todo*. Again and again he returns to the gospel text, "Unless you give up everything that you possess, you cannot be my disciple" (Lk 14:33). And just as self-emptying *(kenosis)* brought Jesus to resurrection—"Therefore God also highly exalted him and gave him the name above every name"—so the self-emptying of the Christian mystic leads to the highest wisdom, the Greek *sophia*, the Latin *sapientia*.

Yet the Christian mystical path has one distinctive feature. It is above all a path of love. Christian mystics speak constantly of the inner fire of love. The Orthodox speak of "the burning of the spirit" and the divine energies. *The Cloud of Unknowing* speaks of "the blind stirring of love." St. John of the Cross speaks of "the living flame of love." Lonergan says that one's being becomes being-in-love. Nor is this love something that the mystic arouses in his or her heart by human effort; it is the answer to a call: "Arise, my love, my dove, my beautiful one and come away" (Sg 2:10).

Francis, the mystic who inspired the Assisi event, was an ecstatic lover. He was in love with God, with the universe, and with the human family. The living flame of love so filled his mind and heart that it overflowed on his body; and blood flowed from his hands and feet and side, just as it flowed from the five wounds of the Crucified. For mystical love is a wound, a delightful wound, a sweet cautery, as St. John of the Cross knew so well when he cried: "O living flame of love, that tenderly wounds my soul in its deepest center!"

Mystical love, moreover, is not only fire; it is also light. So intertwined are the fire of love and the light of wisdom that St. John of the Cross can speak of "lamps of fire." In this book I distinguish between Christian *contemplation,* which is characterized by the sense of presence, and Christian *mysticism,* which is characterized by fire and light.

From this it will be clear that while Buddhist and Christian mysticism have much in common, both being forms of transcendental wisdom, one cannot say that they are the same. At the end of his long life Bede Griffiths, comparing Christian mysticism with the mysticism of Hinduism and Buddhism, came to a significant conclusion: "Perhaps the fundamental difference is this: that the heart of Christian mysticism is a mystery of love, whereas both in Hinduism and in Buddhism it is primarily a transformation of consciousness."[3]

To say that these two forms of mysticism are different, however, is not to say that they are mutually exclusive. It is possible that they are complementary. The twentieth century witnessed the first stages in the search for a marriage between East and West; and the mystical experience of people yet unborn will surely throw further light on this challenging encounter.

Assisi gives us hope for the third millennium. Chaos and conflagration and catastrophe may come, but the united prayer of the nations will prevail. "And all will be well, and all will be well, and all manner of thing will be well." The Beloved speaks and says: "Arise, my love, my dove, my beautiful one and come away; for winter is past, the rain is over and gone."

PART I

The New Consciousness

ONE

New Era

DECLINE OF THE WEST

At the beginning of the twentieth century prophetic men and women were already talking about the decline of the West. The great colonial nations that had planted triumphant flags at strategic points throughout the globe were now retreating to their legitimate borders. On the eve of October 1, 1949, Mao Ze Dong was to utter words that may still prove ominous for the Western world: "The Chinese people, one quarter of humanity, have stood up . . . From now on, no one will ever humiliate us again." Similar sentiments had been expressed by Mahatma Gandhi in India and would be expressed by Ho Chi Minh in Vietnam and by Nelson Mandela in Africa. The days of Western imperialism were over.

Yet Western decline went deeper than the loss of colonies. Psychologists like Freud and Jung, both of whom were physicians, pointed to a spiritual or psychological decline. Western people had lost their sense of meaning; they had lost their myth; they were tired and effete; they were sick; they needed therapy. Under the guidance of analysts countless numbers of depressed people plumbed the depths of their unconscious, often to find themselves more insecure, more uneasy and more anxious. Jung, with great insight, observed that in his experience disturbed people in the second half of life only found meaning by a return to the religion of their childhood.

But what really destroyed Western civilization, as it has destroyed all civilizations, was violence. Millions died in wars that saw the destruction of whole armies and whole cities, while millions more died in death camps. And all this was followed by inhuman guerilla warfare, international terrorism, meaningless murder in the streets, systematic slaughter of the unborn, and finally by the exploitation and violent rape of our good Mother Earth. Truly it was a century of violence. Until the end of time the names of Auschwitz and Hiroshima will remain etched on the pages of history, never to be erased.

As the century proceeded, however, it became clear that the crisis of violence was not confined to the West. Asia and Africa had more than their share of carnage and bloodshed. A world that had watched with horror the atrocities of the Japanese armies as they ran amok in Nanking later heard the tragic story of innocent Asian women torn from family and home to serve the Japanese armies as prostitutes and "comfort women." No less terrible was the communist regime in China, which liquidated millions of its own people and initiated a cultural revolution that encouraged the youthful red guard to torture and to kill. Then there were the rivers of blood and the killing fields of Cambodia and the millions slaughtered by the Khmer Rouge; the attempted genocide in Tibet; the turmoil in Sri Lanka, Kashmir and Afghanistan; the massacres in Timor; the internecine strife in Africa. It is a tragic tale of worldwide violence. Small wonder if bewildered people cast dust on their heads and quoted the Apocalypse: "Alas, alas, the great city, Babylon, the mighty city! For in one hour your judgment has come" (Rv 18:10).

APOCALYPSE NOW

The end of the first millennium in Europe saw widespread and hysterical interest in the Apocalypse. There people read how an angel from heaven seized the dragon, that ancient serpent, who is the devil and Satan, and bound him for a thousand years, and threw him into the pit, and locked and sealed it over him. And then the sacred text continues with alarming words: "When the thousand years are ended, Satan will be released from his prison and will come to deceive the nations at the four corners of the earth, Gog and Magog, in order to gather them for battle" (Rv 20:7, 8). The thousand years were ended, said the fundamentalists. Satan was coming. The great and final battle was in sight.

And now, as we enter the third millennium, we once again hear alarming stories about Armageddon and the Great Beast and the Great Whore. "Fallen, fallen is Babylon the great! It has become a dwelling place of demons, a haunt of every foul and hateful bird, a haunt of every foul and hateful beast" (Rv 18:2). When the Apocalypse was written, the Great Beast was Rome and the Great Whore was Rome. "All the nations have drunk of the wrath of her fornication, and the kings of the earth have committed fornication with her" (Rv 18:3). But at this point in history, we are told, the Great Beast and the Great Whore are not just Rome, not just the Western world, but a whole world civilization on the verge of collapse. Our planet is endangered. The human species faces extinction. The end of the world is at hand. And this apocalyptic vision is brought to a credulous public by stories of apparitions that warn us of catastrophe to come.

Yet apocalyptic predictions are not limited to narrow fundamentalists. Wise and reasonable people speak of our age as a time of tumultuous transition. Late in life the visionary and mystical Benedictine monk Bede Griffiths (1906-93) wrote in apocalyptic terms about coming disaster. Quoting the Epistle to the Ephesians that "we are not contending with flesh and blood, but against the principalities, against the powers, against the world rulers of this present darkness" (Eph 6:12), he maintained that these principalities and powers were the dark forces of the unconscious that were out of control at the end of the twentieth century. He went on to say that a new age might come gradually but "it is more likely that there will be a general catastrophe as the economic, social and political structures of the present civilization break down."[1] Truly a remarkable prophecy.

But let me return to Rome. Alas, alas for the mighty city! Why did this great city collapse?

Paul was quick to point to the root cause. The people had rejected God: "For though they knew God, they did not honor him as God or give thanks to him, but they became futile in their thinking and their senseless minds were darkened" (Rom 1:29). They had exchanged the truth about God for a lie and worshiped and served the creature rather than the creator. "And since they did not see fit to acknowledge God, God gave them up to a debased mind and to things that should not be done. They were filled with every kind of wickedness, evil, covetousness, malice" (Rom 1:29). All the evils of the Roman empire stemmed from rejection of God.

And the twentieth century? Did it not also reject God? Friedrich Nietzsche's cry that God is dead echoed through philosophy and literature and even through a death-of-God theology. Materialism spread through the world—in its communist form in Russia and China, in its capitalistic form elsewhere. An atheistic existentialism drove millions to despair. Is it surprising if prophets of doom make a powerful appeal as they talk of global disaster? Is there hope for the future, or must we succumb to global despair?

PROPHET OF HOPE

In the middle of the twentieth century there arose a prophet of no mean stature. Angelo Giuseppe Roncalli (1881-1963), known to the world as Pope John XXIII, took his seat on the chair of Peter and spoke powerfully to the world. He was supposed to be an interim pope. After the death of the authoritarian and controversial Pius XII in 1958, the cardinals in conclave wanted a quiet caretaker who would not rock the boat of Peter. Angelo Roncalli seemed to be the man. A smiling Italian peasant, he had shown himself to be an astute, broad-minded and compassionate diplomat in Eastern Europe where he established good relations with the Orthodox world. Then he was papal nuncio in Paris, and in 1953 he was appointed cardinal and patriarch of Venice. Now, at the age of seventy-seven, he could occupy the see of Peter for a short time before joining the saints in heaven.

It is said that the cardinals seldom know whom they are electing. Little did they know that Angelo Roncalli was a mystic and a visionary who would sow the seeds of revolution in the seemingly unchangeable Catholic church. To the consternation of the Roman Curia he quickly summoned an ecumenical council. He did so after a sudden flash of enlightenment that recalls the light that blinded St. Paul on the road to Damascus. For while he was addressing the cardinals in the basilica of St. Paul and on the feast of St. Paul, he was surrounded by light and found himself saying unexpectedly, "An ecumenical council!" He himself tells the story. "It will suffice to repeat as historical documentation," he says, "our personal account of the first sudden bringing up in our heart and lips of the simple words, 'Ecumenical Council.'" And he goes on:

> We uttered those words in the presence of the Sacred College of Cardinals on that memorable January 25, 1959, the feast of the conversion of St Paul in the basilica dedicated to him. It was completely unexpected, like a flash of heavenly light, suddenly shedding sweetness in eyes and hearts.[2]

Earlier, when convoking the council, he had spoken of the living presence of God in the church in the gravest periods of humanity. "Today," he said, "the Church is witnessing a crisis under way within society. *While humanity is on the edge of a new era*, tasks of immense gravity and amplitude await the Church as in the most tragic periods of her history."[3] In this tumultuous and disturbed world, he tells us, distrustful souls see only darkness burdening the face of the earth. "They say that our era, in comparison with past eras, is getting worse; and they behave as though they had learned nothing from history which is, nonetheless, the teacher of life."[4] He then makes an important statement:

> We feel we must disagree with those prophets of doom, who are always forecasting disaster, as though the end of the world were at hand . . . In the present order of things Divine Providence is leading us to a new order of human relations which, by our own efforts and even beyond our very expectations, are directed toward the fulfillment of God's superior and inscrutable designs.[5]

God is present in all the turmoil and *is leading humanity to a new era and a new order* in a mysterious yet superior way. One is reminded of the English poet who put on the lips of the dying King Arthur the immortal words: "The old order changeth yielding place to new, and God fulfills Himself in many ways." Pope and poet alike, living in different ages, saw the mysterious action of God in the turmoil of human history.

"RETURN, O ISRAEL . . . "

For Pope John, the council was not just an academic statement of orthodox Christian doctrine. It was primarily a call to prayer and conversion of heart. Previous ecumenical councils had made dogmatic statements and had anathematized those who refused to accept them. Pope John did not want such a council. He spoke of a "pastoral council" that would have compassion on the whole world and would heal with the medicine of mercy.

And so he asked for prayer, especially for the prayer of innocent children and of the sick. He himself prayed for an outpouring of the Holy Spirit: "Renew your wonders in our time as though for a new Pentecost." During the council the bishops and theologians were to pray, discerning the action of the Spirit in their own hearts and in the heart of humanity—"Come and abide with us. Deign to penetrate our hearts . . . Be the guide of our actions, indicate the path we should take."[6]

A characteristic of the council was that it spoke not just to Catholics, not just to Christians, but to the whole world, calling for a conversion of heart and a return to God. This was a world so fascinated by its mindboggling achievements that it had forgotten God—"a world which exalts itself with its conquests in the technical and scientific fields, but which brings also the consequences of a temporal order which some have wished to reorganize excluding God."[7] Excluding God! That was the problem. But what could be the nature of the conversion?

A glance at Angelo Roncalli's autobiography, *Journal of a Soul*, reveals the inner life of a pious seminarian deeply influenced by the Spiritual Exercises of St. Ignatius. Here the future pope learned to build his spiritual life on "the principle and foundation" that states that we human beings are created to praise, reverence and serve God and by this means to save our souls, and that all other things on the face of the earth are made to help us to attain this end. Pope John applies this principle to the modern world, stating it in his own words:

> All human beings, whether taken singly or united in society, today have the duty of tending ceaselessly during their lifetime toward the attainment of heavenly things and to use for this purpose only, earthly goods, the employment of which must not prejudice their eternal happiness.[8]

So the challenge of today's world is what Ignatius called "the use of creatures." We are to make use of our astounding scientific and technological innovations for the service of God and for our eternal happiness. We are to see God in all things, never viewing anything apart from God. Is this message any different from that of Paul to the Romans? Surely it is the message of the Hebrew prophet who cried:

> Return, O Israel, to the LORD your God,
> for you have stumbled because of your iniquity. (Hos 14:1)

Return to God! This is the primary and indispensable condition for a new age of peace.

ONE WORLD

As there is no love of God without love of neighbor, so there is no conversion to God without conversion to the world. Following the inspiration given by Pope John, the council focused its attention on the world, on the whole human family along with the sum of those realities in the midst of which that family lives.

> It gazes upon that world which is the theater of human history, and carries the marks of human energies, human tragedies, and

human triumphs; that world which the Christian sees as created and sustained by its Maker's love, fallen indeed into the
bondage of sin, yet emancipated now by Christ.

Thus spoke the council in its last great document, *Gaudium et Spes*.[9] It
spoke of entering into conversation with the world about its various
problems; it wanted dialogue. Powerful was the council's message for
the world, but it also spoke (what humility from a Catholic council!)
about learning from the world.

In a world torn by violence and strife, priority must be given to the
task of reconciliation. From the beginning Pope John had prayed for
unity among Christians, making his own the prayer of Jesus "that they
may be completely one, so that the world may know that you have sent
me" (Jn 17:23). The first task was to heal the sad rift between East and
West, which went back to the eleventh century. Such healing must be a
process and would take time. Nevertheless, the world watched with awe
and admiration when, on January 1, 1964, Pope Paul VI and Ecumenical Patriarch Athenagoras I met in Jerusalem. The loving embrace of
these two Christian leaders powerfully symbolized reconciliation. And
later, on December 7, 1965, Paul in Rome and Athenagoras in Istanbul
issued a common statement committing to oblivion the regrettable excommunications that had cruelly severed the silken cords that had bound
East and West together. Sincere and friendly dialogue had begun.

Then there was the movement toward healing the wound of the sixteenth century with its legacy of bitterness, hatred and strife, the recognition that we are already united in Christ and that we long for the time
when together we will celebrate the Lord's Supper, becoming one bread
and one body.

Even more dramatic was the movement toward reconciliation between Jews and Christians, the confession of the distinguished Cardinal
Bea that anti-Jewish ideas in Europe had helped the Nazis, the plea for
forgiveness. Equally dramatic was the appeal for dialogue with the Muslims and the effort to heal the long history of crusades and holy wars
and mutual recrimination. The renewed realization that Jews and Muslims and Christians believe in the one God, look to a common father
Abraham, and read the same Bible with love and devotion opens up
possibilities for spiritual friendship hitherto undreamed of.

Dialogue with Hindus and Buddhists was an afterthought. The European bishops and theologians, most of whom were still rooted in Greek
philosophy and Roman law, paid little attention to Asia until their colleagues from the East spoke about the indigenous religions of their countries. The council handled the subject briefly. Yet the few pages of *Nostra*

Aetate devoted to these religions have already had earth-shaking repercussions.[10] A hundred years from now, when theologians look back,
they may well conclude that these pages were the most significant achievement of the council.

Dialogue is an ongoing process. Reconciliation is an ongoing process.
Conversion of heart is an ongoing process. We cannot expect instanta-
neous results. Nevertheless, the fact that dialogue has begun marks the
beginning of a new era in the history of religions and opens up limitless
spiritual vistas. While each religion is determined to preserve its identity
and refuses to be absorbed by another, the ideal of becoming a single
people dedicated to the salvation of humanity is gradually emerging.

Indeed, as the process of dialogue goes on, it becomes increasingly
clear that the religions are called to collaborate in the task of humaniz-
ing the new world culture that is coming to birth before our eyes. In
1986 Pope John Paul invited leaders of world religions to unite in prayer
for world peace at Assisi. At that time he made clear, as the council had
made clear, that while each religion has its message for the world, the
Christian message is Christ. In its final document, after outlining the
anguishing problems of the contemporary world, the council takes an
unambiguous stand:

> The Church believes that Christ, who died and was raised up
> for all, can through His Spirit offer us the light and the strength
> to measure up to our supreme destiny. Nor has any other
> name under heaven been given to us by which it is fitting to
> be saved. She likewise holds that in her most benign Lord and
> Master can be found the key, the focal point, and the goal of
> all human history.[11]

To teach Christ while recognizing the teaching of others, to follow Christ
while collaborating joyfully with those who walk another path—this is
the challenge confronting Christians today as we struggle to build one
world.

"AY, THERE'S THE RUB . . . "

Few will deny that the Second Vatican Council was a great prophetic
event. The call to return to God, the call to reconciliation, the call to
serve the suffering world—believers see here unmistakably the revolutionary action of the Spirit of God. But *this message must be brought to
a turbulent world on the verge of a new era by a church speaking a*

language that that world would understand. "Ay, there's the rub!" The gospel must be brought to the teeming masses of Asia and Africa. It must be brought to a frightened world that has seen the nightmares of Auschwitz and Hiroshima, a perplexed world that had watched a man walking on the moon, an anguished world in which millions starve, an angry world in which millions have been treated with ruthless injustice. Could the good old Catholic church, nurtured in Europe, talking Latin and virtually unchanged since Constantine in the fourth century—could this church measure up to the task? Could a church that represented the declining, dwindling, diminishing, dying West speak to the whole world?

Pope John spoke of *aggiornamento,* usually translated "updating" or "renewal." He talked about opening windows so that fresh air might blow into the old musty building. He even caused theological headaches with his comment that "the substance of the ancient doctrine of faith is one thing and the way it is presented is another."[12] Nevertheless, he seems to have thought that this reform could be enacted within the theological and structural framework of the existing church, in which he had great confidence. He had opened windows without realizing that a hurricane was in the offing.

For as time went on, as thinking and praying people continued to discern what had happened in the council and in the world, *many came to the conclusion that the old European church must die in order that the new global church might be born.* It was not precisely that the council killed the old church to give life to the new. Rather, the council was unconsciously aware of the historical process that we now recognize as the decline of the West. As the West declined, so Western Christianity declined and became progressively irrelevant. The council initiated the process by which a new church might rise from the ashes of the old.

TWO

Age of Revolution (I)

SCIENTIFIC REVOLUTION

In his book *The Origin and Goal of History* the German existentialist Karl Jaspers (1883-1969), looking back on the course of history, speaks of an axial age. This was a time of profound transition, a time of growth in consciousness, a time when humanity came of age. The change took place simultaneously in Greece, Israel, Persia, India and China in the centuries that preceded the birth of Christ. Then humanity took a great leap forward.

Bernard Lonergan (1904-84), referring to Jaspers, claimed that the twentieth century was in the throes of another axial age. This time the transition had its origin in the seventeenth century, when a series of insightful scientists from Galileo to Newton discovered a new methodology and sparked off a scientific revolution that changed the consciousness first of the Western world and then of the whole human family. Quoting the Cambridge historian Herbert Butterfield, Lonergan claimed that the rise of modern science outshines everything since the rise of Christianity, making the Renaissance and the Reformation look insignificant.[1]

The scientific revolution was a revolt against Aristotle, whose thought had dominated Western science since the thirteenth century. The great Stagirite had worked deductively, basing his whole system on first principles. Of cardinal importance was the principle of causality, whereby one argued from effect to cause. One looked to the cause of sensible phenomena, eventually going beyond this world to the First Cause, which the scholastics interpreted as God.

The new method that emerged with the scientific revolution, on the other hand, was practical and empirical, based on observation and experimentation. Galileo looked through his telescope or watched the swinging pendulum. Newton observed falling bodies. Other scientists did ingenious experiments and elaborated theses that were verified in the laboratory. Moreover, this practical, empirical method quickly gave birth to a technology which did such extraordinary things that the world reeled with shock and unbelief.

Soon this powerful methodology spread to all forms of science—history, psychology, sociology, anthropology. All these sciences dropped the deductive approach and began to emphasize observation, collection of data and elaboration of theories, which changed as more data became available. Even the study of religion took on this empirical methodology. Whereas theology had been the science of God, students of religion now began to study not God but the human approach to God. In universities religious studies began to take the place of theology, with students collecting data about the prayer, worship, liturgy and mysticism of peoples everywhere. Religious studies is not concerned with God, even though it may study what people think and say about God; it always remains in this world.

It is hardly surprising if the scientific mentality spread to the masses of the people, creating a new culture and a new consciousness that, abhorring abstract thinking, adopted a practical, empirical approach to life.

Lonergan, in a brilliant lecture at Fordham University in New York in 1968, pointed out that the scientific consciousness—practical, empirical and always remaining in this world—led to "the absence of God in modern culture."[2] After all, there is no sensible data on God, nor can the existence of God be verified in the laboratory. Who or what is God? Though most of the founders of the scientific method believed in God, the method itself and the mentality it engendered made a transcendent God irrelevant. The monotheistic religions were shocked to the core. Muslim, Christian and Jew could identify with the psalmist, who cried, "My tears have been my food day and night, while people say to me continually, 'Where is your God?'" (Ps 42).

The traditional way to God through metaphysics is, I believe, still valid. However, there is another way that might appeal to the men and women of today: the way of love. This is the way of the mystics. It is the way of the First Epistle of St. John, where we hear that *everyone who loves knows God.* "Beloved let us love one another, because love is from God; everyone who loves is born of God and knows God. Whoever does not love does not know God, for God is love" (1 Jn 4:7).

Later in his life Lonergan became interested in love and in mysticism. He who had written dull, dense and highly technical theology began to use the erotic language of the Song of Songs. What had happened? His many admirers were astonished; some were amused.

KNOWLEDGE-LOVE-WISDOM

Lonergan's theory of knowledge is now widely known. He saw knowing as a process of experiencing, understanding and judging in obedience to the transcendental precepts *Be attentive, Be intelligent, Be reasonable*. He was fascinated by the scientific method, which he analyzed carefully, seeing it as a practical application of these transcendental precepts. The good scientist is attentive to the data (attentive); he or she understands it (intelligent), and then he or she makes a theory (reasonable). Science, moreover, is ongoing. As one gets more and more data, one gets more and more insights, and one makes better and better theories. So the process goes on. Science has transformed our view of the universe, has revolutionized our lives. It will continue to transform our view of the universe and to revolutionize our lives. Science fiction is not a joke; it reminds us of the awe-inspiring things that might happen in the third millennium.

Yet the scientists' fidelity to these precepts could lead to world disaster if it were not complemented by yet another precept: *Be responsible*. Without this precept the end could be in sight.

Lonergan further saw that these precepts would not lead to self-transcendence, to the fullness of humanity and to wisdom *unless they were complemented by love*. Cognitional self-transcendence is not enough; human beings aspire to actual self-transcendence, which comes through love. It is in this context Lonergan uses the language of the Song of Songs:

> That capacity (i.e., for self-transcendence) becomes an actuality when one falls in love. Then one's being becomes being-in-love. Such being-in-love has its antecedents, its causes, its conditions, its occasions. But once it has blossomed forth and as long as it lasts, it takes over. It is the first principle. From it flow one's desires and fears, one's joys and sorrows, one's discernment of values, one's decisions and deeds.[3]

This is the all-consuming love of the bride and the bridegroom. It is also the all-consuming love of the mystic and God. Lonergan continues:

"Being in love with God, as experienced, is being in love in an unrestricted fashion. All love is self-surrender, but being in love with God is being in love without limits or qualifications or conditions or reservations."[4] He goes on to speak movingly of a loving God who is both immanent and transcendent, "When someone transcendent is my beloved, he is in my heart, real to me from within me."[5]

Love is primarily a gift and only secondarily a precept. Lonergan quotes St. Paul that the love of God is poured into our hearts by the Holy Spirit, who is given to us. Love is a call: "Arise, my love . . . "; and the bride, fired with the gift of love, goes forth into the night.

And just as the candle sheds light, so does love lead to wisdom. Here Lonergan refers to Pascal's "the heart has its reasons that reason does not know." This wisdom or loving knowledge is not clear-cut and conceptual; it transcends reasoning and thinking and imagining to enter a cloud of unknowing. It is the obscure knowledge of the mystics (though Lonergan does not use this terminology) and is frequently accompanied by "the sense of presence" that the Christian mystics interpret as the presence of God. The Christian tradition has always taught that wisdom is a gift of the Spirit.

THE MYSTICAL TRADITION

In all this Lonergan is faithful to the Christian mystical tradition. *The Cloud of Unknowing* speaks of a "thinking power" by which we can know creatures and a "loving power" by which we can know God:

> For of all other creatures and their works—yea, and of the works of God himself—may a person through grace have fullness of knowing, and well can one think of them; but of God himself can no one think. And therefore I would leave all that thing that I can think, and choose to my love that thing I cannot think.

God can be loved; but God cannot be thought. Love goes directly to God. Some mystics say that it "wounds" God. It brings the highest wisdom—*sophia* or *sapientia*—which is knowledge of God in a cloud of unknowing.

Now St. John of the Cross speaks of two kinds of love. There is *active love*, which is an act of the will, as when I help another person, or when I cry out with the psalmist, "I love you, O Lord, my strength" (Ps 18). In time, however, as this love comes to possess the very core of one's being, it becomes *passive love*. Now it is an inner fire or light, a living flame of love, a compound of love and wisdom. Poetically and ecstatically St. John of the Cross addresses this exquisite gift, crying out, "O Lamps of fire!" This gift of love is like a spring that rises within and flows out on the surrounding world, showering living water upon friend and foe— upon the whole human family and the whole universe, our home. The Orthodox mystics speak of this inner fire as "divine energy," and they speak of "the uncreated energies." St. John of the Cross says that *this living flame of love is the Holy Spirit who is purifying and divinizing the human person*. No doubt Lonergan is speaking of passive love when he says that one's being becomes being-in-love and when he speaks about being in love with God.

Through love the indwelling Spirit is so closely united with the true self that some mystics have been tempted to say, "I am God." Others have been tempted to deny the very existence of a transcendent God and have feared that they might be atheists or pantheists. They have had great difficulty in recognizing a God distinct from themselves, a God "out there." They like to speak of God as "Mystery" and to insist on the words of the fourth gospel: "No one has ever seen God" (Jn 1:18). So close is the mystical union of love between God and the soul.

So much for Lonergan's theory of love and wisdom. The question now is, Has this anything to do with science and the scientific mentality?

SCIENCE AND LOVE

That love plays a role in the life of many scientists cannot be denied. Were we to ask a group of scientists why they chose this profession, some would surely say that they were motivated by love: they wanted to help humanity or to preserve the environment or to explore the universe. Some might say that they were motivated by love of truth. Some might say that from childhood they had experienced a mysterious call or vocation. Surely great scientists like Einstein or Teilhard de Chardin were lovers.

Furthermore, we know that some scientists have recently become interested in mysticism. Fritjof Capra, in his well-known book *The Tao of Physics,* has a chapter entitled "Modern Physics—A Path with a Heart?" He describes, a little dramatically, how some outstanding scientists, shocked by the discoveries of relativity and quantum theory, look to the Oriental mystics for an answer to the riddle of existence.

And yet Lonergan, who wrote so enthusiastically about love, did not add love to his transcendental precepts: he did not try to incorporate love into the scientific method. Unrestricted love, the very basis of all religious experience, is central to his method in theology, but it has no place in his understanding of the scientific method. Why?

I have already said that love is primarily a gift and only secondarily a precept. "We love because God first loved us" (1 Jn 4:19). Love is the answer to the call of the beloved, "Arise, my love . . . " This holds true also for human love. It is precisely because God loves us that we must love one another. "Beloved, since God loved us so much, we also ought to love one another" (1 Jn 4:11). Loving does not come from human effort alone. It cannot be programmed. Love may be very alive in the world of science, but for Lonergan the unconditional, unrestricted love that goes on and on and on until one's being becomes being-in-love *is essentially a religious phenomenon.* Indeed, it is the very core and center of all authentic religion.

Love then is not part of the scientific method. But it can, and must, be *united with* the scientific method if this method is to be fully human. Through love there can be a marriage between science and religion. And how fruitful that marriage will be! Elsewhere I have spoken of such a loving union, saying that the transcendental precepts could ideally be read: "Be lovingly attentive. Be lovingly intelligent. Be lovingly reasonable. Be lovingly responsible."[6] In this way love can permeate the scientific enterprise making it truly human.

But does divine love play a role in the very research of the scientist?

The question sounds outrageous. What part could the love of God play in the research of the mathematician or the physicist? What role has God in the study of the subatomic world or in the investigation of the outer reaches of the universe?

And yet the Second Vatican Council indicates that divine love is indeed active in the heart of the sincere and humble researcher. Stating that earthly matters and the affairs of faith derive from the same God, the council writes:

> Indeed, whoever labors to penetrate the secrets of reality with a humble and steady mind, is even unawares being led by the hand of God, who holds all things in existence, and gives them their identity.[7]

The Spirit of love, ever active in the world, is leading the scientist who humbly labors to penetrate the secrets of reality. What a meeting between science and religion! What a marriage!

I have said that for the mystics God, who is Love, is the mystery of mysteries, the Source of all existence, the Being who cannot be encapsulated in words or letters or images. I believe that many scientists and many people influenced by the scientific mentality, without using the word *God,* are searching for such a Being and are even united with such a Being. Modern men and women, influenced by the scientific method, are drawn to the God of love, the God of the mystics.

In an important book entitled *The Marriage of Sense and Soul* Ken Wilber writes that "there is arguably no more important and pressing topic than the relation of science and religion in the modern world."[8] How true! I have said that there must be a marriage. And the key to this marriage, as to all successful marriages, is love.

THREE

Age of Revolution (II)

A REVOLUTIONARY CULTURE

I have mentioned the scientific revolution. It is one of a series of revolutions that have shocked the human consciousness. There was the enormously influential French Revolution. There was the intellectual revolution that we call the Enlightenment. There was the industrial revolution. The twentieth century witnessed a sexual revolution, a feminist revolution, a revolution in human relationships, a mystical revolution, a technological revolution, a communications explosion—a series of ongoing revolutions that have indeed *revolutionized* the way of thinking and feeling of people throughout the world, making them rethink the religion of their childhood. These revolutions have so molded society that we can be said to live in a revolutionary culture.

The Second Vatican Council, committed to the task of scrutinizing the signs of the times, was aware of these revolutions. It saw that "the human race has passed from a rather static concept of reality to a more dynamic and evolutionary one."[1] In a passage that shows the influence of the once-suspect Pierre Teilhard de Chardin, it declares that "the human race is passing through a new stage in its history so that we can already speak of a social and cultural transformation, one which has repercussions on religious life as well."[2] Indeed, the council says explicitly that the new age has already come—"The living conditions of modern people have been so profoundly changed in their social and cultural dimensions, that we can speak of a new age in human history."[3] Today's culture is no longer static. Revolution is the order of the day.

We who live in this revolutionary age have awesome responsibility. The process of evolution is now entrusted to us, and we must guide it aright. Such is the message of the council:

The modern world shows itself at once powerful and weak, capable of the noblest deeds or the foulest. Before it lies the path to freedom or to slavery, to progress or retreat, to friendship or hatred. Moreover, we are becoming aware that it is our responsibility to guide aright the forces which we have unleashed and which can enslave us or minister to us.[4]

Already in the 1960s the council could say that we are at a turning point in history, and "the whole human family has reached an hour of supreme crisis in its advancement toward maturity."[5] As we enter the third millennium, we are still at that turning point, and we still face that crisis. The challenging questions are: How are we to guide aright the forces we have unleashed? What is the role of religion in this rapidly changing world?

Bernard Lonergan claims that Christianity has had a vitally important mission in the Western world. It has transformed successive cultures. "But the fact of the matter is," he writes, "that the ancient Church set about transforming Greek and Roman culture, that the medieval Church was a principal agent in the formation of medieval culture, that the Renaissance Church was scandalously involved in Renaissance culture."[6] And he goes on to say that a modern church is called to transform the new culture that is coming to birth.

That the new culture needs transformation no one will deny. For all its mighty achievements, the modern world is crying out for help. Apart from the violence, the injustice, the hunger, the despair, the anguish, the systematic suicide, apart from this there is the need to transform and humanize the television, the radio, the press, the Internet and all the media that are telling us what to think and how to act. Can Christianity transform this world?

Much water has flowed under the bridge since Lonergan lived and sang. And now it becomes clear that one religion alone cannot do this task. This must be the work of the people of God taken in the widest sense of these words. That is to say, it must be the work of Jews and Christians, Muslims and Buddhists, Hindus and Sikhs together with people of all religions, collaborating and praying together as they did at Assisi. The council already saw this. It urged Catholics to work for peace in international organizations, joining hands with people of good will:

This Council desires that by way of fulfilling their role properly in the international community, Catholics should seek to cooperate actively and in a positive manner both with their separated brothers and sisters, who together with them profess the gospel of love, and with all people thirsting for true peace.[7]

This seemingly obvious statement was in fact quite revolutionary. It helped bring to an end the isolation and separation from other religions and from the world that had characterized the Tridentine Catholic church. Indeed it lets us see that interreligious cooperation for the building of a new world is the only way forward. It lets us see that to be religious in today's world is, in the enigmatic words of the Asian bishops, to be interreligious. To work with others while maintaining and deepening one's unique religious commitment is today's challenge.

NEW WINESKINS

Revolution and rapid change are always a threat to established religion. For authentic religion must belong to the world it serves. It must be inculturated. That is to say, it must resonate with the joys and the hopes, the fears and the anxieties of the people, giving them consolation in their sufferings, answering their existential questions, teaching them a truly human way of life. It must understand their lifestyle; it must learn from the culture. When the culture changes, the religion must change with it. Otherwise the religion quickly becomes irrelevant and withers away.

Established religion always has difficulty in changing. It clings to the past. This is particularly true of the traditional religions—Hinduism, Buddhism, Islam, Judaism and Christianity—which came to birth and grew to maturity in cultures that no longer exist. If they wish to survive and continue to serve the people, these religions must extract themselves from their old cultures to become incarnate in a new culture without sacrificing one iota of their sacred core. They are called to find new wineskins for the new wine. And this is all the more difficult because the new wine of today's tempestuous culture is not yet old enough to be palatable. Humanity, still reeling from the series of revolutions I have listed, is faced with mind-boggling social, political, psychological and religious problems. It is hardly surprising if the traditional religions, unable to enter into twentieth-century culture, have found themselves isolated and irrelevant.

Here in Japan, however, where I write these lines, Buddhism is facing the problem of inculturation with varying degrees of success. While the traditional sects of Pure Land, Nichiren, Zen and the rest, which wonderfully served the people of a different era, are dwindling and in decline, new Buddhist sects have arisen, attracting millions of adherents. Some of these sects, faithful to the enlightenment of the Buddha, the Four Noble Truths, the Eightfold Path and the Lotus Sutra, are attempting to humanize modern Japan with its anguishing alienation caused by high-powered technology and debilitating wealth. Moreover, at least one of these sects is open to interreligious dialogue and shows true Buddhist compassion to the suffering Third World in a practical way.[8]

But here my main task is to speak about Christianity, where the problem of inculturation is very acute.

CULTURE IN TRANSITION

Karl Rahner distinguishes three cycles of inculturation in Christian history. The first cycle is that of Jewish Christianity, which quickly gave way to a second cycle when Christianity was inculturated in a Hellenistic and European civilization. The third cycle began at the time of the Second Vatican Council, when Christianity was challenged with the task of inculturation in a world civilization.[9]

The transition from a Jewish to a Hellenistic culture cost blood and tears and sweat and toil. Paul encountered fierce opposition from those who were clinging to the Jewish law, insisting on circumcision. Indeed, this dispute, settled at the Council of Jerusalem, might have continued vehemently and acrimoniously had not the Jewish Christians been massacred and persecuted by the Romans after the destruction of Jerusalem, thus opening the infant church to Gentile domination. The Hellenization of Christianity reached a peak with the reign of Constantine. Rooted in Greek philosophy and Roman law, the medieval Church embraced a scholasticism to which it clung tenaciously until the middle of the twentieth century.

Yet another inculturation was called for in the sixteenth century when Christianity went to Asia. At this time the Catholic church confidently maintained that it was the one true religion. Even more, it maintained, at least implicitly, that it was the one true culture. Its culture was the culture of the world. Consequently, when Catholic missionaries brought the gospel to Asia and Africa they also brought Hellenism and scholasticism. In spite of the heroism of many self-sacrificing men and women this missionary attempt met with only limited success. Now, in the third millennium, Asia still faces the titanic task of inculturation.

But let me return to Lonergan, who was particularly anxious that Christianity should be inculturated in the world civilization that is fast coming to birth. The great Canadian maintained that Catholic theology fought against the new consciousness, clinging to Aristotle and the Greeks—to a philosophical system that it considered timeless, immutable and normative for the whole world. Only belatedly did Catholic theology "come to acknowledge that the world of the classicist no longer exists and that the only world in which it can function is the modern world."[10] With a touch of dry humor Lonergan comments on the church's fight against modernity: "When Churchmen were greeted with a heresy that logically entailed all possible heresies, they called the new monster modernism."[11] Here, of course, Lonergan is referring to a Catholic church that condemned Galileo, treated Teilhard de Chardin with suspicion and took an intransigent stand against Darwin, Freud, Marx and the architects of the modern world. This was the church that insisted that seminarians study only the philosophy of Aquinas and follow the dogmatic method of Melchior Cano, while sheltering the faithful from the pernicious winds of modernity with a copious index of forbidden books.[12]

In a perceptive article written in 1972, "Revolution in Catholic Theology,"[13] Lonergan claimed that conservatives who fought against change were losing the battle. Theologians who, open to God's gift of love, followed the transcendental precepts to be attentive, intelligent, reasonable and responsible—these theologians would carry theology into the brave new world.

SUPERSTRUCTURE AND CORE

It is important to remember, however, that when Lonergan speaks of decline and breakdown, he is speaking not about the heart of Christianity, which does not change, but about the *cultural superstructure*. This he makes clear:

> The crisis that I have been attempting to depict is a crisis not of faith but of culture. There has been no revelation from on high to replace the revelation given through Christ Jesus. There has been written no new Bible and there has been founded no new church to link us with him. But Catholic philosophy and Catholic theology are matters, not merely of revelation and faith, but also of culture.[14]

This important distinction between faith and culture was also made by the Second Vatican Council with unmistakable clarity. After describing the changing world of the twentieth century the council goes on:

> The Church . . . maintains that beneath all changes there are
> many realities which do not change and which have their ulti-
> mate foundation in Christ, who is the same yesterday and
> today, yes, and forever.[15]

But is it possible to transcend culture and meet the Jesus Christ of the
gospel, even when the church fails in its task of inculturation?

It is possible. That is to say, it is possible for the mystics, who can
penetrate the rind of the superstructure to taste the delicious fruit of
eternal truth. And there is evidence that the culture into which we are
entering will have its share of mystics, men and women who will relish
the scrumptious fruit of the gospel and will create a new superstructure
for the third millennium.

But before speaking about this mystical call I will consider the institutional dimension of religion.

INSTITUTIONAL COLLAPSE

When there is a change in consciousness, traditional institutions come
into crisis. This is because the old structures do not suit the new people.
As we enter the twenty-first century, we see widespread dissatisfaction
with old institutions. Whether in politics or in law, in business or in
banking, in social work or in family life, traditional institutions are breaking down. In the world of business how great is the suffering caused by
the process of "restructuring"!

Dissatisfaction with institutions is particularly evident in the area of
religion, where the words *institutional religion* have acquired a strongly
negative connotation. The crisis is deepened because today there is a
new consciousness concerning sin. In the past, sin was an individual act
by which one broke the commandments. But now the world becomes
more and more conscious of *social sin*, of *institutional sin*, of *sinful structures*.

As the world became conscious of sinful structures and corrupt institutions, it necessarily turned its eyes to institutional religion. And with
the communications explosion of the twentieth century the sinfulness of
the institutional Catholic church was proclaimed from the housetops
with a consequent loss of credibility.

First, there was the scandal of the Vatican bank, followed by a spate
of books describing the ugly intrigue and the backstairs politics of the
Vatican. No doubt much of this was inflated by the media, but from
within the church came sincere complaints that could not easily be put

aside. The institution, it was said, wrote beautiful things about human rights while crushing human rights in its own home. Theologians were condemned without a hearing. Legitimate rights of women were not recognized. The voice of the laity was not heard. Appointments were made from the center. There was no consultation. Was this respect for human dignity? Could such a system continue into the twenty-first century?

But let me speak about my own country, where seeming collapse points to a mystical future.

TOWARD THE ERA OF JOHN

Ireland had a love-hate relationship with the institutional church. On the one hand, the people loved and respected the clergy, who had suffered with them in the time of persecution, who had supported their struggle for independence and ministered faithfully to their spiritual needs. On the other hand, they were frustrated and dismayed by the growing authoritarianism of the institutional church. The archbishop of Dublin had more power than the president of the country. When the bishops opposed any upcoming legislation, the government trembled. This created a current of anticlerical feeling that had to break out sooner or later.

But the real crisis came when the sexual misdemeanors of bishops and priests became known and were highlighted in the media. Stories of sexual abuse in schools and orphanages appeared on television throughout the world. Failures of the clergy could no longer be concealed in a world that looked on any coverup as the height of hypocrisy. There was an outcry from the people. Many felt betrayed. Others felt angry that bishops and priests, so severe in their condemnation of sexual sins and radically opposed to contraception, were themselves no better than anyone else. Others, feeling sympathy for priests, attacked a system that imposed celibacy on men who had no such calling. Others decided to leave the institution. Priests left the ministry to get married. Vocations to the priesthood and religious life plummeted. Attendance at Sunday mass went down. Quite suddenly and dramatically the institutional church was in shambles. Catholic Ireland, the island of saints and scholars that had sent to all corners of the globe missionaries who were unwaveringly faithful to Rome, of this Ireland it could now be said: "How like a widow she has become, she that was great among the nations!" (Lam. 1:1) Well might the Hebrew poet who sang of the desolate Virgin Israel now sing of the tearful Kathleen Mavourneen:

> She weeps bitterly in the night
>> with tears on her cheeks;
> among all her lovers
>> she has no one to comfort her. (Lam 1:2)

Committed Catholics began to ask: What is the Spirit saying? Is there any action of God in this? Or is it an unmitigated disaster? This is a time to reflect on Lonergan's distinction between the cultural superstructure and the spiritual core.

In Catholic countries like Ireland fidelity to the structures and obedience to the institution can be so emphasized that people, caught up in the externals, fail to see the core of Christianity. They see the church as a highly successful, if oppressive, organization that has weathered centuries of persecution and continues to preach a rigorous ethic to a corrupt and declining civilization. And they miss the central message: that God so loved the world that he gave his only Son. Or they are sociological Catholics who go to church, not out of conviction but because social pressure allows them no option. That such people should be free to leave the institutional church is no tragedy.

But there are other people who, seeing beyond the cultural superstructure, experience the fire of God's love in the depths of their being. They see their faith as total commitment to Jesus crucified and to the gospel. Neither outdated structures nor clerical sinfulness can conceal this from them. No longer do they romanticize the priest. They love him as a weak human being who, like everyone else, needs help. These are the mystics. Did not Karl Rahner say that the Christian of the future will be a mystic? Is there any truth to such an extraordinary claim?

Following Rahner I have already said that Christian history can be divided into three cycles. The second cycle, ranging from the time of Constantine until our day, was the era of Peter who holds the keys—"To thee I will give the keys of the kingdom of heaven" (Mt 16:19). The third cycle now beginning will be the era of John. That is to say, it will be the era of the mystic, the era of the Beloved Disciple who laid his head on the breast of Jesus. Or perhaps it will be the era of Magdalene, that other mystic who knelt at the foot of the cross. "Jesus said to her, 'Mary!' She turned and said to him in Hebrew, 'Rabbouni' (which means Teacher)" (Jn 20:16).

This is not to say that the era of Peter is over. The bishop of Rome, shepherd of the flock, will always be an important center of unity in Christianity. But the emphasis will shift from law to mysticism, from obedience to charity, from dogmatic theology to mystical theology, from the keys to the heart. And is it not John himself who reminds us that

Peter, who held the keys was also a mystic? "Lord, you know all things; you know that I love you" (Jn 21:17).

Indeed, there are indications that Christianity is moving into an era of mysticism. This does not mean that the Christianity of the future will be for an elite. I cannot accept the pessimistic view that the future church will be a tiny flock, a lonely diaspora. No. The good news will be brought to the masses of Asia and Africa. The good news is for the tax collectors and the prostitutes, the gays and the addicts, the dropouts and the outcasts. It is precisely to these that the gospel will make its greatest appeal, and these will be the mystics of the future. "I have come to call not the righteous but sinners" (Mt 9:13).

The old authors spoke of "the universal vocation to mysticism." Perhaps they were speaking prophetically of Christianity in the third millennium.

FOUR

The Great Search

THE GREAT HUNGER

A great hunger for spiritual experience swept through the twentieth century. Thousands of young people traveled to India, walking beneath the blazing sun in search of a guru who might lead them to enlightenment. Others looked to Zen for awakening and emancipation. Yet others were drawn to Pentecostal communities, where they danced, prayed in tongues and were filled with the Spirit. As the century went on, people became more and more dissatisfied with an institutional religion that asked them to believe lifeless doctrines and dogmas, or taught rules and regulations they must willy-nilly follow. What they wanted was spiritual experience. What they wanted was prayer. And theology, together with the catechism that it taught to the people, seemed to overlook prayer and religious experience in its search for an objective truth. Small wonder if we now hear people say, "I am spiritual but not religious." *Religion* for them is dogmas and doctrines and unwanted ethics.

It was not always so. In the early centuries of Christianity theology was never divorced from prayer. Evagrius of Pontus (345-99) summed it up well with his famous statement that the theologian is one who prays and the one who prays is a theologian. Doctrines and dogmas and ethics were born from prayer and led to prayer. Reading the scriptures, the word of God, was a religious experience, like the "lectio divina" of subsequent monastic life. Mystical theology (and mystical theology originally meant mystical experience) was the center of all theology. In short, prayer and theology and catechesis were all of a piece and could not be separated.

It should be noted that this union between theology and prayer was never lost in the Eastern tradition. In the thirteenth century St. Symeon the New Theologian was dismayed that anyone should dare talk about the Trinity without having seen the Taboric light that comes to advanced mystics. To this very day Orthodox theology is mystical theology. Theologians must never forget the Jesus prayer of the hesychasts, while the veneration of icons is an integral part of Orthodox theology.

In the West, however, there was a split, a great divide, between theology and spirituality. Theology claimed to be a rigorously objective science, while spirituality was relegated to pious literature or devotional books. What had happened?

THE CHRISTIAN SEARCH

Medieval theology from the time of Anselm of Canterbury (1033-1109) put great stress on the religious search. "Ask, and you will receive; search, and you will find; knock, and the door will be opened for you" (Mt 7:7). The theologian—or, if you wish, the Christian—was searching for truth. Aquinas stands like a mighty giant in this tradition. Building his *Summa Theologica* on the question *(quaestio),* the angelic doctor keeps asking questions as he searches for truth in the universe, in the scriptures, in the teaching of the church and even in Aristotle. Part of this Christian search (and, indeed, the principal part) was prayer in which one turned over in one's mind and heart the great mysteries of faith, eventually coming to a profound grasp of their inner meaning.

The Second Vatican Council refers to this kind of prayer. Speaking of "a growth in the understanding of the realities and the words that have been handed down,"[1] the council goes on to describe how this growth takes place: "This happens through the contemplation and study of believers, who treasure these things in their hearts (cf. Luke 2:9, 51), through the intimate understanding of spiritual things they experience."[2] The people of God, like Mary, turn over in their hearts the words of scripture, the truths of faith and the mysterious action of God in their lives; in this way they grow in wisdom, entering more and more deeply into the mystery. And if this growth in wisdom is part of the vocation of the whole people of God, how crucial it is for the theologian whose sublime task is to see into and to expound the mysteries of faith!

Needless to say, the mystics have profound enlightenments concerning the mysteries of faith. St. John of the Cross at the pinnacle of the mystical life speaks of growing insight into the mystery of the Incarnation. Indeed, he even longs for death in order to have clear knowledge of this great mystery of which he has had a tiny glimpse. Speaking of the mysteries of Christ that holy doctors have discovered and saintly souls have understood he goes on:

> There is much to fathom in Christ, for he is like an abundant mine with many recesses of treasures, so that however deep individuals may go they never reach the bottom, but rather in every recess find new veins with new riches everywhere. On this account St. Paul said of Christ: "In Christ dwell hidden all treasures and wisdom" (Col 2:3).[3]

Here is a mystic who is also a theologian and a spiritual explorer, forever finding new treasures in the mysteries of Christ.

Seen in this way dogmas are dazzling mysteries to be explored by prayer, by faith and by study. They are as baffling as the Zen koan. One turns them over and over in one's mind, seeking light from the Holy Spirit. Or, like Aquinas, one asks questions, questions, questions, never looking back, remembering Lot's wife, finally coming to a tiny enlightenment that will reach fruition only in eternity.

Now the religious search makes a great appeal to the modern world. If many people, young and old, are turning to the religions of Asia, this is because they see that these religions emphasize the spiritual search. In days of old Buddhist monks and Hindu saints traveled throughout Asia in search of a spiritual guide who would lead them to supreme wisdom. They sat in the lotus for days and weeks and months and years; they underwent great austerities searching for an enlightenment that would set them free. Likewise Buddhism and Hinduism of today teach one to search for the true self or for self-realization through meditation and recitation of the Sutras.

Within Western Christianity, on the other hand, the thrill of exploration has been lost. That, alas, is what many spiritual searchers think and feel. Questions are not encouraged. Obedience is stressed. "We already have the answers. Read the catechism. Obey the teaching authority or magisterium of the church. What more do you want?"

Where are the prophets? Where are the original thinkers? Where are the searchers? Where are the creative theologians whose task is to carry the Christian message into the new culture of the third millennium? Where are the mystics?

Thinking people begin to ask if the villain of the piece is the old dogmatic theology.

THE TYRANNY OF DOGMA

Bernard Lonergan claimed that a great revolution took place in Catholic theology at the end of the seventeenth century. This was the time of the Enlightenment, which was a far-flung attack on Christianity from almost every quarter and in almost every style. It was a time, Lonergan claimed, when embattled theologians "began to reassure one another about their certainties." They introduced a new method in theology:

> They introduced "dogmatic" theology . . . It replaced the inquiry of the *quaestio* by the pedagogy of the thesis. It demoted the quest of faith for understanding to a desirable, but secondary, and indeed, optional goal. It gave basic and central significance to the certitudes of faith.[4]

In short, theologians stopped asking questions and began to elaborate sure and certain propositions. The spiritual search came to a standstill. Theologians began to make dogmatic statements defending the faith against the onslaughts of satanic enemies. Of this dogmatic theology Lonergan writes:

> It owed its mode of proof to Melchior Cano and, as that theologian was also a bishop and inquisitor, so the new dogmatic theology not only proved its theses, but also was supported by the teaching authority and the sanctions of the Church.[5]

The inquisitor Melchior Cano! The sanctions of the church! The authoritarian mentality! The poor theologian had to repeat the traditional, orthodox, unchanging formulae—or face the music.

This dogmatic theology was introduced to Catholic seminaries throughout the world. A thesis, usually taken from the magisterium, was clearly stated and defended by quotations from sacred scripture and from the church fathers. Of primary importance, however, was the little manual of Heinrich Denzinger, which set out clearly and succinctly the dogmatic statements of church councils from the earliest times.[6] These statements were true at all times and in all places and in all cultures. They were static and unchanging, equally true in the early Christian centuries and in the world today, equally true in Europe and Asia, in Africa and America. When quoting them, Denzinger always added a theological note indicating the penalty incurred by anyone who denied the dogma. And woe betide anyone who dared question Denzinger!

The serious seminarian was never without his Denzinger. With Denzinger he went to bed at night; with Denzinger he got up in the morning. But in his quieter moments he knew that Denzinger did nothing for his spiritual life. Denzinger helped him give the correct answers in his examinations but did not help his prayer, did not lead him to union with God, did not give him the tender compassion he needed in dealing with strayed sheep. If in the course of his prayer or contemplation he received enlightenment about the Blessed Trinity or the Incarnation or the eucharist or the maternity of Mary—these enlightenments were graces from God, but they had no significance for theology. Even the enlightenments of St. John of the Cross had no theological significance. They were subjective experiences—and subjective experience had no place in the objective science of theology.

Lonergan challenged this Denzinger theology. He claimed that it was outdated, unable to keep in touch with a contemporary culture that is progressive and historical-minded. Its use of scripture and patrology to "prove" a thesis was incompatible with new discoveries in scripture and patristics. It was static in a world that has become evolutionary. It crushed the theological search.

Yet Lonergan's most important criticism concerned the old dogmatic theology's exaggerated view of the objectivity of truth and its neglect of the subject.

In an insightful essay entitled "The Neglected Subject in Catholic Theology" he maintained that whereas modern philosophers like Hegel, Kierkegaard, Nietzsche, Heidegger and Buber put great emphasis on the subject, influential scholastic theologians had had "an exaggerated view of the objectivity of truth."[7] Their view, Lonergan insisted, was at odds with Aquinas, who held that truth was in the mind—in the mind of God or in the mind of persons. But, Lonergan humorously goes on, these theologians "seem to have thought of truth as so objective as to get along without minds."[8] We must pay great attention, he insists, to subjective experience, to the process by which a person comes to the truth and to the conscience of every human person. But, he laments, this exaggerated view of objectivity spread to the whole Catholic church, influencing its catechism and its policy of censorship:

> The same insistence on objective truth and the same neglect
> of its subjective conditions informed the old catechetics, which
> the new catechetics is replacing, and the old censorship, which

insisted on true propositions and little understood the need to respect the dynamics of the advance toward truth.[9]

This same attitude informed the Denzinger theology, which propounded truths that were valid for all people, at all times, in all cultures and in all countries, while paying little attention to the subjective disposition of the person. Such a theology had little need for prayer and religious experience; it did nothing to promote the religious search.

TWO THEOLOGIES

You might say that this talk about objective truth and subjective disposition is for graying scholars and that it is of little importance for the lives of ordinary human beings. By no means! It is an important application of Lonergan's first transcendental precept—*Be attentive*—and it is crucial for two reasons.

First, paying attention to the subjective disposition of a person has very broad implications. It means paying attention to the cultural background—to his or her way of thinking and feeling, to his or her history, education, customs, religious sensibilities and all that goes to make up the mystery of the human person. It may mean paying attention to the poverty and squalor in which the person lives, to the cruel injustice with which the person is treated, to the millions who are dying of hunger and disease. Or it may mean paying attention to the heartrending anguish of people from broken homes, struggling with chemical addiction or with violence in the streets. All this pertains to the subjective dimension of the person. And the old dogmatic theology ignored it.

From the middle of the twentieth century, however, theologians, clerical and lay, women and men, emerged from their secluded classrooms to live in the real world, whether of Asia or Africa or Latin America or the United States. Feeling great compassion for the suffering people to whom they were sent, they immediately saw that the old static Denzinger theology with its unchanging propositions was irrelevant. But the gospel was very relevant. How could they bring the gospel to the suffering masses?

Their answer was *liberation theology*.

The challenge confronting liberation theologians was clear. On the one hand, they must preserve with great fidelity the Christian tradition. On the other hand, they must bring the message and the person of Jesus to the suffering people in a language the suffering people would understand. In his opening speech to the council Pope John spoke clearly about this challenge:

It is necessary first of all that the Church should never depart
from the sacred patrimony of truth received from the fathers.
But at the same time she must ever look to the present, to the
new conditions and new forms of life introduced into the
modern world.[10]

Pope John in the same context went on to say that "the substance of the
ancient doctrine of the deposit of faith is one thing, and the way in which
it is presented is another"[11]—as if to say that old truths can be expressed
in new ways. This was taken up by the council, which spoke of freedom
in the theological elaboration of revealed truth:

While preserving unity in essentials, let all members of the
Church . . . preserve a proper freedom in the various forms of
spiritual life and discipline, in the variety of liturgical rites,
and even in the elaboration of revealed truth.[12]

All this encouraged theologians to dialogue with their cultural environment and to explore new ways in liturgy, new forms of prayer, new
structures, new paths in the elaboration of revealed truth. Some felt that
Christian theology is necessarily prophetic—that the theologian has a
prophetic role in the community.

Yet this way of thinking was not welcomed by an establishment that
wanted no change; nor was it accepted by conservatives who, deeply
attached to the past, wanted, often unconsciously, to preserve Denzinger
and the Tridentine church. And so there arose a bitter conflict within the
Catholic community. Bernard Lonergan saw great tension between two
theological positions, one of which he called "classicist" and the other
"historicist." He writes:

The differences between the two are enormous, for they differ
in their apprehension of man, in their account of the good,
and in the role they ascribe to the Church in the world. But
these differences are not immediately theological. They are
differences in horizon, in total mentality. For either side really to understand the other is a major achievement and, when
such understanding is lacking, the interpretation of Scripture
or of other theological sources is most likely to be at cross-
purposes.[13]

Lonergan said this in 1966. As we enter the new millennium, the same
tension remains. The Catholic church is deeply polarized. Yet I believe

that the Second Vatican Council points the way forward.

At the end of its great document on the church today *(Gaudium et Spes)* the council speaks inspiringly about dialogue among all people, giving pride of place to *dialogue within the church*. Speaking of the mission of Christianity to the whole world, the council goes on:

> Such a mission requires in the first place that we foster within the Church herself mutual esteem, reverence and harmony, through the full recognition of lawful diversity. Thus all those who compose the one People of God, both pastors and the general faithful, can engage in dialogue with ever-abounding fruitfulness.[14]

The full recognition of lawful diversity is indeed the great challenge of today. The council then quotes the beautiful words of Augustine:

> In certis unitas
> In dubiis libertas
> Et in omnibus
> Caritas[15]

In omnibus caritas! Charity in all things! Is not this the gospel of Jesus Christ? "By this shall all know that you are my disciples, if you have love for one another" (Jn 13:35). Without this love for one another, without dialogue within the church, dialogue with other religions becomes a joke.

I have said that a correct understanding of the objectivity of truth is crucially important for two reasons, and I have spoken at some length of the first reason. Now let me address myself to the second.

The fact is that an exaggerated view of the objectivity of truth may lead to that fundamentalism which is one of the greatest evils of the modern world or of any world. In all the great religions—Hinduism, Islam, Judaism, Buddhism and Christianity—one finds people who claim to have absolute truth. Either explicitly or implicitly they confidently say: "The truth is out there to be looked at. I see it, and I am right. You do not see it, and you are wrong. And error has no rights." From this arises the zealous determination to impose this truth on everyone at any cost. Then we have persecutions, excommunications, inquisitions, holy wars, burnings at the stake and all kinds of savagery carried out in the name of God.

While fundamentalism exists everywhere, it has been most virulent and cruel in the monotheistic religions wherein, we know, religious leaders have been guilty of cruelty, savagery, injustice and inhumanity beside which the actions of the bloated plutocrats and the crafty politicians fade into insignificance. If, at the Enlightenment, there was a bitter reaction against Christianity, this stemmed in part from disgust and anger at the spectacle of religious wars, religious persecutions and the awful human suffering caused by institutional religion.

Fundamentalism is spirituality gone awry. It can even be a fanatical mysticism. Often it has theological roots in an erroneous notion of the objectivity of truth. Let us humbly remember that absolute truth exists only in the mind of God. We human beings are forever searching.

"SEEKERS AFTER TRUTH"

The Second Vatican Council made a remarkable attempt to reunite spirituality and theology. So much so, that its documents can be called treatises in spiritual theology and can be profitably read as "lectio divina." Pope John had called for a pastoral council, one that would lead to conversion of heart not just among Catholics but in the whole world. He asked for prayers from the world for a council that would lead to peace, justice and universal love. In its individual documents to bishops, priests, seminarians, laity and religious the council always spoke about community and the eucharist and about prayer. In its document on the universal vocation to holiness it spoke about martyrdom as the supreme act of love. After praising the profound research of scripture scholars it was careful to add: "And let them remember that prayer should accompany the reading of Scripture, so that God and the people may talk together; for 'we speak to Him when we pray; we hear Him when we read the divine sayings.'"[16] In short, a spirit of prayer pervaded the scholarly documents.

When the council came to an end, the fathers described the spiritual experience they had been through *and they spoke of it as a religious search*. Speaking to scientists and people of thought whom they call "seekers after truth" and "explorers of humanity and of the universe" they say that they also are seekers after truth and they understand very well the suffering and frustration that accompanies such a vocation. Their message is inspiring:

> Why a special greeting for you? Because all of us here, bishops
> and fathers of the Council, are on the lookout for truth. What
> have our efforts amounted to during these four years except a

more attentive search for and deepening of the message of truth entrusted to the Church and an effort at more perfect docility to the spirit of truth?[17]

And then they continue with moving words:

> Hence our paths could not fail to cross. Your road is ours. Your paths are never foreign to ours. We are the friends of your vocation as searchers, companions in your fatigues, admirers of your successes, and, if necessary, consolers in your discouragement and your failures.[18]

These are humble words. The council fathers are not standing on a pedestal lecturing dogmatically to the people. They are searching, searching, searching, while undergoing the suffering that this search entails. And yet the fathers are careful to distinguish their search from that of the scientist. They are searching for *a deepening of the message of truth entrusted to the church*. Paradoxically, they are searching for the truth that they already possess. This they make clear:

> Happy are those who, while possessing the truth, search more earnestly for it in order to renew it, deepen it, and transmit it to others. Happy also are those who, not having found it, are working toward it with a sincere heart.[19]

The scientific search and the religious search have subjectively much in common, but objectively they are quite different. For this reason faith and scientific knowledge can complement one another. The scientist and the theologian can walk hand in hand.

As the council fathers are searching, so they encourage the people to do likewise—to engage in a search in which they must enjoy "immunity from external coercion as well as psychological freedom."[20] In the past the church put pressure on people, punishing and threatening. This must not happen again:

> Truth . . . is to be sought after in a manner proper to the dignity of the human person and his or her social nature. The inquiry is to be free, carried on with the aid of teaching or instruction, communication and dialogue . . . Moreover, as the truth is discovered, it is by a personal assent that people are to adhere to it.[21]

This great respect for human freedom with no hint of condemnation is part of the new spiritual theology. The condemnations, excommunications, inquisitions and the rest will, we dare hope, give place to the compassionate gospel of Jesus Christ. It is interesting to recall that at the beginning of the council some bishops, influenced by the current moral and dogmatic theology, called for a clear condemnation of atheistic communism. But the council, following Pope John, did not want to condemn anyone.[22] Instead, it looked into the *causes* of atheism, saying that Christians were not without responsibility. Its only condemnation concerned war. It said that "those actions designed for the methodical extermination of an entire people, nation, or ethnic minority . . . must be vehemently condemned as horrendous crimes."[23]

The council, then, was not just an objective statement of Christian doctrine. It was a call to conversion of heart. It was a call to a conversion that would affect not only Christians but the whole of humanity. What is the nature of such a conversion?

"THIS ABOVE ALL . . . "

Bernard Lonergan, proposing a new method, addresses himself to the problem of fundamental theology. The old fundamental theology made objective statements about the existence of God, the possibility of revelation, the historical existence of Jesus and other truths that formed the basis of Christian theology. Lonergan claims that "the old foundations will no longer do," and he continues, "In saying this I do not mean that they are no longer true, for they are as true now as they ever were. I mean that they are no longer appropriate."[24] Prior to objective statements, he claims, is a subjective experience—and this must be the basis. In his inimitable way he speaks of a foundation that consists "not in objective statement but in subjective reality."[25]

But what is this subjective reality? To this Lonergan replies that it is the experience of conversion:

> It follows that reflection on conversion can supply theology
> with its foundation and, indeed, with a foundation that is
> concrete, dynamic, personal, communal and historical.[26]

Conversion, Lonergan goes on, may take place in a moment when a blinded Paul fell to the ground on the road to Damascus, or it may be extended over the slow maturing process of a lifetime. Elsewhere he speaks of a holistic conversion compounded of intellectual conversion, ethical conversion and religious conversion. Finally, he claims that conversion *is the experience by which one becomes an authentic human being.*

What is highly significant about Lonergan's theology is his claim that conversion is the basis not only of Christianity but of all religion. Conversion, he tells us, coincides with living religion. And this brings the religions together in a remarkable way. For all, the first step is to be authentically human. One is reminded of the immortal words that Shakespeare puts on the lips of Polonius as he bids his son farewell:

> This above all—to thine own self be true.

This above all! This is the first step for the human being of any religion or of no religion. To be true to one's self, to be true to one's inner light, to be true to the inner voice of conscience—was not Shakespeare a theologian of stature?

In its own way the Second Vatican Council seems to say something similar. Writing inspiringly about conscience as the voice of God echoing in the depths of every human person and referring to St. Paul's assertion that what the law requires is written on the hearts of the Gentiles, the council writes:

> In fidelity to conscience Christians are joined with the rest of people in the search for truth, and for the genuine solution to the numerous problems that arise in the life of individuals and from social relationships.[27]

The twentieth century ushered in the age of conscience in the whole world. It is precisely in fidelity to the light of conscience that Christians will be united among themselves and with others. Buddhists, Christians, Hindus, Jews, Muslims, agnostics and atheists of good will—all are engaged in a common search for truth and for a solution to the awful problems that confront us.

The true light enlightens *everyone*. The Spirit of God is at work in the whole universe.

For Lonergan conversion reaches a climax with religious conversion, wherein one's being becomes being-in-love. If reflection on such conversion becomes the basis of fundamental theology, the theology of the future will be mystical theology.

FIVE

The Awakening of Asia

THE MYSTIC EAST

At the beginning of the twentieth century the saintly Jewish mystic Simone
Weil (1909-43) spoke prophetically of Europe's need for Eastern spirituality:

> It seems that Europe requires genuine contacts with the East
> in order to remain spiritually alive. It is also true that there is
> something in Europe which opposes the Oriental spirit, some-
> thing specifically Western . . . and we are in danger of being
> devoured by it.[1]

What is this specifically Western thing that opposes the East and could
devour the European soul? Is it rationalism, materialism, legalism, intol-
erance, arrogance and all those vices that Paul attributes to the ungodly
in the Epistle to the Romans? Be that as it may, the world today needs
the spirituality of Asia. Western Christianity is not enough. We need
Eastern mysticism to help us penetrate more deeply into the gospel of
Jesus Christ. Now more than ever the world cries out for wise men and
women from the East, people who will follow the star bringing gifts of
gold, incense and myrrh to the child who has been born.

HINDU RENAISSANCE

After a period of decline in the eighteenth century Hinduism gave birth
to a galaxy of gurus and spiritual teachers. Sri Aurobindo (1872-1950),

40

Mahatma Gandhi (1869-1948), Rabindranath Tagore (1861-1941)—
these were people of genius who carried the spirituality of Hinduism to
a thirsting world. Among the Hindu saints, however, a special place
must be given to the mystic and visionary Sri Ramakrishna Paramahansa
(1836-86) who claimed to have experienced identity not only with Kali,
Rama, Krishna and Brahman but also with Mohammed and Jesus Christ.
Under the direction of a Muslim guru he repeated the name of Allah,
claiming to realize the God of Islam. Later, fascinated by the person of
Jesus Christ, he read the Bible. He claimed that he had a vision of Jesus
and heard from the depths of his being a voice that cried out: "Behold
the Christ, who shed His heart's blood for the redemption of the world,
who suffered a sea of anguish for love of men. It is he, the master Yogi,
who is in eternal union with God. It is Jesus, Love Incarnate."[2]
Ramakrishna taught that Jesus, Buddha, Krishna and others were incarnations of God. All religions, he claimed, were leading to the same goal—
to Brahman.

Ramakrishna was made known to the West by a devoted and beloved
disciple. The sannyasin Vivekananda (1863-1902) felt called to bring
the treasures of Indian spirituality, particularly those of his saintly Master, to the declining Western world. At the Parliament of Religions held
in Chicago in 1893 he spoke impressively of a universal religion. In 1895
he founded in New York the Vedanta Society, which quickly established
centers in London and Boston and throughout the world, attracting intellectuals and spiritual searchers everywhere. In 1897 he founded the
Ramakrishna mission, organizing his disciples as monks in a religious
order that would work for the poor and underprivileged. Vivekananda's
message was clear. The divinization of the human person through spiritual experience was more important than doctrines, dogmas, rituals,
books, temples or churches. Such a message could not fail to fascinate a
Western world that was weary of religious legalism, dogmatism and
authoritarianism.

CHRISTIAN RESPONSE

At first the response of orthodox Christians, as indeed of orthodox
Muslims, was negative. Neither Christians nor Muslims were impressed
by Ramakrishna's visions. They felt that their religious path demanded
a total commitment, and that one could not switch from one path to the
other as Ramakrishna claimed to do. Besides, Christians were not happy
with the Hindu doctrine of many incarnations. For them, Jesus was the
Word made flesh and was quite unique—"For in him the whole fullness

of deity dwells bodily" (Col 2:9). This made them skeptical about Ramakrishna's meeting with Jesus.

As for Vivekananda's teaching about a universal religion, Christians and Muslims protested that Vivekananda's universal religion was in fact Hinduism and that they were in danger of being absorbed, thus losing their identity. Even Bede Griffiths protested that "Christian faith in India . . . is always in danger of simply being absorbed in Hinduism, just as in the early centuries Christ was in danger of becoming one of the gods of the Roman Empire."[3] Griffiths painstakingly pointed out the difference between the Hindu *avatāra* and Jesus, the Word incarnate.

While these criticisms of orthodox Christians have their validity and must not be dismissed, it is also true that in the light of the Second Vatican Council we can be more positive about the Christ experience of Ramakrishna. For the council states clearly that Christ communicates himself not only to Christians but to the whole human family. In a way known to God alone every human being has the possibility of coming into contact with the paschal mystery. Urging Christians to unite themselves with the death and resurrection of Jesus, the council continues:

> All this holds true not only for Christians, but for all people of good will in whose hearts grace works in an unseen way. For since Christ died for all, and since the ultimate vocation of humanity is in fact one, and divine, we ought to believe that the Holy Spirit in a manner known only to God offers to every human being the possibility of being associated with this paschal mystery.[4]

Pope John Paul II may have had this passage in mind when he writes about the vine and the branches, stating powerfully and poetically that *"the Paschal Mystery is by now grafted onto the history of humanity, onto the history of every individual."*[5] Can we not, then, be open to the possibility that Ramakrishna met Jesus, who shed his blood for the redemption of the world and who is Love incarnate? Is it not possible that he heard the voice of one who said: "I have other sheep that do not belong to this fold. I must bring them also, and they will listen to my voice. So there will be one flock, one shepherd" (Jn 10:16)?

The council, moreover, expresses appreciation and respect for the Muslims' devotion to Jesus and Mary, saying,

> Though they do not acknowledge Jesus as God, they revere him as a prophet. They also honor Mary, his virgin mother; at times they call on her, too, with devotion.[6]

In the same way, many Hindus call on Jesus with faith and devotion. Think of the great Mahatma, whose love for the Sermon on the Mount is well-nigh proverbial. At the end of his life Gandhi visited the *Pieta* of Michelangelo in St. Peter's and wept as he contemplated Jesus in the arms of his mother. His tiny room in New Delhi contained a single picture—a picture of Jesus. Surely this reminds us that the call of Jesus is to the whole of humanity. "And I, when I am lifted up from the earth, will draw all people to myself" (Jn 12:32).

Now this has important consequences for theology. People outside the institutional churches can speak wisely about the gospel and about Jesus. We can learn from them even when they lack the orthodoxy of Denzinger.

And there is an important corollary.

As Western civilization declines and the gospel spreads throughout Asia, we will see (indeed we already see) the rise of an Asian theology rooted in the Bible and the Christian tradition *but also listening to the voice of Asian saints and mystics*. Primarily mystical, this theology will learn from Ramakrishna, Aurobindo, Ramana Maharshi and the rest. It will not neglect the Vedanta and the Upanishads and the Gita, just as a theology further East will not neglect Lao Tzu, Chuang Tzu and the I Ching. It will bring to Christianity an enrichment beyond our wildest dreams, an enrichment beside which the contribution of Plato and the Greeks will look like high school textbooks.

And here a word of caution is necessary.

I have already quoted Simone Weil to the effect that there is something destructive in the West that opposes the Oriental spirit. The incisive words of this wise Jewish mystic are important for the universal church. For if history repeats itself (and well it may) Western theologians will fight against an Asian theology, attempting to impose Western categories on Eastern minds. Alas, they will do so at their own peril. Not only will they fail miserably, but they will find themselves marginalized and isolated by a powerful current of mystical wisdom that is already energizing not only Asia but the whole world.

Now let me address myself to Vivekananda's second point concerning the unity of religions.

THE UNITY OF RELIGIONS

In 1893, while Vivekananda was speaking at the Parliament of Religions about a universal religion, Catholic theologians were anguishing over the thorny problem of the "salvation of the infidel," asking how the nonbaptized could possibly be saved since outside the church there was no salvation. A few centuries earlier St. Francis Xavier had felt obliged to tell the weeping Japanese that their ancestors were buried in hell forever. This was the theology he learned at the University of Paris.

In 1993, at the Second Parliament of Religions in Chicago, Catholic theologians were talking a different language. They were saying that a plurality of religions is in God's plan for the salvation of the human family. Asked why there were so many religions, Pope John Paul II was to say: "You speak of many religions. Instead I will attempt to show the *common fundamental element* and the *common root* of these religions."[7] And he continued: "Instead of marveling at the fact that Providence allows such a great variety of religions, we should be amazed at the number of common elements found within them."[8] John Paul did not say that all religions are the same, but he *did* say that they have a common root. While he was not in total agreement with Vivekananda, he was closer to the Hindu swami than to Francis Xavier. Can we, then, deny the prophetic element in Vivekananda?

John Paul was, of course, following the Second Vatican Council, which from the beginning was greatly preoccupied with questions of world unity and world peace. It was already becoming evident that there could be no world peace while there is strife among religions. In its document significantly called *Nostra Aetate* ("our time") the council appealed to a very ancient Christian tradition giving primary consideration to what human beings have in common and what promotes fellowship among them. "For all peoples comprise a single community, and have a common origin . . . One also is their final goal."[9] One is their final goal! At the eschaton, at what Christians call the parousia, in a way we will never understand, the human family and all its religions will come together in a common mystical experience. The council refers to the colorful, enigmatic and apocalyptic language of the Book of Revelation:

> And the city has no need of sun or moon to shine on it, for the glory of God is its light, and its lamp is the Lamb. The nations will walk by its light, and the kings of the earth will bring their glory into it. (Rv 21:23-24)

This apocalyptic city is the final goal of humanity and all its religions.

But what about union in this world? What do we have in common while we remain in this vale of tears?

The council indicates that there is a profound wisdom and a profound religious sense that is common to all humanity and has been so from the earliest times:

> From ancient times down to the present, there has existed among diverse peoples a certain perception of that hidden power which hovers over the course of things and over the events of human life; at times, indeed, recognition can be found of a Supreme Divinity and of a Supreme Father too.[10]

From the dawn of history human beings have had a sense of the great mystery, of the hidden power that hovers over things. Is this the cloud of unknowing? Is this the emptiness and the darkness of the mystics? This the council does not say. It simply remarks that "such a perception and such a recognition instill the lives of these peoples with a profound religious sense."

About this "ultimate and unutterable mystery" I will speak at length in a later chapter.

UNIVERSAL WISDOM

The council, then, speaks of a wisdom and a religious sense that has been living in humanity from the earliest times and is still alive today. St. Paul refers to it when he writes to the Romans: "Ever since the creation of the world his eternal power and divine nature, invisible though they are, have been understood and seen through the things he has made" (Rom 1:20). The Roman Empire is without excuse, writes Paul, because although the people knew God they did not worship him as God and did not give thanks. God has revealed himself to the whole human family. First to Adam and Eve in paradise. And then, pointing to the rainbow, God said to Noah: "This is the sign of the covenant that I have established between me and all flesh that is on the earth" (Gn 9:17). There is a covenant with all flesh. There is a covenant with all religions. No one is excluded.

The notion of a universal revelation is in fact quite deep in the Christian tradition, even though it was not taught to Francis Xavier at the University of Paris. The great John Henry Newman (1801-90) wrote a remarkable dissertation, "The Dispensation of Paganism," claiming that all religions were included in the plan of God. And Newman was one of the great influences on the Second Vatican Council.

As the world shrinks and as religions and cultures draw closer together, more and more thought is given to the notion of a universal wisdom—which is quite different from a universal religion—that is the heritage of the whole human family. Already in the middle of the twentieth century the brilliant Aldous Huxley (1894-1963) was writing about the perennial philosophy *(philosophia perennis)* that he claimed was "immemorial and universal." Gathering quotations from all religions and cultures, Huxley pointed to a wisdom that goes beyond reasoning and thinking, beyond dogmas and doctrines. He was not, he claimed, quoting learned theologians and intellectuals but simple people who had experience. Characteristically, he writes: "It is a fact confirmed and reconfirmed during two or three thousand years of religious history, that ultimate Reality is not clearly and immediately apprehended, except by those who have made themselves loving, pure in heart and poor in spirit. This being so, it is hardly surprising that a theology based upon the experience of nice, ordinary, unregenerate people should carry so little conviction."[11] One is reminded of the gospel: "I thank you, Father, Lord of heaven and earth, because you have hidden these things from the wise and intelligent and have revealed them to infants" (Mt 11:25).

In the twentieth century, however, the person who spoke most eloquently and wrote most prolifically about universal wisdom was Bede Griffiths. At the end of a long life spent mostly in his tiny ashram in south India, Griffiths saw that the wisdom of the great religions was necessary for the survival of a world in crisis. There must be a marriage of East and West—a marriage, I might add, that was painfully enacted in his own mystical psyche. There must be a rediscovery of the wisdom of India, China, Africa, Europe. This wisdom, he insisted, must dialogue with a new physics that was searching for the mystical dimension of reality. And all must collaborate in the building of a new world. It was a remarkable vision of unity. It need hardly be said that Bede Griffiths himself was a deeply committed Christian with unwavering faith in the Incarnation. He had a profound devotion to the Jesus prayer which he recited unceasingly throughout his life and in the agonizing days that preceded his death.

UNITY IN DIVERSITY

After speaking of the universal wisdom that is common to all the religions, the council goes on to speak of diversity. Hindus, Buddhists, Muslims and Jews have their distinct paths. Christianity has the greatest respect for these paths, even when they differ from what she holds and sets forth. But the Christian path is clear. Of the Catholic church the council states unambiguously:

> Indeed, she proclaims and must ever proclaim Christ, "the way, the truth, and the life" (John 14:6), in whom people find

the fullness of religious life, and in whom God has reconciled all things to Himself (cf. 2 Cor 5:18-19).[12]

Nor is Christianity alone in stating clearly the differences between religions. All the religions, with the possible exception of Hinduism, are clear on this point. At a seminar held in London in 1994 the Dalai Lama said that to achieve a meaningful dialogue "we need a foundation that is based on the clear recognition of the diversity that exists among humanity."[13] He went on to tell Christians that "when it comes to a philosophical or metaphysical dialogue I feel that we must part company";[14] and he said, citing a Tibetan proverb, that to try to be a Buddhist and a Christian at the same time is like putting a yak's head on a sheep's body. The Parliament of Religions in 1993 was equally clear:

> By a global ethic we do not mean a global ideology or a single unified religion beyond all existing religions, and certainly not the domination of one religion over all others.[15]

The fact is that the religions value their unique faith commitment. The Jew is committed to love the One True God with mind and heart and soul and strength. The Christian is committed to have this love for Jesus, who is the Word incarnate and Savior of the world. The Muslim is committed to the Prophet and to Allah. The Buddhist is committed to the Buddha and the dharma in which he or she finds salvation. None of the religions wants this commitment trifled with. That is why we can only have sincere dialogue by recognizing diversity.

CHALLENGE OF BUDDHISM

Until the middle of the twentieth century most Western philosophers and theologians spoke of Buddhism, and indeed of all Asian thought, as pessimistic, negative and life-denying. After all, did not Buddhism end with the blowing out of the candle?

This way of thinking influenced even the distinguished and influential Swiss theologian Hans Urs von Balthasar, who made negative comments about Asian religion and culture without any knowledge of the most basic texts. It also influenced the "Letter to the Bishops of the Catholic Church on Some Aspects of Christian Meditation," promulgated by the Congregation for the Doctrine of the Faith in 1990.[16] This document, which got wide coverage in the media throughout the world, was a veiled attack on Eastern methods of meditation. It contained an impressive array of references to European texts and European authors but not one reference to any Asian text or any Asian author. It was a purely European document. The author was obviously an excellent Western theologian, but what did he know about Asian meditation?

In *Crossing the Threshold of Hope* Pope John Paul II devoted an excellent chapter to the plurality of religions. Following the council, he stressed what the religions have in common. And then John Paul, who had spoken enthusiastically about interreligious dialogue and had cordially invited religious leaders to common prayer at Assisi—this same John Paul made an unfortunate blunder. When his book comes to treat of Buddhism he says that the Buddhist tradition, and the methods deriving from it, are almost exclusively negative, that the enlightenment experienced by the Buddha comes down to the conviction that the world is bad. The world, moreover, is the source of suffering and evil; to liberate ourselves from this evil we must break the ties that bind us to external reality. The negative "atheism" of Buddhism is contrasted with the theism of a Christianity that has a positive approach to the world and to civilization. As for mysticism, the pope asserts that "Carmelite mysticism begins at the point where the reflections of Buddha end, together with his instructions for the spiritual life."[17]

Buddhists throughout the world were hurt and angry, claiming that this was a caricature of true Buddhism. When the pope visited Sri Lanka in 1995, Buddhists boycotted an interreligious meeting held in his honor; the pope, obviously hurt, made the significant remark that "it is dangerous for us not to be together." But he did not apologize or take back what he had written.

The Second Vatican Council, however, had been cautiously positive about Buddhism. And behind this lies a story I heard from my friend and colleague Heinrich Dumoulin, whose scholarly work on Zen is internationally recognized.

In the document on non-Christian religions *(Nostra Aetate)* the council fathers at first adopted the old notion of a pessimistic Buddhism. However, the Japanese bishops, when they returned to Tokyo between the sessions, submitted the first draft to three Jesuit scholars of Sophia University: Heinrich Dumoulin, Hugo Enomiya-Lassalle and Paul Pfister. These three put their heads together in Dumoulin's room and rewrote the section on Buddhism, which was subsequently accepted by the council and reads as follows:

> Buddhism in its multiple forms acknowledges the radical insufficiency of this shifting world. It teaches a path by which people, in a devout and confident spirit, can either reach a

state of absolute freedom or attain supreme enlightenment by their own efforts or by higher assistance.[18]

Later in his life Dumoulin was not completely satisfied with this statement. Shortly before his death in 1995 he told me that if he had to do it again he would be more enthusiastic about Buddhism and would add something about Buddhist compassion.

ONGOING DIALOGUE

From what has been said it is clear that dialogue between religions, like marriage between a man and a woman, can be tempestuous, even when it is loving. Christianity has a history of such dialogical storms.

In the sixteenth century the Catholic church made an attempt at dialogue with Asia. But Madurai and Beijing were far from Rome and Geneva. How could Romans understand Robert de Nobili and Matteo Ricci? How could they sympathize with the so-called infidels? Little progress was made.

Even more tragic was the controversy over the Chinese rites that lasted throughout the seventeenth century. Most of the missionaries seem to have agreed that it was imperative to practice adaptation; the Holy See, however, condemned the rites in a decree of 1704, a condemnation that was reiterated by Pope Benedict XIV in 1742.

After this there was little dialogue. Rome continued to hold tight control of Asian theology, liturgy, seminary training, church law, ecclesiastical structures, clerical dress, the use of money and even the building of churches. Just as most Asian countries were colonies, dependent upon London or Paris or Amsterdam, so the Asian churches were like colonies dependent upon Rome. This lasted until the Second Vatican Council, which coincided with the collapse of colonialism.

The council ended on December 8, 1965.

In 1970 Pope Paul VI made a historic visit to the Philippines. One hundred and eighty Catholic bishops from all over Asia gathered in Manila; and the Federation of Asian Bishops Conference (FABC), which was to meet at intervals to discuss evangelization in Asia, was duly founded. This was an occasion of *Christian awakening*.

Though the bishops were from all parts of the vast continent—from Bangladesh, China, India, Indonesia, Japan, Korea, Laos, Kampuchea, Malaysia, Singapore, Brunei, Myanmar, Pakistan, the Philippines, Sri Lanka, Thailand and Vietnam—they nevertheless felt a bond of unity. Asking the same questions and facing the same problems, they formed a community or, as they said, "a community of communities," that radiated the joyful spirit of the Gospel.

Moreover, it became clear that just as the Greek Fathers—Origen, Gregory of Nyssa, Basil and the rest—loved their Hellenistic culture and wanted to unite it with their Christian faith, so the Asian bishops loved their heritage and felt closely united with their ancestors. Seeing that Asian culture cannot be separated from Asian religion, they made a sincere plea for dialogue. The First Plenary Assembly, held in Taipei in 1974, gave expression to their feelings about the traditional religions of their countries:

> Down through the centuries the ancient religions of the orient
> have given light and strength to our ancestors. They have ex-
> pressed the noblest longings in the hearts of our people, our
> deepest joys and sorrows. Their temples have been the home
> of contemplation and prayer. They have shaped our history
> and our way of thinking. They are part of our culture. For us
> in Asia, they have been the doorway to God.[19]

In Buddhism the bishops discerned unerringly the action of the Spirit. "We recognize in the personal lives of the Buddhists, as well as in their total religious life, the activity of the Spirit," they wrote. And they spoke of the urgent promptings of the Spirit of Christ:

> We feel the urgency for dialogue because of the promptings
> of the Spirit of Christ, moving us in love to open ourselves
> to Buddhists in new ways, respecting them so that we may
> help one another to grow together to the fullness of our total
> reality.[20]

The pronouncements of the FABC had great influence on the Asian churches.

With the Synod of Asian Bishops held in Rome in April-May 1998 it was clear that the Asian churches had come of age. The bishops spoke frankly and confidently about interreligious dialogue, about the woeful lack of inculturation, about their frustrations in asking Rome for little "permissions." The Indian bishops were positively scathing about the instruction on non-Christian forms of meditation issued by the Vatican in 1990. Why were they not consulted? Much unnecessary embarrassment and pain could have been avoided by "timely dialogue." Likewise the Sri Lankan bishops complained that the pope's book with its remarks about Buddhism had "triggered a host of unpleasant feelings and seriously hampered the work of dialogue."[21] All in all, one is reminded of Paul confronting Peter: "If you, though a Jew, live like a Gentile and not like a Jew, how can you compel the Gentiles to live like Jews?" (Gal 2:14). But the Asian bishops were less angry than Paul.

And just as Paul wrought a change in Peter, so the Asian bishops may have changed John Paul II. In his encyclical letter *Faith and Reason,* published six months after the synod, John Paul spoke in glowing terms of Asian religion and philosophy. About this and about the Asian Synod I will speak at length later in this book.

I have spoken about the Asian Catholic hierarchy. Equally important is the voice of the laity, calling for dialogue between East and West within the church. And among the laity the notion that a European theology does not suit Asian people persists. Let me say a word about one spokesman for an Asian Christianity.

The Japanese novelist Shūsaku Endō (1923-96) was a deeply committed Christian with a special love for the despised and rejected Jesus. Yet throughout his life he insisted that the Greco-Roman Christianity brought by the missionaries did not suit Japan. He, a Japanese, found himself wearing Western clothing; he would feel more comfortable in a kimono. Endō frequently said that he had no problem with Christianity as such. Distinguishing between faith and culture, he kept searching for a Christianity that would be culturally acceptable to the people of Japan. Later in life his search brought him beyond Japan to India.

Endō's last novel, *Deep River,* is the story of five Japanese who converge on the Ganges in search of "something." One of these, a young Japanese Catholic priest, is a misfit, dissatisfied with the rationalism and legalism of the institutional church and longing for the mysticism of Asia. In India he finds Christ, the suffering servant of Isaiah. We see him carrying the bodies of the dead at the Ganges. We see him celebrating the eucharist in an Indian cultural setting. We see him die as a martyr of charity. Endō quotes Isaiah: "Surely he hath borne our griefs" and "He hath no form nor comeliness."

Such was Endō's poignant appeal for an Asian Christianity. He has brought the problem of inculturation vividly not only to Japan but to the whole Christian world.

LEARNING FROM HISTORY

In his "Opening Speech to the Council" Pope John XXIII spoke of history as "the teacher of life." If we listen attentively to this teacher she will guide us in the path of wisdom and preserve us from repeating the disastrous mistakes of the past.

One of the most unfortunate tragedies of Christian history was the great schism that separated Rome and Constantinople. The definitive break came with an act of excommunication. On July 16, 1054, the papal legate Humbert hurled on the altar of Hagia Sophia in Constantinople a document that excommunicated Patriarch Michael Cerularius. The patriarch, in turn, anathematized the papal delegation. Violent language was used on both sides—"wild pigs," "impious men," "cockle of heresy," and so on. In this way the Christian world was tragically divided. At the time of the Second Vatican Council, Pope Paul VI and Patriarch Athenagoras made great efforts to heal the wound, and efforts for reconciliation continue. But complete union has not yet been achieved. We must be careful not to repeat such a tragic mistake. What lesson does history teach us?

First: One of the greatest discoveries of the twentieth century was the art of dialogue. We have learned, at least in principle, that problems are solved not by violence but by listening and talking. Western theologians who wish to dialogue with Asia (and in particularly those who feel called to investigate Asian theologians) must apply to Asian religions the teaching that the Second Vatican Council applies to dialogue with other Christians:

> We must come to understand the outlook of our separated brethren. Study is absolutely required for this, and should be pursued with fidelity to truth and in a spirit of good will.[22]

Who can deny that these wise words apply to our dialogue with Hinduism and Buddhism? Study, carried on with fidelity to the truth and in a spirit of good will, is absolutely required. Did not the council urge us "to learn by sincere and patient dialogue what treasures a bountiful God has distributed among the nations of the earth?"[23]

Second: As problems are not solved by violence, neither are they solved by excommunication.[24] The council, giving pride of place to dialogue within the church, deliberately avoided anathemas. If the Roman Catholic Church, forgetful of the council, were to excommunicate and anathematize Asian theologians, it could cause a rift even more tragic than that which separated East from West in the eleventh century.

As Rome seeks reconciliation with Constantinople, with Geneva and with Canterbury, we hope that the task of deepening its union with the emerging Christianity of Delhi, Beijing and Tokyo will not fall into the background. The Asian church, once a small mustard seed, will soon become a huge tree and the birds of the air will build nests in its branches. We hope that Rome will be open to dialogue, manifesting a love that "bears all things, believes all things, hopes all things, endures all things" (1 Cor 13:7) "so that they may be one, as we are one, I in them and you in me, that they may become completely one, so that the world may know that you have sent me" (Jn 17:23).

SIX

Asian Meditation

———— ————

THINKING AND NO-THINKING

In the twentieth century Asian meditation swept into the Western world captivating the minds and hearts of millions of people. For meditation is built into the very culture of Asia. Whether one practices yoga in India, or t'ai-chi in China, or Zen in Japan, whether one practices the way of tea, the way of the bow, or the way of flower arrangement, one begins with, or ends with, a meditation that draws one into deep areas of psychic life that are ordinarily unconscious. In this way one comes to the state of *seishin tōitsu* (usually translated into English as "one-pointedness") and acquires great psychic power.

精神統一

In this process there is no discursive thinking. One lets go of all reasoning and imagining in order to enter into a new world of silence where with great joy one discovers one's original face, one's true self.

There are many kinds of meditation in Asia, but basic to all is the breath. One learns deep, rhythmical, abdominal breathing. This takes time. Many years pass before one learns to sit like Mount Fuji, getting in touch with the life force and allowing the energy (the *ki* or *chi*) to flow freely through the body. Now one is in touch with the energy of the vast cosmos. This energy flows through the top of the head to the outermost reaches of the universe and down through the spine and the anus to the inmost depths of the earth.

The development of Western culture was quite different. Here from the time of the Greeks the emphasis was on thinking. Western meditation was enacted at the level of analytical thought, discursive reasoning and rigorous logic—all of which led to remarkable cultural achievements in mathematics, science, philosophy and theology. The art of no-thinking, it is true, was not totally absent. Teresa of Avila taught her sisters that in contemplative prayer one should not think much but love much. But she was talking to mystics or potential mystics.

Until the middle of the twentieth century religious meditation was an activity of the rational mind. Novices and seminarians were taught to think, to use "the three powers of the soul"—the memory, the understanding and the will. Practically, they were asked to recall a scene from the gospel, to reflect on its inherent teaching and to make prayers or colloquies to Jesus or Mary or to the Father. Very good prayer. But seldom were they guided into those deep areas of the psyche where silence and wordlessness reign and one experiences the presence of the living God. Contemplative prayer was for a few chosen souls. Fools must not rush in where angels fear to tread.

THE MARRIAGE

As the twentieth century went on, Western people began to feel surfeited with rationality and thinking. Like the frustrated Hamlet they cried, "Words, words, words." Like Hamlet's distressed mother they said, "The lady protests too much, methinks." Too many words, too much protesting, too much of what people called a head trip. This frustration became more and more neurotic as society was deluged with information, information, information—from television, radio, Internet, e-mail, mobile phones and the rest. Yes, information is fine. But what about the richness of silence? What about wordless wisdom? What about the human capacity to wonder? Perceptive people began to ask if traditional Asian culture had something to offer, the traditional Asian culture that is fast disappearing in the communications explosion and the craze for money.

First on the scene were the psychologists.

Early in the century Jung had pointed to the split between the conscious and the unconscious mind in the Western world. The conscious mind, he maintained, was highly developed while the unconscious lagged behind. Bede Griffiths saw this well. As an Oxford don he was living from one half of his soul, the conscious, rational level, and he needed to discover the other half, the unconscious, intuitive dimension. "I wanted to experience in my life," he writes, "the marriage of these two dimensions

of human existence, the rational and intuitive, the conscious and unconscious, the masculine and the feminine. I wanted to find the way to the
marriage of East and West."[1] He goes on to make an extraordinary, if
characteristic, claim: "The future of the world depends on the marriage
of these two minds, the conscious and the unconscious, the rational and
the intuitive, the active and the passive."[2] Griffiths then immersed himself in Indian spirituality to find integration and a deeper understanding
of the gospel.

Then the scientists.

With the discoveries of relativity and quantum physics scientists became increasingly dissatisfied with the old analytical thinking that made
divisions, distinctions, separations, and led to a radical dualism. Their
research was leading them to see reality whole, to reject a naive objectivity that saw the universe "out there" and made a clear-cut separation
between the observer and the observed. Now they were impressed and
astonished at the oneness of all things, the interconnectedness of all things.
They began to describe the universe with words like *web* and *net*. Furthermore, they became more and more preoccupied with consciousness
and energy, seeing the universe as a field of energy somehow penetrated
by consciousness. We human beings have too long been alienated from
the universe from which we have been born and which is our home.
Such were the conclusions of some thoughtful scientists. And much of
what they said seemed to fit with the perennial wisdom of pre-Renais-
sance Europe and with the intuitions of Eastern mystics.

Then the religious people.

Many Jews and Catholics who felt drawn to mysticism became Buddhists and are now leaders in a vibrant meditation movement that is
gaining momentum in the Western world. Other Catholics with mystical inclinations felt frustrated by an institutional church that had failed
to introduce them to the rich mystical tradition of Christianity. Their
leaders, they claimed, were quite incapable of guiding them along the
path of mysticism. The institutional church itself, after a brief period of
enlightenment under the inspiration of Pope John XXIII, had fallen into
the old legalism, putting its emphasis on ethics, particularly sexual ethics, and ruthlessly insisting that theologians subscribe to the right formulas and use the correct words, or pay the price. While paying eloquent lip service to dialogue, church leaders made Freudian slips that
revealed their abysmal ignorance of anything Buddhist. Where was the
mysticism? Was the church, a religion of the spirit under Pope John, was
this church becoming a religion of the law? Such was the anxious questioning of mystically inclined Catholics.

Yet many prophetic Christians were open to dialogue and willing to learn. Following the Second Vatican Council they saw the work of the Holy Spirit in the rich culture and ancient religions of Asia. They studied in Asia or under Asian teachers. They set about integrating Zen and yoga, vipassana and transcendental meditation into the Christian life, drawing inspiration from Thomas Merton, Bede Griffiths, Enomiya-Lassalle and others.

The great challenge was to unite Asian meditation with a deep commitment to Jesus Christ, to the scriptures and to the Christian tradition. This these pioneers did by rediscovering the Christian mystical tradition. They turned to the desert fathers, the apophatic mystics, the hesychasts, Eckhart and Tauler, Teresa and John. Now we see the growth of a new mysticism at once deeply traditional and deeply influenced by Asia. Already innumerable Christians pray by repeating a mantra. Others imitate the Russian pilgrim by reciting the Jesus prayer. Others are drawn into the mystical silence of the cloud of unknowing. Others gaze with faith at the icon, the window through which they see the imageless God. Others breathe, or remain breathless with adoration, before the mystery of the eucharist.

In this great encounter between East and West we see that the Semitic tradition has much to offer to Asia. In *Awakening to Prayer* the Japanese Carmelite Ichirō Okumura tells us how the French writer Andre Malraux, visiting Engakuji, the exquisite Zen temple in Kamakura, was deeply impressed by the lofty spirituality of the place but remarked that *he did not find the sacred.* Okumura then distinguishes between the spiritual and the sacred. "The Oriental sages climb the lofty mountain of detachment from the world; they breathe the pure air of the heights"— but true holiness is beyond all this and belongs to God.[3] Here is the contribution of the Semitic religions. "Come no closer! Remove the sandals from your feet, for the place on which you stand is holy ground . . . And Moses hid his face, for he was afraid to look at God" (Ex 3:6). "Holy, holy, holy is the Lord of hosts; the whole earth is full of his glory" (Is 6:3).

Perhaps the vocation of Jews and Christians is to bring the sense of the holy to Kyoto and Kamakura without destroying the lofty spirituality that is there. The consummation of the marriage between the sacred and the spiritual is the great ideal in the meeting of East and West.

ZEN GOES WEST

At the Parliament of Religions in 1893 the spokesman for Zen Buddhism, the Rinzai Abbot Shaku Sōen (1859-1919), made little impression because of his inadequate command of English. With him, however, was a young disciple who was to shock the religious world with powerful books and eloquent lectures. Suzuki Daisetsu, known to the West as Dr. Daisetz T. Suzuki (1870-1966), was at once a profound scholar and a brilliant popularizer. Married to an American, he studied the psychology of William James and while writing learned commentaries on the Buddhist Sutras he told amusing and outrageous Zen stories to a fascinated American audience. Together with Heinrich Dumoulin I attended one of his lectures in Tokyo shortly before his death in 1966. He spoke about Pure Land Buddhism. To hear his simple yet profound words about the mercy of Amida and about death and rebirth in the Pure Land—this was a moving and unforgettable experience for both of us. I subsequently learned that though Suzuki spoke to the world about Zen, the Pure Land was his first love.

While Suzuki was speaking to the Western world, a group of Japanese philosophers in Kyoto were reflecting on Zen in the context of German philosophy and Christian thought.[4] These Kyoto scholars were not mere armchair philosophers. Practicing Zen in Buddhist temples or in their own homes they wrote about emptiness and nothingness and the Self both from personal experience and from study of Nagarjuna, Dōgen and the Mahayana tradition. They were familiar with Hegel and Kant and Heidegger. For mysticism they turned to Meister Eckhart, whose writings, they claimed, were close to Zen. And, of course, they quoted the Bible. Mystical theology might have responded to them, but alas, mystical theology in the West was at a low ebb. The Kyoto school has not yet received the theological attention it deserves.

THE PRACTICE OF ZEN

In the middle of the twentieth century the emphasis shifted from philosophy to practice. Westerners flocked to Japan. They sat for hours or days in the lotus, grappling with *mu* and with Zen koans, enduring the rigors of the intensive retreat known in Japanese as *sesshin*. Some claimed that they reached enlightenment and found the true self. At the same time Zen masters moved to the West, setting up meditation halls where they trained disciples. Zen became an important spiritual movement, attracting the attention of Thomas Merton and other spiritual searchers.

As time went on, Catholic priests and sisters began to practice Zen under the guidance of Buddhist masters, causing raised eyebrows in some parts of the world. The pioneer was a German Jesuit. Hugo Lassalle

(1898-1990) became a Japanese citizen, taking the name Enomiya (which means "Temple of Love") and is sometimes called Enomiya-Lassalle. The Zen group Sanbōkyōdan, in which he and many Christians practiced, is little known in Japan, though it has become famous in the West. It has special characteristics that I will outline briefly.

The Sanbōkyōdan (Three Treasures Association) is rooted in the teaching of a very powerful and charismatic Zen Master. Harada Sogaku (1871-1961), whose temple was at Hosshinji near the Japan Sea, was at the same time professor and priest. He broke with tradition by making a synthesis of Sōtō and Rinzai Zen, claiming that in this way he was faithful to Dōgen Zenji, the illustrious founder of Sōtō. Moreover, he reacted against clericalism and opened his *sesshin* to lay people and to foreigners, though many of these, unable to endure his uncompromising severity and his insistence that "nothing means nothing," abandoned their practice. I can recall how Lassalle, who made many *sesshin* under Harada's direction, pursed his lips and said, "He was a mystic!"

Yasutani Hakuun (1885-1973), the successor of Harada, devoted himself more and more to the training of the laity, including foreigners. Like Harada he was an ordained priest, but he severed all ties with established Zen to create Sanbōkyōdan, which became an independent Zen organization. Famous for his unrestrained and almost poetic attacks on the establishment, he talked of professors in Buddhist universities who cheat and bewilder beginners. These professors, he said, were thieves and devils who must fall into hell after death. Yet Yasutani was a great master who led many to enlightenment.

Yasutani's successor Yamada Kōun (1907-1989) was a layman, a businessman who was never ordained priest and had little or no monastic experience. He remained chairman of the board of directors of a large medical clinic till shortly before his death. Under his direction Sanbōkyōdan was more and more oriented toward the laity. Most significant was his insistence that to practice Zen and get enlightenment one need not be a Buddhist. This reassured Catholic priests and sisters as well as other Christians who came in growing numbers to his meditation hall. Yamada wanted Christians to remain Christians. More than once he warned that Zen was on the verge of disappearing in Japan because the monastic leaders were not truly enlightened; but, he went on to say, Zen has a great future within the Catholic church.

From the beginning of his practice Lassalle always found time to celebrate the eucharist in a quiet corner of the Buddhist temple. Now, under Yamada, practicing Catholics were given a separate room where they celebrated the eucharist while the others were chanting the Sutras. It is not surprising, then, that the Zen of Sanbōkyōdan made great progress within Christianity. It seems that it has entered the Catholic church to stay.

Like every prophetic movement, however, Sanbōkyōdan has had its critics, both Buddhist and Christian.

First, let me speak of Buddhist criticism.

Obviously Buddhists of the establishment were not happy with teachers of Sanbōkyōdan who claimed to be the bearers of the only authentic Zen. They did not relish the invectives of a Yasutani, who cried that his Rinzai and Sōtō rivals were unenlightened fools and frauds; nor did they appreciate Yamada's insistence that monastic Zen in Japan is all but defunct. Nevertheless, such invectives are not uncommon in the Zen tradition, and most Buddhists passed them over with a dignified silence.

More important was their insistence that true enlightenment is the profound wisdom that comes to privileged people after many decades of monastic life. A beautiful liturgy, chanting of the Sutras, assiduous study of the scriptures, work in the fields, a vegetarian diet, submission to a rigorous training, the direction of an enlightened master—all play their part. Sanbōkyōdan, they claimed, had plucked enlightenment out of its context and reduced it to a momentary, transforming experience that was open to anyone after a relatively brief training. In short, Sanbōkyōdan had "democratized" Zen and made it look like a New Age experience.[5]

As for Yamada's distinction between Zen and Zen Buddhism and his claim that one need not be a Buddhist to get enlightenment—about this they had (and still have) profound reservations. Before sitting in Zen one makes a deep commitment to the Buddha, the dharma and the sangha—that is, to the Buddha, the teaching and the community. This commitment, orthodox Buddhists claim, enters into the Zen experience and even gives birth to enlightenment. They are skeptical about the Zen of Lassalle and other Christians who are primarily committed to Jesus Christ and the gospel. Such Zen the Buddhist tradition calls "Gedō Zen," which means "heretical Zen," literally "Zen outside the way of the Buddha."

外道禅

So much for the criticisms of Buddhists.

In speaking of Christians I need not mention those who reject all dialogue with Buddhism. Only let me speak of Yamada's Christian disciples. Almost all of these had the highest esteem and reverence for the master. However, some did say that he was not ecumenical in the ordinary sense of the word. He was not really interested in interfaith dialogue. This was because he was convinced that the Zen enlightenment to which he led his disciples was the core and center of all religions, including Christianity. He found plenty of Zen in the gospel, but he did not see that the gospel had something to offer to Zen. Probably he thought that Zen had nothing to learn from the mysticism of Hinduism, Islam, Judaism and Christianity.

Such were the criticisms or hesitations of Buddhists and Christians.

And yet, however valid these criticisms may be, the fact remains that many people, East and West, Christian and Jew, have been led by Zen to a self-realization they did not find in their own tradition. Christians have claimed that, far from weakening their commitment to Jesus Christ and the gospel, this experience has deepened their Christian faith, even giving them new insights into the words of sacred scripture. Some Jews make similar claims. All in all, it is difficult to deny that Zen will play an important role (indeed, is already playing an important role) in the new religious consciousness that is slowly evolving in the whole world.

At the same time, Christians who practice Zen are faced with theological problems that cannot be sidestepped. For we see here the meeting of two living traditions in living people. Zen puts great store on a tradition that stems from Shakyamuni the Buddha and has been transmitted through a long line of patriarchs and teachers to the present day. Christianity—particularly in its Orthodox and Catholic forms—puts great stress on a tradition that has been transmitted through the centuries from the apostles of Jesus. When these two traditions meet in one person who takes direction from a Buddhist teacher while celebrating the eucharist and living the gospel—what happens? Can it be said that Buddhist and Christian share a common experience? Or must we agree with Buddhists who say that the Zen of the Christian is Gedō Zen, different from that of the bodhisattva who walks the path of the Buddha?

Let me now consider this question.

EMPTINESS

One of the most important scriptural texts for the Buddhist-Christian dialogue is the second chapter of the Epistle to the Philippians, where St. Paul, probably quoting an ancient Christian hymn, speaks of the *kenosis* or self-emptying of Jesus. The context is practical. Paul is telling the Philippians to be unselfish, to think about others, and to put on the mind of Jesus by emptying themselves as Jesus emptied himself.

It is easy to see why this text appeals to Zen Buddhists. For central to all Zen practice is the process of emptying oneself of attachment and clinging and grasping of any kind. One even lets go of imagining and thinking and reasoning. One may sit in the lotus just breathing, lengthening the exhalation so as to empty oneself all the more. Or one may repeat the word *mu* with the output of the breath—muuuuuuuuu. Just that. And eventually, when one has reached a point of radical emptiness, the true self rises up with the overwhelming joy of enlightenment. The process is one of total emptiness leading to total fullness like the *todo y nada* of St. John of the Cross.[6]

Now the hymn in the Epistle to the Philippians tells us the story of Christ Jesus who, though he was in the form of God, emptied himself totally, taking the form of a slave and becoming human. So radical was the self-emptying of this divine person that he embraced death—and what a death! And then God highly exalted him with the overwhelming joy of resurrection, giving him a name that is above all names so that at the name of Jesus every knee should bend. What a story of total emptiness leading to total fullness!

For the Zen Buddhist this story of the total self-emptying of Jesus is a powerful and inspiring myth, and Jesus is a powerful and inspiring symbol. By imitating the radical self-emptying of Jesus, the Zen Buddhist may die the great death and rise to the highest enlightenment while remaining totally faithful to his or her basic commitment.

For the person with Christian faith, however, this Pauline text is not only a powerful myth, it is also the record of an event that we call the Christ event. Furthermore, Jesus is not only an inspiring symbol, he is also an inspiring historical person who, Christians believe, died on the cross, rose from the dead and is now alive in the world interceding for the human family. This belief in the Incarnation as a historical event is the distinctive feature of Christianity; it leads to a whole spirituality whereby we die and rise with Christ. Paul puts it clearly: "For if we have been united with him in a death like his, we will certainly be united with him in a resurrection like his" (Rom 6:5).

But the question that confronts us here is: How does all this affect one's practice of Zen?

To me it is of the greatest significance that Lassalle insisted on celebrating the eucharist during *sesshin* and that in his Zen center outside Tokyo he placed a massive rock, a truly impressive altar, on which he celebrated the eucharist and expected his successors to do likewise. For it is precisely in the eucharist that the Christian dies with Christ and rises with Christ crying out, as Christians have cried out from the beginning:

"Dying you destroyed our death! Rising you restored our life! Lord Jesus, come in glory!"

The eucharist, then, was at the heart of Lassalle's Zen.

I am aware that many Buddhists do not accept Lassalle Zen and call it Gedō Zen. I am also aware that many Christian practitioners say that Lassalle's experience of Zen was shallow. Nevertheless, I believe that for all his defects he had the true Christian vision. He was open to the marriage of Christianity and Zen in the depths of his own being.

INTERRELIGIOUS MEDITATION

In the challenging search for one world, interreligious dialogue has already played a significant role, one that will become more and more important as time goes on. But even more challenging than interreligious dialogue is the next step: interreligious prayer and meditation. Here John Paul II gave great leadership to the world when, in October 1986, he invited leaders of all religions to pray together for peace at Assisi. His bold initiative opened the way for religious gatherings in which Buddhists and Jews and Christians sit together in an imageless meditation that goes beyond words and letters and doctrines to the great mystery that unites us and makes us one. I have already spoken of the universal wisdom and the perennial philosophy that are the common heritage of humanity. In meditation we can search for this wisdom and relish it, always retaining our cherished identity and our personal commitment.

Let me give an example of meditation that is interreligious and can be practiced by men and women with no formal religion whatever.

Elaine MacInnes is a Canadian Catholic sister who practiced Zen for many years, first under the direction of Enomiya-Lassalle and then under the direction of Yamada Kōun. Now she teaches meditation to prisoners in the U.K. She maintains that in order to meditate one has only to be a human being. She, and those who work with her, teach the meditators to count the exhalations of the breath until they can "just sit" with a silent body and a silent mind. In this way the light that dwells within everyone is awakened. Sister Elaine quotes a prisoner's letter: "I know now that the spiritual child is sleeping inside all of us. All beings, no matter how reactionary, fearful, dangerous or lost, can open themselves to the sacred within and become free even in prison. Prison is the perfect monastery."[7] Sister Elaine speaks of remarkable transformations of consciousness, or, if you will, conversions of heart.

And let me describe a personal experience.

While teaching in Sophia University in Tokyo I offered a course in meditation. It was open to everyone, and Buddhists, Hindus, Muslims, Jews, Christians and agnostics turned up. I assured them that it was not my intention to interfere with the religious convictions of anyone. My aim was that we should meditate together to find what we had in common.

We began with Thich Nhat Hanh's miracle of mindfulness. There are two ways to wash dishes. The first is to wash dishes in order to have clean dishes, and the second is to wash the dishes in order to wash the dishes. So wash the dishes in order to wash the dishes. Be mindful! Do what you are doing! When you walk, walk. When you sit, sit. When you breathe, breathe. And so on. "Do not be anxious about tomorrow, for tomorrow will be anxious for itself. Today's trouble is enough for today" (Mt 6:34). Live in the here and now like the flowers of the field and the birds of the air. This is meditation in action.

We also used mantra meditation, repeating a word or a sound. Some students liked the word *Love* or *Good*, or some who believed would repeat the word *God*. I explained that there are two levels in the human psyche, an upper level of anxious thinking and dualistic reasoning and a deeper level of unitive and peaceful silence. Think of the hand with its five fingers and one palm. Human consciousness is like that. The top level is dualistic; the deeper level is unitive. And so amid the swirl and noise of central Tokyo one can breathe gently and rhythmically or quietly repeat one's mantra, thus moving from the dualistic phenomenal world to the unitive silent world.

I found that many students understood this very well. They said they could move to the deeper realm—but only for a moment.

A powerful meditation that was fun for everyone was the Zen koan

Every day is a good day *(Nichinichi kore kōjitsu)*

日 日 是 好 日

I told the students just to repeat the words. "Don't think and reason about them. If you do, you are lost. You'll say: 'It isn't a good day. It is raining. I flunked my exams. I was rejected by my boyfriend or my girlfriend. My mother died. How can you say it is a good day?'"

Thinking has to stop. Just repeat the koan. It is, if you wish, an act of faith.

So we sat silently in class, interiorly reciting these words. Some students went on to recite them all the time, while sitting in the train or standing at the bus stop. "Every day is a good day." And then it happened in a few cases that they broke through with great joy to a deep conviction that *Every day is a good day. It's true! It's true! Life is worth living! Would that the whole world knew it!* Such a breakthrough changed their lives.

That every day is a good day is an act of faith that is common to all the religions and perhaps to the whole of humanity. The sentence itself is Buddhist, being a Zen koan composed by a wise old Chinese master who believed in the universal presence of the Buddha nature. For those who believe in the Bible every day must be a good day because God is good and after creating each of the seven days God saw that they were exceedingly good. But *it is above all an act of faith*. We have no rational proof that every day is a good day and plenty of evidence to the contrary. Perhaps it is a faith etched deeply on the heart of every human being, a faith that made the poet Alexander Pope cry out: "Hope springs eternal in the human breast!"

Be that as it may, meditation that brings us together and leads to universal wisdom without weakening our individual commitment—this is the way of the future. To accept such meditation may demand a leap in consciousness, as I have experienced.

Some decades ago I remember speaking to a French Jesuit in Paris. He told me that the great religious danger in France was what he called "an atheistic mysticism." At that time I was impressed. But now, after my experience in Sophia University, I heartily disagree. I believe that this seemingly atheistic mysticism can lead to universal wisdom, to transformation of consciousness and ultimately to God.

Let me add a corollary.

After "Every day is a good day" I suggested my own koan: Every person is a good person. This was more challenging and difficult; nor was it very successful. Alas, there is something in human nature that rebels against such a koan. Yet it must be true. If only we could come to the conviction that every person is a good person we would be truly wise with the foolishness that is wisdom.

TOWARD MYSTICISM

From what has been said it will be clear that Asian meditation leads beyond the rational consciousness to a deep level of psychic life that is traditionally called mystical. The whole culture of Asia—its architecture, its painting, its calligraphy, its poetry, its religion—proclaims this mystical dimension. Not without reason did Western explorers of earlier centuries speak romantically of "the mystic East."

Now, just as Asia, overrun by industrialization and the craze for money, is in danger of losing its mysticism, Asian meditation is pouring into a Western world that is hungering desperately for the things of the spirit. I have said that we are at a turning point in history, that our present civilization is collapsing, that a new consciousness is evolving, that a new humanism is coming to birth. Who can deny that Asian mysticism, joining hands with a long-neglected Western counterpart, will be a decisive factor in building the new world?

A new mysticism will make its impact on philosophy and theology and law. It will shake the very foundations of the institutional religion we have known. Prophets will appear who, like Jeremiah, are called "to pluck up and to pull down, to destroy and to overthrow, to build and to plant" (Jer 1:10).

Yet "all will be well, and all will be well, and all manner of thing will be well," for "there shall once more be heard the voice of mirth and the voice of gladness, the voice of the bridegroom and the voice of the bride, the voice of those who sing, as they bring offerings to the house of the LORD" (Jer 33:11).

SEVEN

Searching for Mysticism

HUNGRY SHEEP

When Vivekananda went West to teach the wisdom of India, he found a society of men and women who were like sheep without a shepherd. The decline of traditional religion and the consequent loss of faith had created a spiritual vacuum and a great hunger for meaning. Confronted with the baffling mystery of existence and dissatisfied with the answers they had received from their forbears, people were searching, searching, searching. Nor has this search come to an end. It continued throughout the twentieth century, it continues today, and it will undoubtedly continue in the twenty-first and twenty-second centuries. It has led many searchers to the mystical religions of the East and the esoteric tradition of the West.

And the question immediately arises, Why did these earnest searchers not find answers in the orthodox Jewish and Christian traditions? Why did they desert their religious heritage? What had happened?

To answer this question it is helpful to return to Lonergan's distinction between the cultural superstructure and the mystical core of a religion. Religious people can be so preoccupied with the cultural superstructure that they miss the mystical core. Or the cultural superstructure can decline and become corrupt. Or it can simply become the irrelevant, outdated product of another age. Then people whose faith was pinned to the cultural superstructure find themselves rootless and lost. They are like hungry sheep who look up and are not fed. They look elsewhere for nourishment, wisdom, truth and meaning.

Now Christianity was originally a Semitic religion, but its cultural superstructure for almost two thousand years was largely the work of

Greece and Rome. Consequently, it contained both the pearls and the garbage of Greco-Roman civilization. It produced treasures of philosophy and theology that will never die. It created art, music, poetry and architecture that have captivated the civilized world. It gave birth to a spiritual literature that will forever nourish the mystics of the world. Truly magnificent were its achievements.

Yet this same civilization had its shadow side, its ugly characteristics that came more and more to the surface as time went on: a history of religious wars, the cruelty of the Inquisition, the injustice of the witch hunts, the sins of the clergy, the clerical craze for money and power, the hypocrisy of the churches, the covert political involvement of religious leaders. Furthermore, as the philosophy of Plato and Aristotle was superseded and as the structures of the Roman Empire collapsed, unenlightened religious leaders seemed to make desperate efforts to preserve the cultural superstructure by excommunicating, anathematizing and persecuting prophetic people who dared criticize the externals of their religion.

The decline of the cultural superstructure began early in the history of Christianity, reaching a climax with the Protestant Reformation. Decline continued through the twentieth century, and the end of the century witnessed a dramatic collapse of the church in traditionally Catholic countries like Ireland and Poland. I am reminded of Mark Antony, "O, what a fall was there, my countrymen! Then I, and you, and all of us fell down."

Let me emphasize that I am speaking of the cultural superstructure, not of the essence of faith. There were, and are, plenty of committed Christians, lay and clerical, who pierce through the rind to taste and relish the delicious fruit. They see that the cultural superstructure is striving, however poorly, to express the central message that God loves us and we are called to love God. They grow in their love for Jesus Christ yesterday, today and the same forever. They commemorate the death and resurrection of Jesus as they chant at the eucharist: "Christ has died; Christ is risen; Christ will come again." They find mysticism in Christianity. If the old cultural superstructure collapses, they see that their task is to build a new one.

But, as I have said, there were other serious searchers whose faith was pinned to a superstructure that they saw collapsing around them. Disillusioned and thinking that Judaism and Christianity had no mysticism, they looked for spiritual nourishment in the Oriental religions and in the esoteric tradition of the West. About these I will now speak briefly.

JOURNEY TO INDIA

In the middle of the twentieth century thousands of young men and women flocked to India. They were, if you will, rootless and restless—hippies and drop-outs from society—but they were searching for something they could not find in their own culture. Some wandered around India with packs on their backs, as free from care as the flowers of the field and the birds of the air that our heavenly Father loves and protects. They wanted to savor the spirituality and the poverty of India, so different from the wealthy and anxious sophistication of the declining West. Others, like the Beatles, visited the ashram of the Maharishi Mahesh Yogi, whose transcendental meditation had captivated and inspired thousands. Others visited the Ramakrishna Mission in Calcutta. Others sought wisdom at the ashram of Aurobindo in Pondicherry. Yet others went north to Dharmsala to listen to the wise teaching of the exiled Dalai Lama. They were searching for the holy man or woman—the sadhu or the sannyasin—who would guide them in the way of wisdom and peace.

Many found what they wanted at two Christian centers that radiated to the world the spirituality of India.

One was at Calcutta where Mother Teresa and her sisters gave their lives to serve the poorest of the poor. Here Jews and Christians, Buddhists and Hindus, Muslims and agnostics worked side by side with hippies and doctors and nurses and scholars—caring for the destitute and the dying. Mother Teresa did not speak of a new cultural superstructure (she had not read Lonergan), yet the structure she created was eminently contemporary. No one said that her lifestyle was irrelevant. It was a way of life that talked to the twentieth century in a language the twentieth century understood.

Nor was Mother Teresa's work just humanitarian. She and her sisters spent many hours in silent prayer; they celebrated a vibrant liturgy; they read the scriptures; they modeled their lives on the gospel. They were concerned with the eternal salvation of the dying, who were about to meet their God. Mother Teresa said clearly that in embracing the bodies of the sick and dying they were embracing the body of Christ.

And so the Calcutta of Mother Teresa and her collaborators spoke powerfully to the whole world. It was not that their heroic compassion did a lot to relieve the grinding poverty of India. Rather, it was a witness to the Transcendent. Many anguished searchers found meaning and peace, even when they did not share Mother Teresa's faith.

Another spiritual center that attracted eager searchers was Shantivanam (Forest of Peace), an ashram in South India. Here an English Benedictine monk, once an Oxford don but now a sannyasin, lived a life of prayer and poverty, welcoming all who came.

Bede Griffiths (1906-93) came to India to find the other half of his soul—the intuitive, contemplative, feminine dimension that was much neglected in the West but richly present in traditional India. He grew in the conviction that Western Christianity, like the Western world, was lopsided and overly masculine. It needed the culture and the spirituality of India. Realizing that the westernized church of India must undergo a radical transformation, he writes:

> It has to rethink its theology in Indian instead of Greek terms, and to adapt its organization to Indian instead of Roman models. Even its Semitic base cannot go untouched . . . It has to learn . . . what Hinduism, Buddhism, Taoism and Confucianism have to teach it. Then only will the "marriage" take place between East and West.[1]

As time went on Griffiths became more and more convinced that this marriage was necessary not only for the church of India but for the universal church and for the world. Indeed, the fate of the civilized world, he claimed, depended on the consummation of this marriage.

I spent some time at Griffiths's ashram in the mid 1980s. Every morning after breakfast I visited him in his tiny hut and we talked about everything. For all his saffron robes and bare feet, he remained the English gentleman, the Oxford don—charming, intelligent and witty. When he heard I was a Jesuit, he said with an impish smile, "A vow of special obedience to the pope? That's practically immoral these days!" And he cupped his hand over his mouth like a naughty boy who has said too much. Then he went on more seriously, "The present pope is the last of the 'big popes.' After him the church will decentralize."

But how to explain the broad influence of Shantivanam? Why did it attract such a motley group of searchers?

Surely it was that Bede Griffiths enacted within himself the marriage of East and West. He retained all that was good in Western Christianity, down to the philosophy of Aristotle and the scholastics; and he united this with a profound grasp of the Vedas, the Upanishads and the Gita. He was at once the brilliant Western intellectual and the Indian sadhu (holy man). He saw that Christianity could only meet the Asian religions at the level of a mysticism that goes beyond words and images and forms to the cloud of unknowing, the hidden power from which all created being comes forth.

Griffiths himself recited the "Jesus prayer" all through his life until it spontaneously recited itself and continued to do so while he lay dying. I was at Shantivanam during Holy Week and took part in the liturgy. The outer forms, the cultural superstructure of flowers and incense and chanting—all this was beautifully Indian; but the mystical core was transcultural and perennial. In union with Christians of the first centuries we proclaimed the mystery of faith: "Christ has died. Christ is risen. Christ will come again."

The marriage between East and West may well be stormy. Even when bride and bridegroom long for union, wicked outside forces may strive to keep them apart. But the marriage will be consummated, and it will bear much fruit.

A PERILOUS JOURNEY

But let me return to the pilgrims who flocked to India with bright hopes and high ideals. I have said that some found the spirituality they sought in Hindu ashrams or in close encounters with gurus like Bede Griffiths or at Mother Teresa's center in Calcutta. Others, however, came to grief, misled by false prophets or deceived by the wiles of satanic powers.

For the fact is that one who aspires to enter the mystical path must be prepared for conflict of a subtle kind. Bede Griffiths speaks of the *asuras*, which in Hinduism are the equivalent of the evil spirits and demons of the Christian tradition. That these powers of darkness are at work in the world of today Griffiths does not doubt:

> It cannot be too strongly affirmed that these are real powers
> which act on the unconscious . . . that is, on the lower levels
> of consciousness, bringing man into subjection to the powers
> of nature. The fact that modern man does not recognize them
> is one of the many signs that he is under their power; only
> when they are recognized can they be overcome.[2]

In speaking this way Griffiths is faithful to both the Hindu and the Christian traditions. Until the scientific revolution of the seventeenth century, believing Christians lived in a world that was filled with the presence of God, a world in which conflicting forces of good and evil were at work. The Book of Revelation was not forgotten. The Pauline epistles, which speak of "the elemental spirits of the universe" (Col 2:20) and "our struggle against the cosmic powers of this present darkness, against the spiritual forces of evil in the heavenly places" (Eph 6:12) were not regarded as outdated mythology. The Second Vatican Council taught this unequivocally, stating graphically that "a monumental struggle against the powers of darkness pervades the whole history of humanity."[3] And elsewhere the council tells us that "all of human life, whether individual or collective, shows itself to be a dramatic struggle between good and evil, between light and darkness."[4]

This is the world into which many searchers, sometimes sincere searchers, naively entered.

Now the forces of evil, as Griffiths remarked, influence the lower levels of consciousness, and for this reason their action has to be carefully discerned. When it comes to unmasking the wiles of evil spirits few have been more insightful than Ignatius of Loyola. The enemy of our human nature, he tells us, is like the astute commander of an army who explores the fortifications of a city and makes his attack at the weakest point. What were the weak points of the spiritual searchers who went to India?

Some were led to believe that one can enter mystical states through drugs. The brilliant Aldous Huxley had experimented with mescaline and LSD, claiming that he had found a way to mysticism for the denizens of the brave new world. When the doors of perception are cleansed, he held, one has a vision of naked existence, like that of Adam on the morning of his own creation. What an ideal!

Again, some gurus taught a mysticism of sexuality. Liberated from sexual taboos one can enter, they claimed, into deeply loving relationships that are nothing short of mystical.

Again, some searchers were deceived by the psychic powers or *siddhis* of self-styled gurus. How easily extrasensory perception can masquerade as mysticism! And the desire for such psychic powers can be very powerful, even addictive. It led Faust to do a deal with Mephistopheles. And isn't Faust an archetypal figure?

Many Western searchers were particularly vulnerable because they had rejected their own tradition. Unlike Bede Griffiths, who contracted a marriage with Indian culture and religion, these pilgrims wanted not marriage but divorce. They became rootless and lost. Jung, who watched contemporary psychological development with the greatest interest, insisted that this journey to India was perilous indeed. We human beings cannot reject our past. The consciousness of the West, he held, was different from that of India. The Western person approaches reality with his or her understanding; the yogi approaches reality with breathing, belly and blood. Dialogue, yes; imitation, no. Such was his astute observation.[5]

Be that as it may, while the journey to India led some searchers to wisdom and enlightenment, others ended their journey in disillusionment, psychological collapse and even insanity.

THE ESOTERIC TRADITION

The end of the nineteenth century saw a surge of interest in the occult. Some scholars took a new look at gnosticism, alchemy, astrology, magic, spiritualism, witchcraft and the mystery religions of the Mediterranean world. Others turned East and asked about reincarnation. Others were interested in psychic powers and extrasensory perception. The prophecies of Nostradamus and the writings of Paracelsus became popular reading. Thus began a spiritual movement that has reached a climax today with a New Age that teaches every kind of spirituality from mysticism to Satanism, speaking about psychic healing, channeling, crystal gazing, divination, palmistry, ouijiboards, tarot cards, numerology and anything that might appeal to the disillusioned and rootless searchers of today.

All this has roots in the nineteenth century.

Of great significance was the founding of the Theosophical Society in New York in 1875 by a Russian aristocrat, a colorful personality with more than ordinary psychic powers. Helena Petrovna Blavatsky (1831-91), married at the age of sixteen, quickly fled to Constantinople where she became a bareback rider in a circus. Subsequently she traveled throughout the world, witnessing voodoo ceremonies in New Orleans and studying the Eastern esoteric tradition in Tibet. Her close friend and collaborator, Colonel Olcott, tells us that her first book, *Isis Unveiled,* was written rapidly in a tempestuous burst of inspiration. It shows the somewhat confused influence of Buddhist, Hindu and Tibetan thought and opens the way for *The Secret Doctrine,* which traces the evolution of humankind from a mythological race that inhabited the lost continents of Atlantis and Lemuria. Her seemingly prophetic writings are now discredited, but they appealed greatly to a confused generation that was searching for meaning in the exotic.

Madame Blavatsky died at the house of Annie Besant (1874-1933), who subsequently became president of the Theosophical Society and remained president for twenty-six years. Originally a social reformer, she devoted herself to the task of uniting the occult tradition of the West with Hindu philosophy. At the end she rejected the materialism of her youth and spoke of the human person as "a fragment of the Divinity clothed in matter."

Together with her collaborator, Charles W. Leadbeater, a former Anglican priest, Annie Besant taught that a world teacher, the Lord Maitreya, would become incarnate in this age, just as Krishna and Jesus had become incarnate in their ages. And in their search for this world teacher they found at Madras a young Indian who was to become one of the great spiritual leaders of the twentieth century. Jiddu Krishnamurti (1895-1985), after briefly accepting the messianic role, rejected all organization, all religion, all dogma, to walk his own unique and independent path. Krishnamurti undoubtedly had deep religious experience, accompanied by intense interior suffering. A fascinating speaker, he lectured widely throughout the United States and Europe. His aim was to liberate men and women from the "cages" of institution and dogma through the practice of mindfulness or awareness, a way of meditation that led to the true self.

Today the Theosophical Society, based in Madras, is active in some sixty countries throughout the world. It still speaks of the divine wisdom "channeled" through Madame Blavatsky; its motto is that "there is no religion higher than truth." The Theosophical Society aims at integrating science, religion and philosophy while studying psychic powers, particularly powers of healing. It has developed its own anthropology in dialogue with the esoteric tradition, Eastern philosophy, modern psychology and modern science. Theosophical literature speaks of the gross body, the subtle body, the astral body. It speaks of the chakras through which flows the vital energy known as *prana, ki* and *kundalini*. Together with scientists it investigates psychic phenomena like telepathy, bilocation and out-of-the-body experience. The study goes on.

THE NEW AGE

The search for gurus and sadhus in India and the revival of the esoteric tradition in the West set the stage for the spiritual movement that we call the New Age. This began in California and quickly spread throughout the world. It is very much alive in Japan where I now write, and it is seriously studied by scholars in universities everywhere.[6]

It is difficult, perhaps impossible, to define the New Age because it has no dogma or doctrine that everyone must believe, no institution to which everyone must be committed, no leader whom all must follow, no committee that governs the whole movement. Therefore, it is only partly true to say that New Ageism claims that we are approaching a new stage of evolution, that we are entering into the age of Aquarius, that we are discovering hitherto unknown psychic powers, that we are encountering visitors from outer space, and so on. Some New Agers may hold these things, but not all. The very essence of New Ageism is freedom to follow one's inner light without pressure from exterior dogmas or teachers. The distinguished mythologist Joseph Campbell (1904-87) summed it up in his famous advice to young people, "Follow your bliss!"

One who browses in a New Age bookshop will find information about the occult, about mysticism in all religions, about witchcraft, about tantra and about Satanism. One will find books about Madame Blavatsky, Annie Besant and the Theosophical Society. Krishnamurti, with his rejection of dogma and his total openness, is an important figure. One may find books about science and mysticism. The writings of Stephen Hawking and Fritjof Capra may be there. There will be books about Tibetan Buddhism and the Dalai Lama and about dreams with special reference to Jung. Nor is Christianity neglected. In New Age bookshops I have seen books about Fatima and Medjugorje and the Italian Capuchin Padre Pio together with the works of John of the Cross, Teresa of Avila, Thomas Merton and Teilhard de Chardin. And then there are the gurus of modern India—Bhagwaan Shree Rajneesh, Sai Baba, Mother Meera and others.

From a large variety of guides and teachers and gurus one is free to choose.

POWERS OF DARKNESS

The twentieth century, then, has seen serious and scientific study of the esoteric tradition and of the occult. Thanks to scholars like Carl Jung, Joseph Campbell and Ken Wilber we have a growing knowledge of gnosticism and alchemy; we have new insight into extrasensory perception and the deeper states of consciousness. Historical studies have brought to light the appalling injustice of witch hunts that tortured and killed thousands of innocent women. This increased knowledge can only be helpful in the forward march of humanity.

At the same time the new knowledge has created problems. It has encouraged naive searchers to dabble in the occult, sometimes with horrendous consequences. Krishnamurti's total openness, the New Age rejection of dogma, Joseph Campbell's advice to follow one's bliss—all sound attractive, prophetic and life-giving, but these ideas can leave innocent searchers unprotected and vulnerable before dark forces of evil, making them easy prey to false prophets, who are ravening wolves in sheep's clothing.

Let us remember that Eve was following her bliss when she sank her teeth into the delicious fruit in the Garden of Eden. And Adam followed suit. "You shall be as gods!" What greater bliss could there be?! And was it not a glorious thing to reject the oppressive dogma that crushed their freedom, "Of the tree of the knowledge of good and evil you shall not eat"? Alas, they were tricked by the cunning serpent, who was later called the father of lies; instead of bliss they found themselves ejected from paradise, torn and broken and miserable. Follow your bliss!

And the wily serpent is still slithering around.

In a well-researched book on the powers of darkness and the powers of light John Cornwell devotes some disturbing chapters to a consideration of the demonic.[7] Not that he goes along with the hysterical talk that so often accompanies such writing. He discounts the melodrama, even telling an amusing story of Evelyn Waugh, who thought he was possessed by demons when in fact he was suffering from the alcohol and barbiturates that made up his nightly sleeping draught. But John Cornwell did encounter scholarly and saintly people who spoke of the reality of Satan, of diabolical possession and of the necessity (in rare cases) of exorcism. One is led again to ask the meaning of that story in Mark where Jesus expels the unclean spirits from the demoniac and sends them into a great herd of swine, which rushes down the steep bank and is drowned in the sea.

But John Cornwell is most disturbing when writing about Satanism in today's world. He traces its beginnings to the hippie movement of the late 1960s and early 1970s. At that time it became popular to dabble and experiment in Eastern religions, voodoo, channeling, astrology and all forms of the occult. In 1966 a Church of Satan was founded in California, disseminating a Satanic Bible and elaborating a whole "theology" with the claim that Satan is a much maligned, much misunderstood spiritual reality. Then came the New Age.

Yet the real evil comes to the surface in the Satanic practices and rituals investigated by the Christian Exorcism Study group based in London. We are told of ceremonies in which children have been sexually abused and even murdered and of rituals that are so revolting that they cannot be printed. Most distressing of all is the fact that the people caught up in these Satanist groups were not bad at the beginning. Many of them were young high school or university students who were lonely or sexually deviant or fascinated by the occult. Like Adam and Eve they were deceived.

John Cornwell refers to some of the cults that shocked the Western world, such as the mass suicide of almost a thousand devotees at Jonestown, Guyana. Another such cult shocked Japan in the 1990s.

FALSE PROPHET

On March 20, 1995, Japan was shocked by the news that sarin poison gas had been released on the Tokyo subway during the morning rush hour, killing twelve people and injuring thousands. Police quickly attributed the crime to a new religion, Aum Shinrikyō (Aum Teaching of Supreme Truth), which had stockpiled weapons and chemicals in its commune at the foot of Mount Fuji. The sect was accused of kidnapping, drugging and murdering helpless people and conspiring to commit armed insurrection to overthrow the government. Japan was shocked to the core. What was going on?

Aum Shinrikyō was founded in 1984 by a young acupuncturist who had studied traditional Taoist medicine and who, like many masseurs, was partially blind. Asahara Shōkō was committed to the search for meaning. "What am I living for? What must I do to overcome this sense of emptiness?" he asked. And later he wrote about his search:

> I tried all kinds of practices, such as Taoism, Yoga, Buddhism, incorporating their essence into my training. My goal was supreme spiritual realization and enlightenment. I continued the austere practices with Buddhist texts as my only resort. Finally, I reached my goal in the holy vibration of the Himalayas; I attained supreme realization and enlightenment.[8]

He goes on to say that he attained absolute freedom, happiness and joy, and that he acquired paranormal powers of levitation and of leaving the physical body anywhere and at any time.

Claiming that the Dalai Lama had commissioned him to teach authentic Buddhism in Japan, Asahara began by teaching meditation with special emphasis on the awakening of the *kundalini* and the acquisition of *siddhis* or paranormal powers. Most important of all was *gedatsu*, the highest form of enlightenment. Pictures of the bearded guru sitting splendidly in the lotus attracted many young and highly qualified graduates of Japan's leading universities.

Esoteric Buddhism speaks of a mythical country called Shambhala, from which, some Sutras say, will come the savior who will defeat the infidel and establish the reign of Buddhism. Asahara now claimed that Japan was Shambhala, from which the messiah would come. Furthermore, he read and commented on the Book of Revelation and saw the approach of the great battle of Armageddon. He and his followers who had attained to *gedatsu* must hasten this battle, which was coming at the end of the millennium, a battle in which millions of peopie would die. Hence the weapons of destruction at his compound.

As time went on, guru worship was more and more emphasized. No opposition to the guru was tolerated. Frightening stories of violence, murder, kidnapping and torture have since been told. Then came the subway attack of 1995.

When the police entered the commune near Mount Fuji to arrest Asahara, they found the bearded guru sitting in the lotus, absorbed in meditation.

After this incident and until this very day there was great soul-searching in Japan. Why had this happened? Japan, the safest country in the world, the most highly disciplined country in the world, the country where one could go anywhere without fear of violence—this Japan had overnight become frighteningly dangerous. Questions were asked not only by popular magazines but also by scholarly journals and learned professors. Among the many explanations offered by competent people let me here select the one that seems to me most plausible.

In 1945 Japan collapsed. The Shinto myth of Great Japan (Dai Nippon) descended from the gods and ruled by a divine emperor—this myth for which millions had given their lives—was smashed by the atomic bombs and the American occupation. The emperor was humiliated. Disillusioned soldiers returned from a shattered empire. The military leaders were summarily executed or imprisoned. Left without a myth the country united in the search for one thing: money. Money! money! money! "Economy first" was the slogan. Japan must overtake Britain, overtake Germany, overtake the United States. Total devotion to the company was the ideal, even if family life suffered drastically.

Japan performed its economic miracle. But at what a price! People do not live by bread alone. The leaders of Japan, like the emperors of Rome, had given the people bread and circuses; and the people were not satisfied. They wanted more. *Japan found itself in a great spiritual vacuum that the traditional religions were unable to fill.* Buddhism was in decline. Christianity was hopelessly foreign. People turned to newly founded religions that gave hope with promises of spiritual experience and psychic power.

Into this vacuum stepped Asahara. He himself had been a searcher in the Himalayas; now he restored the myth of Great Japan while teaching yoga and awakening paranormal powers. Sincere people came to him to learn meditation. Some donated all their money to this new sect, only to find themselves trapped in a situation from which they could not escape.

But what was the Buddhist reaction?

There was an outcry from orthodox Buddhists who said that the doctrine of Asahara was *heretical teaching* or *jakyō*.

邪教

Buddhists, it should be noted, place great importance on correct teaching. The dharma, handed down from teacher to disciple through many generations, is all important. The true Buddhist makes a total commitment to the Buddha *and the dharma*. Without the dharma there is no Buddhism.

Now Asahara, Buddhists claimed, had departed from the dharma to teach a mishmash of esoteric Buddhism, Hinduism and Christianity. His teaching could not be called Buddhist. It was heretical. It was not the way of the Buddha.

And here there is an important message. For it is fashionable today to say that spirituality is necessary, but not religion. Or to say with Krishnamurti that all authoritative teaching or dogma is useless baggage. Or to say with Joseph Campbell that we must follow our bliss without the constraint of religious teaching. The story of Asahara gives the lie to this. Teaching is important.

The fact is that there is no authentic Buddhist experience without the dharma, as there is no authentic Jewish experience without the Torah, no authentic Islamic experience without the Qur'an, no authentic Hindu experience without the Vedas, no authentic Christian experience without the gospel. The cultivation of experience without sound teaching can lead to disaster.

Thinking people in Japan know that the problem is not solved by the dissolution of Aum Shinrikyō and the trial of its leaders. Japan needs its myth. Money is not enough. Nor is Japan alone in this frightening predicament. Other wealthy countries are saying with the Book of Revelation, "I am rich, I have prospered, and I need nothing," without realizing that they are wretched, pitiable, poor, blind and naked. And, alas, China as it moves into the twenty-first century is following in the footsteps of Japan. Money! Money! Money!

DISCERNING THE SPIRITS

The Second Vatican Council reminds us that the Holy Spirit is at work in the whole world. In all authentic religion, in art and music and poetry, in science and technology—everywhere we can find the action of the Spirit. The Spirit, moreover, is at work in the hearts of all men and women—the voice of conscience is always echoing in the depth of the human mind and heart, telling us what to do and what not to do.

At the same time there are other spirits at work in the world and in our hearts. These are the dark forces of evil. "A monumental struggle against the powers of darkness pervades the whole of human history." "All of human life, whether individual or collective, shows itself to be a dramatic struggle between good and evil, between light and darkness."[9]

At times this struggle may be a pitched battle—"like a roaring lion your adversary the devil prowls around, looking for someone to devour" (1 Pt 5:8); but more often the forces of evil are like a crafty enemy who deceives his adversary in order to destroy. "But I am afraid that as the serpent deceived Eve by its cunning, your thoughts will be led astray from a sincere and pure devotion to Christ," writes Paul (2 Cor 11:3); he goes on to say that "even Satan disguises himself as an angel of light" (2 Cor 11:14). And the First Epistle of St. John warns us to discern the spirits with great care: "Beloved, do not believe every spirit, but test the spirits to see whether they are from God: for many false prophets have gone out into the world" (1 Jn 4:1).

From all that has been said in this chapter it will be clear that many sincere people have been deceived, sometimes with horrendous consequences. This makes it necessary to look once again at the traditional science of discernment and to apply its rules to ourselves and to the world around us.

To understand the science of discernment it is useful to consider the human person not just as body and soul, as in the Aristotelian tradition, but as

> Body
> Mind
> Spirit

This terminology is used by St. Paul and by some of the early fathers. Particularly helpful is the distinction between the human mind and the human spirit.

By the mind I mean the reasoning and thinking faculty that receives its data from the senses. It is here at the gateway between mind and spirit, said the old science of discernment, that the evil one takes his stand. By the human spirit, on the other hand, I mean the center of the soul, the inner sanctum, the true self, the cave of the heart, the mystical core, the point at which the human meets the divine. This is for God alone. The evil spirit cannot enter unless invited to do so by a free act of the will. Such was the traditional teaching.

The old authors insist that the evil spirit is like a chained dog. He can bark and howl, but he cannot harm the person who ignores his existence. Ignatius says something similar. The enemy, he tells us, is a weakling. Face the tempter boldly, do the opposite to what he suggests, and you have nothing to fear.

But why should anyone invite the evil spirit to enter the inner sanctum?

Here we are faced with the great mystery of evil. People advanced in the mystical life sometimes say that they have experienced the freedom to choose evil. At the very core of their being they have felt existentially that they could change their fundamental option and turn from God to Satan. This is a harrowing experience. Yet more often those who deliberately open their minds and hearts to the forces of evil are people with powerful addictions or compulsions, people who are willing to pay any price to get what they want. Faust sold his soul for psychic power. Indeed, lust for power is the greatest temptation, much more dangerous than addiction to alcohol or drugs or sex or gambling. Such is the doctrine of Ignatius, who speaks of the two standards—the standard of Satan calling to pride and power, and the standard of Jesus calling to humiliation and powerlessness.

One who well understood the occult was Shakespeare. "Caesar, beware the ides of March," cried the soothsayer. And then Macbeth! Crossing the windswept heath amid thunder and lightning the brave Scottish soldier met the foul and ugly witches. "All hail, Macbeth, that shalt be king hereafter." It matters not whether the witches were "out there" or whether they were invisible forces. What matters is that powers of darkness were acting on the unconscious of Macbeth, focusing on his tragic fault, his desire to become king. And as time went on, the gallant soldier became a ruthless tyrant, destroying anyone who stood in his way.

In this way forces of evil, like the astute general, look for the tragic fault in the human unconscious, deceiving those who listen and get involved. The end is destruction.

Yet it would be a mistake to think that forces of evil act only on people like Macbeth. The Christian tradition insists that Satan is active in the mystical life, trying to deceive those who have given their all to God. Indeed, St. John of the Cross tells us that the fall of the mystic is of more value to Satan than that of thousands of others. Satan is particularly active, the Carmelite saint tells us, in the lives of those who claim to see visions and hear voices. Such people are easily deceived.

It is not possible here to enter into the role of Satan in the mystical life. Only let me say that in today's world many visionaries claim to have seen the Virgin Mary, to have heard voices and to have been entrusted with secrets about the future. In accordance with the Christian tradition all such claims must be subjected to the most rigorous discernment.

TOWARD A NEW MYSTICISM

The twentieth century, then, has witnessed a spectacular spiritual search throughout the world. This search has had its pitfalls, its dangers, its aberrations. At times it has been infiltrated by powers of evil. But it will certainly lead us to profound wisdom, for the words of sacred scripture must be fulfilled, "The one who asks receives, the one who searches finds, and to everyone who knocks the door will be opened" (Mt 7:8). We do not doubt that good will triumph, for we have been assured that "the one who is in you is greater than the one who is in the world" (1 Jn 4:4).

I believe that through all the revolutions and turmoil we have witnessed, and are still witnessing, there is a search for a new mysticism. Let me then explain what I mean by *mysticism*, and what I mean by *new*.

I have already said that it is useful to speak of the human person as body, mind and spirit. Corresponding to this, we can speak of three levels of consciousness,

> the sensible
> the rational
> the spiritual

The sensible and the rational were greatly developed in the twentieth century. Think of the computer! Even as I write these lines, the Pathfinder spacecraft sends more and more information from Mars, and my morning paper claims that a robot is doing a better job than the brightest graduates of Harvard or Yale. This may well be true. And what is it telling us?

Surely it is telling us to grow, to develop, to move toward an area of experience that is peculiarly human, that is to say, toward the spiritual. Are we not now called to save ourselves from enslavement to robots by moving toward a transcendental consciousness—toward ultimate reality, the ground of being, the true self, the ultimate concern, the great mystery that envelops the universe and dwells at the core of our being? The spiritual search that began in the early part of the twentieth century and continues in our day, does it not stem from an immense human hunger for this world of the spirit?

As in the interior castle of Teresa of Avila there are many mansions or dwelling places, so in the world of the spirit there are many levels or realms. The deepest realm I call mystical. This is the center into which no one enters by human effort but only by the call of God. To enter the world of mysticism is a gift. And God, who shows no partiality, offers this gift to people of all religions or of no religion.

I speak of a new mysticism. Not that mysticism in itself is new. It is very old. But certain circumstances in today's world make it possible to speak of a new mysticism.

First is the fact that whereas the mysticism of the past was for an elite of monks or nuns, sadhus or sannyasins, the mysticism of today is for millions of people who are searching. Whereas the mysticism of the past was for celibates who lived in monasteries, the mysticism of today is for married people who work in factories or business corporations or classrooms or kitchens. The mystic of today can no longer separate himself or herself from our harrowing problems of peace and justice and ecology and violence and racism. Indeed, we now know that these problems can never be solved at the level of the mind but only at the level of spirit.

Again, whereas the mystics of the various religions lived separate from one another in splendid isolation, the mystics of today are united in dialogue. Well they know that silent, supraconceptual enlightenment is the place where the religions can meet.

This is not to say that mysticism in all religions is the same. In fact, each religion has its own scriptures, its own commitment and its own path. Even the silent, imageless entrance into the mysterious cloud allows for varieties of experience. But the goal is the same, as the Second Vatican Council said so clearly:

> For all peoples comprise a single community, and have a single origin, since God made the whole human race dwell over the entire face of the earth (Cf. Acts 17:26). One also is their final goal: God.[10]

For this reason we can join hands in the journey toward a common goal where we will together enjoy a final mystical experience. Here we will be the same and different, one and many. Here we will experience unity in diversity.

The challenge, then, that faces the institutional religions is to guide the people to this supreme wisdom. This is not the calling of clerics alone. Everyone has his or her gift. "The wind blows where it chooses, and you hear the sound of it, but you do not know where it comes from or where it goes. So it is with everyone who is born of the Spirit" (Jn 3:8).

PART II

The New Mysticism

EIGHT

Journey of Prayer

PRAYER FOR ALL

If prayer is a hunger, there are many hungry men and women in today's world. So great is the longing for prayer. In a little book about awakening to prayer the Japanese Carmelite Ichirō Okumura writes about the prayer of atheists, claiming that many self-styled atheists—people who would never dream of kneeling in a church or bowing in a temple—are practicing a kind of incipient prayer. Unconsciously they are searching for God. Unconsciously they are seeking the self-transcendence without which their life would have no meaning.[1]

While the great contribution of Buddhism has been its life-giving meditation, prayer is by no means absent from Buddhist life and practice. This is particularly true of Pure Land Buddhism, which advocates calling on the name of the Buddha in a practice known as the *nenbutsu*, represented by the characters

念仏

With great faith and trust in the Buddha Amida the believer recites or chants the words *Namu Amida Butsu*

南無阿弥陀仏

The saintly and greatly loved Shinran (1173-1262), founder of the Pure Land, taught that one is reborn in the Pure Land (that is to say, one attains salvation) by reciting the *nenbutsu* even once, so boundless is the mercy of Amida. Deeply conscious of his own unworthiness and filled with compassion for the sinner, Shinran could say: "If even the just person is saved, how much more the sinner!" Whereas Zen was, and still is, a religion of the elite, millions of humble working people throughout Japan, with or without prayer beads, called fervently on the name of the Buddha. Their prayer was not unlike that of devout Christians who call with faith on the name of Jesus. The renowned Dr. D. T. Suzuki, famous for his research on Zen, made no secret of the fact that Pure Land Buddhism was his first love. He further taught the interesting and somewhat revolutionary doctrine that constant recitation of the *nenbutsu* leads to the same *satori* or enlightenment as hours of silent sitting in zazen. So powerful is the prayer of the Pure Land.

It is not surprising, then, that in 1986 the Dalai Lama and other Buddhists enthusiastically joined Pope John Paul in prayer for world peace at Assisi. The Catholic organizers of that interreligious prayer meeting, in an act of unprecedented generosity, removed the blessed sacrament from its place of honor in a church and replaced it with a statue of the Buddha, so that Buddhists could raise their minds and hearts to the great compassionate mystery in accordance with the dictates of their conscience.

At Assisi everyone realized that human effort alone will not bring peace to the chaotic world in which we live. However valuable our social, economic and political endeavors, they alone will not bring peace. The same holds true for our other mind-boggling problems—destruction of the environment, pollution of the atmosphere, violence in the streets, the breakdown of family life, racial and sexist discrimination, inhuman torture and cruel injustice. To find some kind of solution to these problems (for we will never solve them completely) we must pray together. More than the knowledge that comes from research we need the wisdom that comes from prayer.

TALKING TO GOD

The chief characteristic of the Semitic religions is prayer to a transcendent God—prayers of praise, thanksgiving, petition, sorrow for sin. "Incline your ear, O Lord, and answer me, for I am poor and needy" (Ps 86:1). In this prayer one of the great models for Jews, Christians and Muslims is the gigantic personality of Moses, who climbs the mountain and enters into the cloud, Moses, who encounters God in the tent of meeting. This is the Moses to whom God spoke face to face as one might speak to a friend. So radiant was his countenance after this mystic meeting that the Israelites could not bear to look at him. So he covered his face with a veil to protect them from the blinding light of God.

Moses talked intimately to God as to a friend. He could complain and grumble, "Why have you treated your servant so badly? Why have I not found favor in your sight, that you lay the burden of all this people on me?" (Nm 11:11). With words of remarkable intimacy he goes on:

> Did I conceive all this people? Did I give birth to them, that you should say to me, "Carry them in your bosom, as a nurse carries a sucking child," to the land that you promised on oath to their ancestors? . . . I am not able to carry this people alone, for they are too heavy for me. (Nm 11:12-14)

Here the prayer of Moses rises up from his femininity—from his Jungian *anima*. He identifies with the mother who conceives and gives birth—and with the nurse who carries the sucking child at her bosom. How different is this Moses from the rugged lawgiver of Michelangelo! Yet this short passage speaks volumes about prayer and the feminine. It supports Pascal's thesis that all human beings are feminine before God. It lets us see how St. John of the Cross can identify with the bride who caresses her lover as he lies sleeping on her flowering breast.

Nor is the prayer of Moses a monologue. The great lawgiver is not engaging in soliloquies like Hamlet. God answers him, telling him to come to the tent of meeting and gently assuring him: "Is the Lord's power limited? Now you will see whether my word will come true for you or not" (Nm 11:23). God defends him vigorously against the carping criticism of Aaron and Miriam. How beautiful is the intimacy between Moses and his God!

Prayer like that of Moses echoes through the Hebrew scriptures, in the psalms and in the prophets. It is the prayer of Job and of Jonah. Today it is practiced everywhere by Jews and Muslims and Christians who, feeling deep intimacy with God, cry out to their Creator as to a loving and merciful friend. Indeed, the prayer of talking to God is practiced by innocent children, by anguished sinners and by consummate mystics. Is not this the great contribution of the monotheistic religions to a world that hungers for the love of God?

In the New Testament the same theme continues. Jesus, who was once the master, becomes the friend. "No longer do I call you servants . . . but I have called you friends" (Jn 15:15). Intimate friendship with the risen Jesus who walks with us, as he walked with the disciples on the road to Emmaus, has always been central to the spiritual life of Christians.

Speaking to priests the Second Vatican Council advocates such friendship in a eucharistic context:

> They should prize daily conversation with Christ the Lord in
> visits of personal devotion to the most Holy Eucharist.[2]

In this short sentence the council describes a prayer that is practiced wherever there is a Catholic church throughout the world. There one can see men and women, boys and girls, rich and poor, people of every profession or of no profession talking to the risen Lord about their joys and fears, their hopes and desires, interceding for their relatives and friends, living and dead.

In short, the prayer that spontaneously cries out to God is practiced everywhere. It is part of the existential experience of the human family.

GROWTH

People who pray regularly begin to see that prayer is a process or, in the terminology of the old masters, a journey. It has its ups and downs, its bright days and dark nights, its consolations and desolations. The tiny seed sown by the Divine Sower struggles to grow and become a mighty tree.

After some time people may find themselves repeating one short ejaculatory prayer again and again. It may be the famous Jesus prayer of the Russian pilgrim: "Lord Jesus, Son of God, have mercy on me, a sinner." Or it may simply be the word "Jesus." Or it may be "Come, Holy Spirit." Sometimes people feel that they have their own word—"my word"— which has been given to them from they know not where. Again, people may like to repeat a phrase from scripture, like the Johannine words, "Dwell in my love." Short prayer, says the author of *The Cloud of Unknowing*, pierces heaven.

Such ejaculatory prayer may be practiced morning and evening, but after a time one finds that it continues during the day. The phrase goes on, even in the midst of a busy schedule. One discovers existentially that one's psyche is multi-layered. At the top level one is busy with work; at a deeper level the phrase is repeating itself. In fact, a profound awakening is taking place: areas of psychic life that were previously dormant are now becoming conscious. Eventually the great awakening will take place when, as St. John of the Cross says, the Word will awaken at the divine center.

Furthermore, just as human intimacy can lead to a blissful silence in which lovers are united in wordless and loving communion, so friendship with the risen Lord can lead to a similar blissful union. This is the *silentium mysticum*. Quite often simple people experience this loving silence after receiving holy communion. Then they cry out with Paul, "I live, now not I, but Christ lives in me" (Gal 2:20). Or they say with conviction, "Anyone united to the Lord is one spirit with him" (1 Cor 6:17). This union may eventually lead to the mystical marriage. But about this I will speak later. Here let me pause to dispel an unfortunate misconception.

ONE AND NOT ONE

It is sometimes said that prayer to a transcendent God is dualistic—that it is prayer to a God "up there," separated from the universe and from the human family. Prayer to a "separate God" is quite unacceptable to Buddhists, to Hindus, to philosophers and even to many scientists, who become increasingly aware of the oneness of existence.

But prayer to the transcendent God of the monotheistic religions is not dualistic. We pray to God with whom we are one. *The Book of Privy Counselling* puts it starkly when it says of God, "He is your being and in Him you are what you are."[3] God is at the same time immanent and transcendent. This is already clear in the psalms: "If I ascend to heaven you are there; if I make my bed in Sheol, you are there" (Ps 139:8). The universe is penetrated with the presence of God, who is at the same time its Creator. God is the very ground of a universe that God has created.

All this is, of course, very paradoxical. But one who enters the world of contemplation must be prepared for paradox. All is nothing; light is darkness; wisdom is foolishness; the two are one; we know by unknowing; we are familiar with a God who is the mystery of mysteries. To the intellectual who lives solely in the rational consciousness this is fantastic, but to the simple person who prays at the level of spirit this reconciliation of opposites is a non-problem. Think of the paradoxes of the gospel. Jesus says, "Whoever sees me sees the Father" (Jn 14:9), and then the gospel tells us that "Jesus looked up to heaven and said, 'Father, the hour has come'" (Jn 17:1). The Father is both immanent and transcendent.

In fact, as prayer develops, one more and more transcends dualism to live a life of union in love—not just union with God but union with people and with the whole universe. One may transcend the before and after of time to live in a world of the eternal now. One realizes existentially, "I am one with God and all things, and I am not one with God and all things." If I were to say that I am totally one with God and all things, this would be monism. If I were to say that I am separated from God and all things, this would be dualism. But in fact I am one and not one. And is not this the non-dualism or *advaita* of Asian thought?

If scientists become increasingly interested in Asian philosophy and religion, this is because they now see the universe as a web or a net, and they further see that we human beings are part of this web or net. We cannot stand outside and look in. We cannot be pure observers, for we are necessarily involved. Such is the unity of existence.

Yet one must distinguish carefully between the ontological unity that is always present and the loving union that comes from prayer and can, alas, be broken. "Apart from the surd of sin," writes Bernard Lonergan, "the universe is in love with God."[4] By the "surd of sin" he means the irrationality of evil, which can break the spiritual, but not the ontological, union with God.

GIFT

The old mystical theologians spoke of *acquired* and *infused* contemplation, using a distinction that is still quite useful.[5]

Acquired contemplation is the consequence of human effort aided by ordinary grace. One repeats a sacred word again and again with great consolation and joy; or one enters into a silence much like the one-pointedness of the martial arts. Acquired contemplation is the ordinary development of a life dedicated to prayer and meditation.

Infused contemplation, on the other hand, is all gift. It does not come through the senses, even though it overflows on the senses. In the words of St. John of the Cross, God communicates himself "by pure spirit." Human effort is of little importance. Contemplatives, sometimes quite unexpectedly, become conscious of a mysterious and loving presence in themselves and in the whole universe. They have entered a new state of consciousness characterized by what they call the "sense of presence." If asked to describe or define God they may answer, "For me, God is presence." Karl Rahner may have enjoyed infused contemplation, for he spoke constantly of "presence to the mystery."

When contemplatives become aware of this all-embracing presence, they may say with amazement and gratitude, "I did not cause this, nor do I deserve it. It is pure gift." Ignatius of Loyola called it "consolation without previous cause." He saw that there is no sensible cause for this state of consciousness that opens us to infinite presence and leads us to see God in all things. Such a state of consciousness just happens. Like the quality of mercy, "it droppeth as the gentle rain from heaven upon the place beneath." And so we call it infused.

In our world of earth-shaking technology where observable data is all important and where scientific knowledge is frequently regarded as the *only* knowledge, people find it difficult to believe in a knowledge that does not come from human endeavor and does not depend upon the senses. Yet such gift knowledge (better called wisdom) is well known in the perennial philosophy, the universal wisdom that undergirds all religions and all civilizations. Let me give some examples.

Buddhists hold that enlightenment is a gift. It does not depend upon human endeavor. It is quite unpredictable. Enlightened people often cry out in ecstatic gratitude and with deep humility, thanking Buddha and the patriarchs for an undeserved gift of which they are unworthy and which they could not have obtained by the most rigorous religious practices. Likewise the Upanishads, speaking of ultimate wisdom, state clearly: "Not through much learning is this spirit reached, nor through the intellect, nor through sacred teaching. It is reached by the one it chooses, to such a one does the spirit reveal itself."[6] In short, enlightenment is sometimes given to those who work all day in the vineyard and at other times to those who come at the eleventh hour. It is a free gift that no human being deserves.

Since this contemplation is a gift, one must wait humbly. One must not enter the sheepfold until one hears the call of the good shepherd. The mystics quote the Song of Songs,

> I adjure you, O daughters of Jerusalem,
>   by the gazelles or wild does:
> do not stir up or awaken love
>   until it is ready! (Sg 3:5)

Do not awaken contemplative love until the time has come! Just as the sensitive and tender bridegroom does not hasten to awaken the bride lest the hymen be broken violently or too soon, so the bride (and all human beings are the bride) must not invite the divine lover until the time has come. But the time does come for the awakening of love. Then there arises in the depths of her being a tiny flame. This the author of *The Cloud* calls "the blind stirring of love." It is a movement of divine energy, which will become a living flame of love, the center of the bride's mystical life.[7]

A NEW VISION

With the awakening of love the prayer of the bride enters a new stage. She becomes increasingly passive—just waiting, doing nothing, allowing the Spirit to act. Or she may enter into the prayer of quiet, a form of contemplation in which the upper layer of the psyche runs wild with all kinds of distractions, while the deeper layer quietly enjoys the sense of divine presence. At this time incompetent directors can do untold damage when, as St. John of the Cross says, they hammer and pound like blacksmiths, telling the contemplative to give up this laziness, to get busy, to think, to use her faculties; or when they force their methods or mantras on one who is called to rest quietly and effortlessly in the embrace of God. Little do they know that the principal director now is the Holy Spirit. The human director must stand back in awe, admiring the Spirit's work.

For the tiny flame of love is surfacing in the contemplative's consciousness, and at this early stage it could be smothered by human effort and rational activity. Furthermore, the spiritual senses are emerging. The bride sees, but not with the eyes of the flesh. She hears, but not with the ears of the flesh. She touches and is touched, but not with fleshly hands. She is tenderly embraced, but with an eroticism of the spirit. She may be surrounded with a sweet fragrance. Inner words may arise from the core of her being, filling her with joy. She enjoys the Pauline fruits of the Spirit, which are love, joy, peace, patience, kindness, generosity, faithfulness, gentleness, and self-control. What a wealth of spiritual experience is now born!

Born anew also are the Pauline spiritual gifts, traditionally associated with contemplative prayer. "To each is given the manifestation of the Spirit for the common good" (1 Cor 12:7). Gifts of wisdom, healing, prophecy, discernment, tongues, working of miracles—these or other gifts now manifest themselves in the contemplative's life. With joy she reads the scriptures, tasting the sweet inner fruit and transcending the outer crust of exegesis.

With contemplation comes a new vision of reality. One becomes conscious of the spirit world. One is united not only with the entire cosmos but with the dead—with those who have gone before, some of whom are being purified while others are in glory. "We look not at what can be seen but at what cannot be seen," writes Paul. "For what can be seen is temporary, but what cannot be seen is eternal" (2 Cor 4:18). Paul likewise speaks of "things visible and invisible, whether thrones or dominions or rulers or powers" (Col 1:16). Let us remember that this invisible world of saints and angels and cosmic powers is central to the vision of Dante and Shakespeare and Aquinas. Indeed, it is central (with a different terminology) to the vision of traditional Hinduism and Buddhism. Only with the scientific revolution of the seventeenth century were we robbed of an invisible world. But now science itself shows interest in what cannot be seen.

Sometimes, as contemplatives are liberated from addictions and attachments, they acquire a certain clarity of vision that manifests itself in telepathy, clairvoyance, reading of minds and other psychic powers that Hinduism calls *siddhis*. These psychic powers make a deep impression on curious searchers, but genuine contemplatives make little of them and conceal them from public view.

"DO NOT BELIEVE EVERY SPIRIT"

With infused contemplation, then, a new and rich consciousness is born. The contemplative is truly privileged. Yet (and here again we face paradox) the spiritual teachers of the Christian tradition state unhesitatingly that the path of visions and voices and extraordinary experiences is filled with danger. The possibility of deceit is very great. Teresa of Avila knew well that she needed guidance from a prudent person well versed in mystical theology.

For the psychic world into which the contemplative enters contains cosmic forces of good and evil. Moreover, the evil forces appear as angels of light, as St. Paul himself said, leading contemplatives astray in subtle ways. St. John of the Cross, the great mystical doctor, is clear:

> Among locutions and visions there are usually many that come from the devil. For he commonly deals with the soul in the same manner as God does, imparting communications so similar to God's that, disguised among the flock like the wolf in sheep's clothing, his meddling may be hardly discernible.[8]

Note that St. John of the Cross says that "many" locutions and visions "usually" come from the devil. He further says that the action of the evil spirit is quite similar to that of God. Nor is he speaking to renegades but to good contemplative people. St. Ignatius of Loyola says something similar.

The spirit of evil, a fallen angel in the Christian tradition, has a powerful intellect and deep insight. St. John of the Cross tells us that this evil spirit can foresee earthquake and pestilence or the number of years that some person will live. This he can communicate to contemplative men and women whose prophecies, however true, are then diabolical in origin.

Visions also can be diabolical in origin. Think of the mystical vision of Jesus himself: "Then the devil led him up and showed him in an instant all the kingdoms of the world." What a vision! And the temptation, "If you, then, will worship me, it will all be yours." And Jesus firmly unmasked the tempter, "Worship the Lord your God, and serve only him" (Lk 4:5-8). To unmask and reject the tempter is the task of the contemplative and the one who guides. This is discernment in accordance with the First Epistle of St. John: "Beloved, do not believe every spirit, but test the spirits to see whether they are from God" (1 Jn 4:1).

But even when the visions and voices come from God, the possibility of deception remains great. St. John of the Cross distinguishes between the communication of God and *its interpretation by the human person*. A great number of saintly persons misunderstood the word of God because they took it literally: "With a number of ancients, many of God's prophecies and locutions did not turn out as had been expected, because they understood them in their own way, in another literal manner."[9] St. John of the Cross then makes an important statement concerning God's reason for conferring visions:

> God's chief objective in conferring these revelations is to express and impart the spirit that is enclosed within the outer rind. The spirit is difficult to understand, much richer and more plentiful, very extraordinary and far beyond the boundaries of the letter.[10]

A vision is the sensible overflow of a spiritual experience. The saint continues with a strong warning to people who take visions and locutions literally:

> Anyone bound to the letter, locution, form or figure apprehensible in the vision cannot avoid serious error and will later become confused for having been led according to the senses and not made room for the spirit stripped of the letter.[11]

In other words, one must never become attached to the sensible figure or form that one sees. One must transcend the rind to taste the delicious fruit. One must go beyond sense to spirit.

Here it is important to remember what a vision is. Ordinarily the object of the vision is not "out there" but is the projection of an inner experience. In the case of a contemplative person, God self-communicates by pure spirit to the center of the soul, and the contemplative projects this experience in the form of a picture. But no sensible picture is adequate to express the divine communication. Furthermore, the picture necessarily contains subjective elements. The cultural background, education, temperament, the psychological health and the neurotic tendencies of the visionary—all play their part. That is why a literal interpretation of a vision (especially a vision of hell) can be disastrous. The rind obscures the true message, which lies at the level of spirit. Just as dreams cannot be taken at their face value but need to be interpreted, so visions cannot be taken at their face value but must be carefully discerned lest one be led astray.

In short, the great challenge is to distinguish between the sign and the reality. In today's world where visions and prophecies abound, many people, alas, are so caught up in the sign that they miss the reality toward which it points. They keep chewing the coarse rind and never taste the sweet fruit. Sometimes it is the visionaries and prophets themselves who are attached to their experiences. At other times it is their directors who are swept away. At other times it is the masses of the people.

"Beloved, do not believe every spirit, but test the spirits to see whether they are from God; for many false prophets have gone out into the world" (1 Jn 4:1).

SIGNS AND WONDERS

In the early 1990s I made a pilgrimage to Medjugorje. It was an unforgettable experience. Particularly impressive was the atmosphere of prayer that enveloped the whole village, reaching a climax at the eucharistic liturgy in the big basilica. Many people could be seen receiving the sacrament of reconciliation; others received the sacrament of healing. At night we climbed the mountain on which, it was said, the visionaries saw the Virgin Mary and received messages for themselves and for the world. Here, too, there was a hushed silence that reminded me of the contemplative "sense of presence." It was indeed a place of prayer.

What was it all about?

It seemed to me that here was a sign, calling the people of today to prayer and fasting and conversion of heart. It was also a call to world peace with the warning that peace is finally a gift of God, a gift that will

not come as a consequence of economic, political and sociological efforts alone. If we want to create peace we must turn to God and pray.
Such, it seemed to me, was the message.

And yet there was, and is, a great need of a St. John of the Cross. For
caught up in the signs, many people were in danger of missing the Great
Mystery toward which the signs point. Preoccupied with the rind they
were in danger of missing the fruit. So much talk of the sun spinning and
rosaries becoming gold. So much talk of lights and illuminations and
miracles and prodigies. Many people went to Medjugorje in search of
the extraordinary and spectacular. Here, they believed, they would find
evidence for a divine intervention that would bolster their faith. They
wanted to see the sign. "An evil and adulterous generation asks for a
sign, but no sign will be given to it except the sign of the prophet Jonah"
(Mt 12:39).

As in Fatima so in Medjugorje one of the visionaries had a graphic
vision of hell with a detailed description of its inhabitants, and this was
accepted literally and uncritically by thousands. Yet the words of St.
John of the Cross cannot be ignored: "Anyone bound to the letter, locu-
tion, form or figure apprehensible in the vision cannot avoid serious
error and will later become confused for having been led according to
the senses and not made room for the spirit stripped of the letter."[12] If
we cannot take literally the graphic descriptions of the Book of Revelation, how can we take literally the visions of the seers of the twentieth
century?

And then, the messages, the apocalyptic prophecies and the secrets!
Here again it is useful to recall the teaching of the mystical doctor, who
speaks of three kinds of locutions—substantial, formal and successive.

Substantial locutions are the most reliable. It seems that another is
speaking brief words in the substance or center of the soul without the
use of the senses. These words may rise to consciousness quite unexpectedly at any time or in any place, and they achieve their effect at once.
"For example, if our Lord should say formally to the soul, 'Be good,' it
would immediately be substantially good . . . or if he should say to a
soul in much fear, 'Do not fear,' it would without delay feel great fortitude and tranquillity."[13] Such inner words are a wonderful gift of God.
"Happy the soul to whom God speaks these substantial words. 'Speak,
Lord, for your servant is listening' (1 Sm 3:10)."[14]

Formal words are also spoken interiorly without the use of the senses.
Again, it seems that another person utters them. They may teach or shed
light on some truth, or they may be prophetic. "When bestowed, this
kind of knowledge is so embedded in the soul—without anyone telling it
anything—that if someone were to assert the opposite it would be unable

to give interior assent even by force, for it has a spiritual knowledge of this truth that resembles clear vision."[15] Yet even in this case, says St. John of the Cross, one must submit to the judgment of a prudent person, thus walking by faith and not relying on one's inner experience.

Successive locutions are more prolonged and usually come to consciousness when one is absorbed in prayer or meditation. These, too, seem to be spoken by another person. They may come from God, or from the spirit of evil disguised as an angel of light, or from oneself. "I knew a person who in experiencing these successive locutions," writes St. John of the Cross, "formed, among some very true and solid ones about the blessed sacrament, others that were outright heresies."[16] The mystical doctor tells the contemplative to ignore these successive locutions. "We should pay no heed to them, but be only interested in directing the will, with fortitude, toward God." [17]

From all this it can be seen that the work of discernment in today's world is very challenging. Holy men and women have written whole books, claiming that every page was dictated by our Lord or the Virgin Mary. St. John of the Cross would turn in his grave! Then there are the predictions of impending cosmic calamity, the secrets entrusted to a chosen elite, the miraculous signs in the heavens. What are we to think of this? Or again, the talk at Fatima about the spread of communism throughout the world and the eventual conversion of Russia. Can we take all this literally or must we take it with a grain of salt?

It seems to me that with St. John of the Cross we must distinguish between the communication of God and its interpretation by the human person. We must recall that "with a number of the ancients, many of God's prophecies and locutions did not turn out as had been expected, because they understood them in their own way, in another literal manner."[18] For "the spirit is difficult to understand, much richer and more plentiful, very extraordinary and far beyond the boundaries of the letter."[19]

Let us be wary of secrets. Let us beware of taking literally the messages of visionaries and prophets, however holy they may be. Let us distinguish carefully between the rind and the fruit.

At Medjugorje the local bishops declared that they saw no evidence for supernatural intervention. They saw nothing that could be said to contravene the ordinary laws of nature. For many people this was disappointing. But need it be so? The statement of the bishops could have the salutary effect of withdrawing our minds from the signs and fixing them on the mystery toward which the signs point.

In *Powers of Darkness, Powers of Light* John Cornwell relates a conversation he had with Graham Greene. The latter had had a mysterious experience while attending the eucharist celebrated by the great Italian mystic Padre Pio. Asked about religion Graham Greene said, "I think . . . it's a mystery. There *is* a mystery. There is something inexplicable in life. And it's important because people are not going to believe in all the explanations given by science or even the Churches . . . It's a mystery which can't be destroyed."[20] This is well said. For the very existence of a man like Padre Pio points to a mystery. It would be a sad mistake to get so fascinated by his stigmata, his out-of-the-body experiences and his powers of mind-reading as to forget the great mystery toward which he points.

Furthermore, if the institutional church has always been wary and even skeptical about visions and wonders and locutions and revelations, this is for reasons that are profoundly theological. The Christian revelation comes from sacred scripture and the tradition that stems from the apostles. Private revelations may help some people, but they are not part of the deposit of faith, and no one is bound to accept them. As for the mystical doctor, he too wants us to walk by faith in the cloud of unknowing, and he sees that visions could be a distraction. "Blessed are those who have not seen and yet believed" (Jn 20:29).

Let us hope, then, that pilgrims will continue to flock to the great religious shrines, praying for peace and for healing, seeking conversion of heart, opening their being to the immense love of God and directing their eyes to the great mystery of faith.

THE WAY OF NOTHING

Those who enter the path of infused contemplation, I have said, may experience an expansion of consciousness, finding the great mystery of God in the whole universe and in the very depths of their being. This is a wonderful gift. Yet it is no more than the first step in a journey that goes on and on, leading to the summit of the mystical mountain.

And on this journey one takes nothing. "Take no gold, or silver, or copper in your belts, no bag for your journey, or two tunics, or sandals, or a staff, for laborers deserve their food" (Mt 10:9-10). One lets go of all reasoning and thinking and imagining. One lets go of all anxieties, living like the flowers of the field and the birds of the air. One is not preoccupied about tomorrow, for tomorrow will take care of itself. One takes nothing. One becomes nothing.

It sometimes happens that people who embark on this journey have spent many years in therapy, analyzing their dreams, plumbing the depths of their unconscious and exploring their life in the womb. To such people

I have sometimes found myself saying: "It is good that you went through all this. It has helped you a lot. But now is the time to let go of psychology and fall into the void." Again, some may have found great help in meditation from a certain methodology that has led them on. To these also the time comes when we must say: "Let go of your methods and fall into the void. Remember how St. John of the Cross said that the way is no way."

One gives up attachment to consolations in prayer, to voices and visions and psychic powers. One even gives up attachment to the joys of silence. One leaves all that is familiar, one abandons all that gave security, to enter into the cloud of unknowing or the dark night where one experiences a deep loneliness like the loneliness that comes before death.

This is the path of the Hindu sannyasin who practices the most radical renunciation to find total liberation and profound wisdom. It is the path of the bodhisattva who leaves all to come to supreme enlightenment and unlimited compassion. It is the path of the mystic who sings,

> nothing, nothing, nothing
> nothing, nothing, nothing
> and even on the mountain nothing

> nada, nada, nada
> nada, nada, nada
> y aun en el monte nada

Even on the mountain nothing! All for love! "If one offered for love all the wealth of his house, it would be utterly scorned" (Sg 8:7).

Since the mystical path in all religions is so similar, we are learning from one another. We in the Christian tradition are learning from Asia the way of the breath and of the lotus posture. We are learning from the exquisite serenity of the Buddha. We are learning from the *Heart Sutra* that "form is emptiness and emptiness is form." We are learning from the paradoxical koan—"Jump from the top of a hundred foot pole." One who *lives* this koan and jumps from the pole loses all security and falls into the nothingness of the void that is enlightenment.

Yet each mystical tradition has its own distinctive features, and the Christian mystical path is above all a following of Christ in love. The *nada* of St. John of the Cross only makes sense in the context of the cross of Jesus, who emptied himself taking the form of a slave. Ignatius of Loyola, speaking of the human addiction to money and reputation, tells us not only to renounce these attachments but positively to desire poverty with Christ poor and humiliation with Christ humiliated. In this way one comes to a humility, a poverty of spirit, an emptiness that is the basis of the mystical life. In short, Christian detachment comes from taking one's cross and following Jesus.

But what is the most basic human attachment? To what do we human beings most of all cling?

The Zen Buddhist does not hesitate. The most basic human attachment is the clinging to life and the fear of death. Zen claims, moreover, that one can be freed from this clinging and this fear. There are stories of liberated Zen monks who died laughing.

In the Christian life liberation from the fear of death comes from contemplating the death and resurrection of Jesus. "O death, where is your victory? O death, where is your sting?" cries Paul after speaking about the resurrection (1 Cor 15:55). And then the martyrs! Thomas More cracked a few jokes and embraced his executioner before putting his head on the block at Tyburn. Total liberation came at the time of death.

I have spoken of the way of active purification in which human effort plays an important role. However, many attachments and addictions (as psychologists know well) are rooted in the unconscious, and no amount of human effort will dislodge them. We need the passive purification that is enacted through the dark night of the soul. This is the happy night that leads beyond the contemplative consciousness to the mystical consciousness.

CONTEMPLATION TO MYSTICISM

As the journey of contemplation goes on, one enters a new stage. One gets a glimpse into another world. This is the world of mysticism. Whereas the chief characteristic of infused contemplation is the sense of presence, the mystical state is preceded by a painful sense of absence. Indeed, it is preceded by a harrowing experience that can bring the mystic to the brink of despair and to nervous collapse. But the dark night does not last forever. Time comes when the log of wood, hitherto damp and sodden, catches fire and begins to burn brightly. The winter is past. The rain is over and gone. "Arise, my love, my dove, my beautiful one and come away" (Sg 2:10).

NINE

The Road to Mysticism

NIGHT MUST FALL

In the early stages of contemplation one walks in glorious sunshine beneath the blue sky of God's presence. But, alas, the sun cannot shine forever. Night must fall.

As time goes on, prayer becomes arid, boring and full of distractions. Teresa of Avila shook the hourglass, hoping that the time would pass quickly. She had no satisfaction in prayer and no satisfaction outside of prayer. God, who had been palpably present, was now distressingly absent. Created things that once gave joy were now uninteresting. Night was beginning to fall.

Those called to mysticism enter more and more deeply into the night. They may fall into a void of fear, anxiety and loneliness, as one who said to his disciples, "My soul is sorrowful, even unto death" (Mt 26:38). This is a time when one sees no meaning in life, when one is tempted to despair, when one cries out with Job, "Why did I not die at birth, come forth from the womb and expire?" (Jb 3:11). One may spend sleepless nights of misery: "But the night is long, and I am full of tossing until dawn" (Jb 7:4). What is happening?

It will be remembered that in contemplative prayer the upper reaches of the mind are swept clean as one grows in detachment from thinking and reasoning and imagery of all kinds. One becomes *empty*. In this time the unconscious begins to surface. One is confronted with one's inner darkness; one comes face to face with one's shadow.

In the shadow lie all the parts of our personality that we have repressed or refused to face. Here lie the fears and anxieties, the frustrations and the traumas, the hurts and the resentments that we accumulated when we were children and even when we slept in our mother's womb. Here lies the terrible fear of death that we have never confronted. How great is the darkness that lies dormant in the human psyche!

And deeper than the personal unconscious is the collective unconscious, which contains the sin and the sadness of the world. This also surfaces, and one gets a glimpse of the shadow of humanity. For the fact is that we are all united. We might like to forget the solidarity of the human race and to think of ourselves as isolated nomads with no responsibility for the murders and massacres, the concentration camps and the torture chambers and the rest. But the human race, let us not forget, is mysteriously united; in some strange way we ourselves are responsible for the horrors and the evil we condemn as we complacently read the morning paper. Somehow we all share in the shadow of humanity. It is not surprising that some mystics, faced with the sin of the world, have spent days and nights with Jesus in Gethsemane.

But if we follow St. John of the Cross we see that something very wonderful is happening. God himself is surfacing in the soul. It is as though the God who dwells in the depth of one's being is (if I may be permitted a crude anthropomorphism) pushing to the surface all the inner garbage and darkness in order that a thorough purification may take place. That is why St. John of the Cross can speak of this night as "dark contemplation" and, when it is all over, he can ecstatically sing, "O night more lovely than the dawn."

But, someone may ask, if God is light, how can God cause such terrible darkness? To this St. John of the Cross, following a long apophatic tradition, answers that God, who is light in himself, blinds the person who is still unpurified, just as the light of the sun blinds the bat and just as the divine light blinded St. Paul on the road to Damascus. The encounter of the human with the divine can be full of suffering.

Yet, as night must fall, so the sun must rise. When the damp and sodden log has belched forth its ugly dirt and smoke, it finally catches fire. "Come, Holy Spirit, fill the hearts of the faithful and enkindle within them the fire of your divine love," pray the people. Their prayer is answered when the Spirit fills the heart of the mystic, bestowing light and enkindling fire. Now he or she, consumed with the spiritual fire of love and flooded with the divine light of wisdom, shouts with joy. "O lamps of fire!" "Oh lamparas de fuego," cries St. John of the Cross, as he sings of the happy purification that has come through the blinding light and the torturing fire that burned into the deepest recesses of his soul.

Yet one who reflects on this dark night must face a question that the psychologist necessarily asks: How does this dark night differ from acute neurosis or psychological collapse? Were the mystics sick people? And, if so, how can they be models for the twenty-first century?

It would seem that quite often mystics, prior to their great awakening, have gone through a period of nervous upheaval bordering on psychological collapse. Confrontation with the unconscious was just too much for them, as it was too much for Jung at one period of his life. They have suffered from insomnia and depression. Sometimes they have exhibited suicidal tendencies. For this reason, visits to a psychiatrist or a counselor have proved helpful and even necessary.

But these counseling or psychiatric sessions deal only with the upper levels of consciousness and the superficial area of the psyche. There is a much deeper level that only a consummate spiritual guide or a psychiatrist of the calibre of Jung will understand. Yet even the wisest guide may feel helpless, knowing that he or she is faced with the awesome mystery of human suffering and the baffling riddle of the void. Face to face with the ordinary neurotic a competent psychologist may quickly put a finger on the cause of the problem, whether some abuse in childhood or some rejection in later life. But faced with the mystic in the dark night the psychologist has nothing to say. His or her years of patient research will not help. Human skill will accomplish nothing. The wise guide waits upon God with faith that "all will be well, and all will be well, and all manner of thing will be well."

And yet another question must be asked today: Do Buddhists and mystics of other religious traditions pass through a dark night on their way to enlightenment?

Before attempting to answer this question, let us reflect that for St. John of the Cross the dark night is not the path of a privileged few. It is the path of human life. All human beings stand in need of purification. All must pass through purificatory fire either in the dark night of this earthly life or in the spiritual fire of purgatory in the life to come. Only through deep purification can humans come to the vision of God that makes them divine.

An experience I had in Japan has made me realize that Buddhists know of the spiritual darkness that one must pass through before reaching enlightenment.

THE DARKNESS OF THE BUDDHA

In 1998, shortly after the winter Olympics, I visited the famous temple of *Zenkōji* in Nagano with a Jesuit friend. After watching the assembled monks reciting the Sutras, we joined a host of pilgrims to climb down a narrow staircase leading to a long, dark corridor or tunnel that runs beneath the temple. Very slowly we walked single file in the pitch darkness, unable to see anything. It could have been a frightening experience, especially if someone had panicked or gone berserk; but I retained my peace of soul, reciting again and again my mantra, "Come, Holy Spirit! Come, Holy Spirit! Come, Holy Spirit!" I felt instinctively that there was wisdom in this darkness. My companion later told me that he also was at peace: for him each step in the darkness was an act of blind trust. In the silence I heard a woman's voice crying, "Become nothing!" *(Mu ni naru)*. And so we walked slowly for ten or fifteen minutes. We heard the crashing sound of pilgrims' fists banging against the wooden paneling, searching for the key to "the door of heaven" that leads to Paradise. And then we saw flickers of light. Finally we turned a corner, came into broad daylight and found ourselves in front of a magnificent statue of the Buddha.

My companion and I walked away in silence, speaking not a word. We had been through a religious experience. When we did eventually speak, we asked one another if we had been through a near-death experience, going through the dark tunnel, knocking on the door of heaven and coming to the light. Or, we asked, in passing through that tunnel were we leaving the phenomenal world of *samsara* and entering into the darkness of the real world, the darkness of the cloud of unknowing, the divine darkness—to meet the light? As I looked at the statue of the Buddha, I realized that Shakyamuni in total silence and stillness had gone through that inner darkness to a glorious enlightenment.

I thought also of the Tibetan Book of the Dead, which claims that death can be a veritable mystical experience.

The Tibetan lamas tell us to prepare for death, meditate on death. "Do not let death take you by surprise" is their important message. If we prepare, the process of dying, however painful, can be filled with joy; but if we do not prepare, it can be a time of very great suffering.

Tibetan Buddhism divides human life into four *bardos* or periods of transition; and the *painful bardo,* which is something of a dark night, lasts from the beginning of the process of dying until the great awakening called "the dawning of the Ground Luminosity." A lama or spiritual friend sits beside the dying person, explaining what is happening and how in death one passes through various states of consciousness. One may pass through a hallucinatory phase, like the *makyō* of Zen,[1] a time when one sees devils and ghosts and grotesque figures; and the task of the lama is to reassure the dying person that these phantasms have no objectivity, being no more than projections of the mind. One who has devoted much time to meditation during life will die meditating and thus be ready to recognize the Ground Luminosity, the Ground of Being, the Ultimate Emptiness. Sogyal Rinpoche tells us that the moment of death can be the supreme mystical experience:

> The reason why the moment of death is so potent with opportunity is because it is then that the fundamental nature of mind, the Ground Luminosity or Clear Light, will naturally manifest, and in a vast and splendid way. If at this moment we can recognize the Ground Luminosity, the teachings tell us, we will attain liberation.[2]

The Ground Luminosity is quite different from the light that appears at the end of the tunnel in the near-death experience. If one wanted to draw a parallel, one might compare it to the beatific vision which, the scholastics held, is the goal of human life.

Can death, then, be a mystical experience?

It seems that it can, whether in Buddhism or Judaism or Islam or Christianity.

In the monotheistic religions the great mystical experience is martyrdom, as we see in the Book of Maccabees. In the New Testament Stephen, filled with the Spirit, gazed into heaven and saw the glory of God and Jesus standing at the right hand of God. And in this way he died. He was the first of many—and, indeed, of many in Japan—whose "glorious martyrdom" was their crowning mystical experience.

BIRTH OF THE TRUE SELF

After death comes life. After the dark night comes the awakening that marks the transition from contemplation to mysticism. Now the true self that lay sleeping at the center of one's being comes to life and cries out, "I am!" This true self is one with God, one with the universe, one with all that is. This is the self that knows no subject and object, no life and death, no light and darkness, no yin and yang. It transcends the changes and the anxieties of *samsara* to live in the world of enlightenment. This awakening, moreover, admits of levels or degrees. At its deepest level it is the earthshaking enlightenment of Shakyamuni, which has shaped the spiritual lives of millions of Asians for more than two millennia.

Some Christian mystics have spoken of "the birth of God in the soul." This may shock pious ears. It is less baffling, however, if one reflects on the anthropomorphism I have already used, saying that God pushes to the surface of consciousness the garbage and the darkness that have cluttered the unconscious mind. Furthermore, it is less baffling if one reflects on the Hindu teaching that the *atman* or true self is Brahman or God. Or if one reflects on the sanjuanist statement that the center of the soul is God. So closely united with God is the true self that the birth of the true self may seem like the birth of God.

Be that as it may, the true self is born with great joy, and a new life begins. After the excruciating birth pangs the sorrow is turned into a joy that no one can take away. Now one enters a mystical life that is in continuity with the life of contemplation but goes far beyond. Now one sees God in all things and all things in God. Whereas previously one saw God through creatures, now one sees creatures through God. One is gifted (and gift it is) with a vision of unity and a reconciliation of opposites. This is great wisdom. This is mystical wisdom.

Ignatius of Loyola had such an awakening when, after his frightening dark night, his gaze fell on the flowing river. But even more important than Ignatius is Paul, who writes to the Corinthians about the wisdom of the cross. "For Jews demand signs and Greeks desire wisdom, but we proclaim Christ crucified, a stumbling-block to Jews and foolishness to Gentiles, but to those who are called, both Jews and Gentiles, Christ the power of God and the wisdom of God" (1 Cor 1:24). After speaking about the foolishness of his message Paul, as though having second thoughts, continues:

> Yet among the mature we do speak wisdom, though it is not a wisdom of this age . . . But we speak God's wisdom, secret and hidden, which God decreed before the ages for our glory. (1 Cor 2:6, 7)

Here Paul speaks of an entirely new wisdom, a wisdom that is diametrically opposed to the wisdom of the Greeks. This is a wisdom that cannot be expressed in concepts and images—"What no eye has seen nor ear heard, nor the human heart conceived" (1 Cor 2:9)—and God has revealed it to us through the Spirit. It is a wisdom that is secret and hidden, formless and empty. It is what we now call mysticism.

It might seem that the Pauline wisdom of the cross is quite different from anything in Buddhism. But not so. Enlightened Buddhists see the total emptiness of the crucified Jesus as an example of the highest wisdom. They understand Paul very well. That is why, as I have said earlier in this book, the *kenosis* of the Epistle to the Philippians is a basis for Buddhist-Christian dialogue. The Pauline emptiness speaks to those who have constantly recited the *Heart Sutra* and have experienced the transcendental wisdom *(prajñāpāramitā)* that is the glory of Buddhist religious experience.[3]

WOOD AND FIRE

The log, then, catches fire and begins to burn brightly. The mystical life has begun. The fire is love; the light is wisdom. St. John of the Cross vividly describes the fire of love progressively engulfing the log that was formerly sodden and wet: "Although the fire has penetrated the wood, transformed it, and united it with itself, yet as this fire grows hotter and continues to burn, so the wood becomes more and more incandescent and inflamed, even to the point of shooting out flames from itself."[4] And so he sings: "Oh llama de amor viva"—"O Living flame of love."

At the end of the dark night new life and a new energy surge into consciousness from the void. Great joy and great pain they give, so that St. John of the Cross can cry, "O sweet cautery, O delightful wound!" And just as the fire and the wood become one, so God and the human self become one in the all-consuming divine love. The goal of creation is that all should become one in God, that the human person and the human family should become divine.

When we speak of divinization, it is necessary to remember that in traditional mystical theology God is present at different levels.

At the level of existence God, the very Ground of Being, is present in all beings. God is present in Satan and in satanic people and places, giving them existence. Without God's presence they could not exist. Yet all beings are different from God and from one another by reason of their essence.

At the level of love, however, God is not necessarily present, since human beings can refuse or reject the love of God, just as they can refuse or reject human love. In the dark night the human person is cleansed or purified from his or her ugly tendency to reject love. As the fire of divine love is applied to the water-logged wood, the smoke and dirt of hatred, of refusal to love and to accept love belch forth. And the ensuing union between the human log and the divine fire is a union of love, not of essences. Mystical theology, careful to avoid any taint of pantheism, made clear that while the human person is divinized and comes to participate in the divine nature, the human person never becomes the essence of God. At the very pinnacle of the mystical life, one can still cry out, "Lord Jesus, Son of God, have mercy on me a sinner," and, "Abba, Father!"

MAGDALENE THE MYSTIC

One of the greatest mystics of the Christian tradition is Mary Magdalene.

The historical-critical approach to the scriptures tells us of three Marys—Mary Magdalene, Mary of Bethany, and the unnamed woman who was a sinner. But the mystics read scripture in their own way, finding therein the highest enlightenment. For them there was one Mary, the repentant sinner and the mystic.

The author of *The Cloud of Unknowing* speaks movingly of the love of Jesus for Mary and of her love for him. "Sweet was that love betwixt our Lord and Mary. Much love had she to him. Much more had he to her."[5] While Martha prepared the meal, Mary sat at his feet, listening to his words.

Now for this English author it is of the greatest importance that Mary sitting at the feet of Jesus enters into the cloud of unknowing in utter detachment from all things. So radical is her detachment that she even pays little attention to the body of Jesus—to "the beauty of his precious and blessed body." Her love goes straight to his Godhead:

> Yea! and full ofttimes I think that she was so deeply disposed to the love of his Godhead that she had but right little special beholding unto the beauty of his precious and blessed body, in which he sat full lovely, speaking and preaching before her; nor yet to anything else, bodily or spiritual. That this be truth it seemeth by the Gospel.[6]

This is a theme to which the author returns, telling us that Mary sitting before Jesus "regarded not the business of her sister . . . nor yet the sweet voice and the words of his Manhood . . . but she regarded the sovereignest wisdom of his Godhead shrouded in the dark words of his Manhood."[7]

That one must go beyond the humanity of Jesus to reach his divinity is an important theme in the Christian mystical tradition. In another treatise the author of *The Cloud of Unknowing*, quoting the words of Jesus to his disciples, "It is expedient for you that I go" (Jn 16:7), goes on to quote Augustine—"Unless the shape of his Manhood be withdrawn from our bodily eyes, the love of his Godhead may not fasten in our spiritual eyes."[8] And Aquinas, commenting on the same text of the gospel, tells us that the humanity of Christ is a way to God and that "we ought not to rest in it as an end in itself, but through it we should reach out to God."[9] Christ took away his physical presence lest the hearts of the disciples be captivated by his purely human qualities. In the *Summa Theologica* Thomas states his position very clearly:

> Things concerning the Godhead are, in themselves, the strongest incentives to love and devotion because God is lovable above all things. Yet, such is the weakness of the human mind that it needs a guide not only to the knowledge, but also to the love, of divine things by means of certain sensible objects known to us. Chief among these is the humanity of Christ . . . Accordingly, things related to Christ's humanity are the chief incentive to devotion, leading us there as a guide, although devotion itself has for its principal object things that concern the Godhead.[10]

This is the traditional theology that the author of *The Cloud of Unknowing* and others apply to the spiritual life. Ruusbroec said that "never creature may be or become so holy that it loses its created being and becomes God; even the soul of our Lord Jesus Christ shall ever remain creature, and other than God."[11] As for St. John of the Cross, also a Thomist, he insists that sensory things, such as sensible visions of Jesus or Mary or the saints, can be an impediment to the spirit, because they detain the soul and prevent the spirit from soaring to the invisible. "This is one of the reasons our Lord told his disciples that it was fitting for him to go so that the Holy Spirit might come (Jn 16:7). And so that Mary Magdalene would ground herself in faith, he refused to allow her to touch his feet after his resurrection (Jn 20:17)."[12]

I may have belabored this point, but I have done so for a reason.

People called to contemplative prayer, after meditating for some time on scenes from the gospel, find themselves drawn beyond the Jesus of history to the emptiness and the silence of the cloud of unknowing. Like Magdalene, they are no longer preoccupied with "his precious and blessed body," for they are drawn to love his person, which is divine. Like Paul, they say, "Though we once knew Christ according to the flesh, we know him no longer in that way" (2 Cor 5:16). Practically, the Jesus to whom they pray is the Jesus to whom God gave a name that is above all names "so that at the name of Jesus every knee should bend, in heaven and earth and under the earth, and every tongue should confess that Jesus Christ is Lord to the glory of God the Father" (Phil 2:10, 11).

Similarly for those who recite the "Jesus prayer." They may begin praying to the historical Jesus of Nazareth who walked by the Lake of Galilee; but as time goes on they no longer use images, for their gaze is fixed on the Word who enlightens everyone, the Son who stands at the right hand of the Father, the Second Person of the Blessed Trinity. Through union with the Son they are divinized. Becoming "participators in the divine nature" (2 Pt 1:4), they cry out to the Father in the Spirit. In short, their prayer is Trinitarian.

MYSTICISM AND INDWELLING

The Christian mystical tradition has constantly appealed to the Pauline text, "I live, now not I, but Christ lives in me" (Gal 2:20). Here Paul remains Paul, but the deepest reality within him is the indwelling Christ, who inspires and moves and directs. Many mystics resonate with this Pauline experience. The inner voice of the Spirit of Jesus dominates their lives.

In the fourth gospel the theme of indwelling is very central. Here the Eucharistic dimension is much in evidence. "The one who eats my flesh and drinks my blood dwells in me and I in him" (Jn 6:56). And again, "Dwell in me as I in you. Just as the branch cannot bear fruit by itself unless it dwell in the vine, neither can you unless you dwell in me" (Jn 15:4). Both individual and community are told to dwell in the love of Christ. If they do so, they will be one with Christ while retaining their identity; and they will bear much fruit.

Jesus dwells in the Father, as the Father dwells in Jesus. "As you, Father, are in me and I am in you, may they also be in us" (Jn 17:21). Jesus is not the Father and the Father is not Jesus; yet Jesus can say, "The Father and I are one" (Jn 10:30). Here we have the most sublime example of unity in diversity.

Furthermore, these deeply significant Johannine words tell us not only about our relationship with Jesus and the Father but also about our relationship with one another. "As I have loved you, you should love one another" (Jn 13:34). Does not this mean that as Jesus dwells in us, so we should dwell in one another? Does it not mean that we dwell in those we love and that they dwell in us? And have not these words the greatest significance for life in community, in marriage and in friendship?

With remarkable insight the Second Vatican Council draws such a conclusion:

> Indeed, the Lord Jesus, when he prayed to the Father, "that all may be one . . . as we are one" (Jn 17:21-22) opened up

vistas closed to human reason. For he implied a certain likeness between the union of the divine Persons, and in the union
of God's children in truth and charity. This likeness reveals
that the human person, the only creature on earth that God
wills for itself, cannot find self except through a sincere gift of
self.[13]

Here the council points to *a mysticism of interpersonal relationships*.
The gospel, it claims, tells us of a dimension of human love that reason
alone could not discover. Earlier the council had spoken of the compan-
ionship of man and woman as "the primary form of interpersonal communion."[14] Now we see this communion in the context of mutual
indwelling. When a man and a woman love one another, they dwell in
one another as the Father dwells in the Son and the Son in the Father.
What sublime mysticism is here! What a challenge to our world! Is not
this the human intimacy that all seek today?

A distinguishing feature of the fourth gospel is its emphasis on communion. Here there is no talk of non-self or non-ego or identity with the
Absolute. Everything centers around communion and indwelling. With
prophetic words the Johannine Jesus points to a glorious eschatalogical
climax, "In that day you will know that I am in my Father, and you in
me, and I in you" (Jn 14:20). Surely these words have special significance today. There is much talk of sexual union and of collaboration
between men and women; and while sexuality and collaboration are
indispensable dimensions of life, affective communion—that is to say,
union of minds and hearts—is the fundamental need, without which
human beings fall into gnawing loneliness and wretched despair. Can
there not, then, be a mysticism wherein people, married or celibate, love
one another to the point of indwelling? And is not such mysticism based
on the mystery that God is three Persons in communion and that Jesus
came to share that communion with the human family?

Obviously such mysticism will be a process, with dark nights,
anguishing struggles and agonizing failures. Yet it may lead to the union
that Shakespeare envisages when, in one of his most religious sonnets,
he cries,

> Let me not to the marriage of true minds
> Admit impediments . . .

A colleague of mine, a Shakespearean scholar, claims that this sonnet's
insistence that love never ends was inspired by Paul's hymn to love in the

Epistle to the Corinthians. Were Paul and Shakespeare alike speaking of the mystical marriage wherein each person finds his or her unique self in communion with the other?

The council makes clear that in the mysticism of loving interpersonal relations one finds one's true self precisely in the gift of oneself. Teilhard de Chardin puts it well in a powerful paradox:

Union differentiates

If this Teilhardian principle is taken seriously, it could revolutionize mystical theology East and West, changing our approach to the self. In union with the other, in becoming the other, in dwelling in the other, in intimacy with the other I find my true self. People who have lived for years in a happy and loving relationship and who have passed through its dark nights bear witness to the truth of this Teilhardian insight. In intimate union with the other they have found their true self, always with ecstatic joy. Union differentiates. "Let me not to the marriage of true minds admit impediments . . . "

MYSTICAL ENERGY

From what has been said it will be clear that mystical experience engenders a very powerful energy. I have spoken of spiritual fire and blinding light and the burning log. I have said that at the end of the dark night an overwhelming energy that may knock the mystic for a loop is released. In the beginning stages the mystic-to-be may have bizarre dreams, frightening hallucinations, grotesque visions and disturbing voices. The great stigmatic Padre Pio could read minds and bilocate, traveling mysteriously to various parts of the world. Similar mystical phenomena are recorded in India and Tibet. All this points to the existence of very powerful energy.

Following St. John of the Cross and the Christian tradition, I have already said that we must always evaluate these psychic phenomena with cautious discernment. Forces of good and evil are at work in our turbulent world, and the possibility of deception is very great. At the same time mystical theology has always taught unequivocally that the ultimate source of energy is God, who is love. St. John of the Cross tells us that the living flame of love *is* the Holy Spirit. Eastern Christianity speaks of the Uncreated Energies, Orthodox theologians distinguishing between the divine essence, which is unknowable, and the divine energies, which are experienced in the mystical life. And Dante, seeing the energy of

God's love as a cosmic force that vivifies the entire material universe, speaks of "the love that moves the sun and other stars."

L'amor che move il sole e l'altre stelle

Dante speaks for the Christian tradition. Forces of evil may plot destruction, but the great energy of the universe, the energy that will finally triumph, is love.

In the twentieth century psychology and physics became increasingly interested in energy. It is said that Jung, while dining with Einstein in the 1920s, began to develop his theory of synchronicity, which postulates a form of energy that mirrors deep unconscious forces of the human mind and explains meaningful coincidences. Einstein had pointed to a staggering amount of energy concealed in the atom, and Jung began to ask if there might be an equivalent energy concealed in the human psyche. And could this energy be released under certain circumstances?

Jung then became more and more interested in Asian meditation and mysticism.

For energy or the life force—*ki* in Japanese, *chi* in Chinese and *prana* in Sanskrit—is central to all Asian culture. This mysterious energy that still baffles the scientist plays an important role in Chinese medicine, in the martial arts, in the way of tea and all the "ways." It is of special importance in meditation and mysticism. This is a cosmic energy that flows through the universe and through all things that exist. Enlightenment, the highest mystical experience, is associated with the flow of energy through the human body.

From time immemorial enlightened Asian masters have taught their disciples to control this energy so as to reach consummate wisdom. They have given their disciples instruction concerning diet, breathing, posture and control of the mind. They have insisted that one who would allow the energy to flow freely must practice the most radical detachment and live a life of compassion toward all sentient beings.

Of special importance is *kundalini*.[15] The serpent, the feminine energy or *Shakti*, lies coiled and dormant at the base of the spine. Once awakened it passes through the various chakras, or energy centers, awakening and giving life. A climax is reached at the crown chakra, where the marriage between Shiva and Shakti is celebrated with great enlightenment and bliss. Yet *kundalini* is more than religious energy. It is operative, we are told, in artists, scientists, poets, musicians and people of genius in every walk of life. It is the evolutionary energy of the universe.

That energy flows through the spine to the crown of the head bringing enlightenment would seem to be a tenet of all Asian meditation from

India to Japan. One must keep the back straight, allowing the energy to flow freely. Sometimes Zen enlightenment comes to the meditator like a psychological explosion, accompanied by bursts of laughter in which the whole body shakes almost uncontrollably for ten or fifteen minutes. So powerful is the energy that has been unleashed.

Thanks to Jung and others the energy of Asia has come to the attention of people in the Western world. Institutes have been founded to study *kundalini* and to investigate what is now called spiritual emergence. Here my question is, What does all this say to the Christian mystical tradition?

It seems to me that the Asian tradition will teach Christians of the third millennium very much about energy and enlightenment. Christians will reflect on the chakras. They will learn breathing and posture and control of the mind. They will be increasingly open to the wisdom of Asia. In this way we will come to a new understanding not only of our Christian mystical path but also of many passages of sacred scripture. The Bible has not a few references to explosive energy and profound enlightenment. Asian exegetes of the future will surely interpret these passages in a new and creative way.

At the same time it seems to me that we must stay with dialogue, retaining our Christian terminology and allowing Hindus and Buddhists to do likewise. I do not think it is helpful to identify *kundalini* with the Holy Spirit. I prefer to say that the Holy Spirit, the *source* of all cosmic energy, is the source of *kundalini*. Nor do I think it helpful for Christians to use the Hindu symbolism of the coiled serpent and the marriage between Shiva and Shakti. Would it not be better if Christians of all denominations were to collaborate with the Orthodox in further developing the theology of the Uncreated Energies? In this way we could enter into an exciting dialogue that would help give birth to a new mysticism.

THE HEBREW PROPHETS

In the twentieth century some scholars distinguished between the mystical religions of Asia and the prophetic religions of the Bible. Mysticism and prophecy, they held, were different charisms.

This is not in accord with the Christian tradition, which sees Moses and Elijah as the greatest of mystics and finds profound mystical experience in the lives of Isaiah, Jeremiah and Ezekiel. The mysticism of the prophets, however, is *kataphatic*, based on a theology of affirmation, whereas the mysticism of Asia is primarily *apophatic*, based on a theology of negation. The Hebrew tradition sees God as the source of all existence; the Hindu tradition says "not this, not this, not this."

Aquinas claimed that the prophets enjoyed the gift of infused contemplation, of which I have already spoken. In this way he understood the formula so often used by the prophets, "The word of the Lord came to me" or the words of the Lord to Jeremiah, "I am putting my words into your mouth" (Jer 1:9). The word of God was a gift. It was, moreover, a dynamic gift that compelled the prophets, often tearing them asunder. "The Lord God has spoken; who can but prophesy?" cries Amos (Am 3:8). And Jeremiah, consumed by mystical fire, laments that "within me there is something like a burning fire shut up in my bones" (Jer 20:9).

Kataphatic mysticism, however, reaches a great climax with the inaugural visions of the prophets. Moses encounters Yahweh at the burning bush and learns that God has a name: "I am who I am" (Ex 3:14). And how powerful is the vision of Isaiah, "Holy, holy, holy is the Lord of hosts; the whole earth is full of his glory" (Is 6:3). And then Ezekiel: "As I was among the exiles by the river Chebar, the heavens were opened, and I saw visions of God" (Ezek 1:1). But in all these visions God is not simply revealing himself to his people; he is *sending* the prophet on a mission. The prophet is not called to live as a solitary in a spiritual world; he is sent into the toil and trouble and hurly-burly of this world. It is here he must suffer and die.

After meeting God, then, the prophets were sent into the world. They were rooted and embedded in this world. They were involved in the economics and politics of their times. They fought for the poor and the downtrodden and the oppressed. They confronted the rich and powerful, demanding social reform. They lived in history, and they made history. They insisted that the rewards and punishments of God come in this life and in this life only. The prophet Nathan did not tell David that he would go to hell after death. He told him that his beloved son would die. We are not told that Job went to heaven to enjoy eternal bliss but that "Job lived one hundred and forty years, and saw his children and his children's children, four generations" (Jb 42:16). The prophets were sent by God, but they were immersed in the nitty-gritty of this world.

Hebrew prophets are needed in our world today, as proponents of liberation theology have seen so well. The human race, conscious that our problem now is survival, cries out for prophetic men and women who are deeply concerned with the suffering of our planet—people who see the evil structures that oppress the poor, the fortunes squandered on weapons of mass destruction, the useless waste of the resources of the earth, the pollution of the environment, the exploitation of women and children. Such prophetic people will feel called to confront ruthless dictators, corrupt politicians, bloated capitalists, scheming tycoons, wealthy playboys, unscrupulous drug barons, wily tricksters and hypocritical religious leaders. To save our world they must have a deep compassion and a strong sense of justice; they must be willing to go to prison and to die. But, above all, they must be men and women who have met God and are sent by God. "The spirit of the Lord God is upon me, because the Lord has anointed me; he has sent me to bring good news to the oppressed, to bind up the broken-hearted, to proclaim liberty to the captives and release to prisoners" (Is 61:1).

The apophatic mysticism of Asia will not solve these problems unless it is complemented by the kataphatic mysticism of the Bible. For India, in its tireless search for God and its profound mystical experience, has always been tempted to deny the reality of this world and to look on the sensible universe as *maya* or illusion. Indeed, many educated Hindus believe that their unworldly mystical tradition is responsible for the grinding poverty and the economic chaos that bedevils their country. Might not Hindu mystics learn the necessity of economic and political reform from the Hebrew prophets? Might they not learn from the Hebrew tradition to become more worldly?

Nor is India alone. The apophatic mysticism of the Christian tradition has similar problems. It will not speak to today's world unless it is complemented by its kataphatic counterpart. Scholars remind us that the Christian apophatic tradition was originally influenced by a neo-platonic "flight from the world." That is why it needed dialogue with Francis of Assisi and Ignatius of Loyola; that is why today it needs dialogue with Teilhard de Chardin and Mother Teresa of Calcutta. Only a marriage between the apophatic and the kataphatic will speak to the third millennium.

THE FUTURE

It is now time to sum up.

Christian mysticism must be faithful to its glorious tradition while learning from the mystical religions of Asia and moving into the future.

In what may be a slight break with the past I have distinguished between *infused contemplation*, which is characterized by the sense of presence, and *mysticism*, which is characterized by the fire of love and the light of wisdom. I maintain that mysticism only begins after a harrowing purification which tradition calls "the dark night," though it may take a variety of forms. Now one's being becomes being-in-love. Now the true self is born. Now there arises in the mind and heart the living flame of love, the divine energy, the burning of the heart. As the candle burns and gives light, so the mystic burns with the fire of love and radiates the light of wisdom.

In mystical experience Christians can dialogue with mystics of Asia, paying special attention to the *advaita* or nondualism of Hinduism and the emptiness of Buddhism. Here we find common ground. Yet each religion has its distinctive features. Most Christian mystics love the Song of Songs. For them, in the terminology of Bernard Lonergan, mysticism is an experience of falling in love with God so that one's being becomes being-in-love. The Christian does not lose his or her unique personality but finds it in a new and profound way. "Those who lose their life for my sake will find it" (Mt 10:39). The gospel teaches a nondualism of love.

And as we move into the future, Christians must pay more and more attention to the kataphatic dimension of their own tradition and share this dimension with others; they must pay more and more attention to the biblical mysticism of prophecy. Only in this way can we save our mysticism from sterile irrelevance; only in this way will we speak meaningfully to the men and women of the third millennium. The answer to our problems is not flight but further involvement.

TEN

Sannyasin, Bodhisattva and Mystic

MYSTICAL DIALOGUE

To Christians living in Asia it becomes increasingly clear that interreligious dialogue must be carried on principally at the level of mysticism. Hinduism and Buddhism and Taoism, profoundly mystical religions, have penetrated Asian culture, leading millions to liberation and enlightenment. Even now these religions live in the unconscious of the people, influencing their way of thinking and feeling and acting, influencing art and architecture, literature and poetry. Early European travelers were not completely off base when they talked about the "mystic East."

It is not surprising, then, if religious people in Asia are little impressed by a wordy philosophy and theology that indulges in extensive reasoning and thinking, or if they are unmoved by a historical-critical approach to the scriptures that tells them in detail about the rind without helping them savor the sweet and delicious fruit. It is not surprising if they are unimpressed by a psychology that stops at the level of dreams and repressed memories without penetrating to the true self, to the void and to the ground of being. While they have unbounded admiration for the thousands of dedicated Christian educators and social workers who have given their all to the masses of the people, they still long for the Buddhist bodhisattva, the Hindu sannyasin and the Christian saint.

Let me first speak about India.

HINDU-CHRISTIAN SANNYASINS

From time immemorial India has had the greatest respect for the saint, the holy person who renounces everything in the world in search of God.

120

Such persons are known as sannyasins and their way of life is called sannyasa. From the time of the saintly Italian Jesuit Robert de Nobili (1577-1656), some Christians in India have always aspired to become sannyasins, adopting a lifestyle at once deeply Indian and deeply Christian. Here I would like briefly to discuss the lives of three such Christian sannyasins whose lives spanned the twentieth century. Jules Monchanin (1895-1957), Henri Le Saux (1910-73) and Bede Griffiths (1906-93) were no doubt the last foreign missionaries to live in India as sannyasins. The future of Christian sannyasa rests with Indian Christians.

Jules Monchanin arrived in India from France in 1939. He was truly a man of God with a great love for India and a strong sense of mission. To his mother he wrote that his aim was "to rethink India in a Christian way and Christianity in an Indian way—and I believe profoundly that it is for that I was born."[1] From the dawn of history India had never wavered in its search for the Absolute; Monchanin, following the theology of his time, was convinced that the spiritual aspirations of India would be fulfilled and reach fruition in the gospel of Jesus Christ. But the gospel preached in India had neglected the mystics. Monchanin wanted to understand and experience the gospel in a mystical way; he wanted to bring the Christian mystics to India.

In 1948 Monchanin was joined by a younger French monk, Henri Le Saux. Now commonly known by his Sanskrit name, Abhishiktananda, Le Saux aimed to introduce into India a monastic life that would be wholly Benedictine and wholly Indian.[2] Together the two founded an ashram where they lived a life of radical poverty, dressed as Hindu sannyasins, sitting and sleeping on the floor, eating vegetarian food and walking barefoot. The ashram they called Shantivanam, meaning "Forest of Peace," or Saccidananda, which is the Hindu name for the Godhead. As *Sat* means "Being," *Chit* means "Consciousness" and *Ananda* means "bliss," they took Saccidananda as a symbol of the Blessed Trinity—the Father as Being, the Word as Consciousness and the Spirit as Love or Bliss. Monchanin insisted that Christian mysticism is above all Trinitarian and that the doctrine of the Blessed Trinity alone would fulfill or complete the Hindu religious quest, which until now had expressed itself in terms of non-dualism or *advaita*.

But, as happens so often, the holy men did not get on together. They were quite different in temperament and ideas. Shortly after his arrival in India, Henri Le Saux, now Abhishiktananda, felt the call to be a wandering sannyasin, to visit the Hindu holy places and to enter more and more deeply into the Hindu religious experience. He met and was deeply impressed by the saintly Hindu mystic Ramana Maharshi, and when Ramana Maharshi died, Abhishiktananda was in some way initiated into Hindu sannyasa by another guru, Swami Gnananda, in a ceremony known as *diksa*. At a thirty-two day retreat he claimed to have experienced the *advaita* of the Upanishads in the depths of his being, the cave of the heart. From now on, his vocation was to be a Hindu Christian monk.

Monchanin watched all this with growing dismay. The younger monk, he felt, had moved too rapidly into a Hindu religious experience that he was unable to integrate, particularly as he had been educated in a somewhat narrow theology in France. In a letter to one of his friends Monchanin laments:

> Fr. Le Saux is incapable of questioning his experience (except verbally). The institutional church is a burden to him (to him who earlier was devoted to Canon Law and Liturgy!); he suffers from its narrowness, realized through his contact with Hinduism. Basically, he comes from a *rigorist* and even *integrist* theology: the change is too sudden.[3]

About his own theological stance Monchanin was clear: "Our task and the task of our successors is the same as that of the Greek fathers: to accept that which is compatible, to reject that which is incompatible with Christianity. And the rest is vertigo or betrayal."[4]

As time went on, Abhishiktananda, feeling that Shantivanam had failed, spent more and more time in the mountains of North India, exploring the possibility of moving permanently to a new ashram in the Himalayas. Again, Monchanin was not impressed. To a friend he writes about the problems of Shantivanam and about the departure of Fr. Le Saux, "who follows his own line and wants to live as a Christian hermit among spiritual Hindus." He goes on sadly, "Serious divergences between us have overshadowed these last years; I think he goes too far in his concessions to Hinduism, and it seems to me more and more doubtful that the essence of Christianity can be recovered beyond *Advaita* (the non-duality of Shankara)."[5]

After the death of Monchanin in 1957 Abhishiktananda built a hermitage in the Himalayas and lived there for sixteen years, praying, meditating and writing until his death from a heart attack in 1973. His books and articles are widely read in the West, and scholarly studies of his enigmatic personality continue. No doubt that study will go on. Even now, as we enter the third millennium, the theological and experiential tension that divided these two men of God is of the greatest significance.

Abhishiktananda's ideal was to become a Hindu-Christian monk. If this had meant living Christianity in a profoundly Indian way, he would have had the full support of Monchanin. But Abhishiktananda meant more. He had been initiated into Hindu sannyasa. Convinced of the validity of his Hindu enlightenment and equally faithful to his Christian prayer, he wanted to be a Hindu monk and a Christian monk at the same time. "The experience of the Upanishads is true—*I know!*" he wrote enthusiastically, at a time when he was celebrating the eucharist and reciting the breviary with fidelity and devotion.[6] The Hindu revelation and the Christian revelation came from the same source. Surely union between the two must be possible. Abhishiktananda wanted to live both of them in the *guha* or "cave of the heart."

Yet this methodology caused him untold anguish. The haunting fear that the two experiences might be irreconcilable appears throughout his *Journal Intime,* published posthumously. "A fear that these two experiences may be irreconcilable is everywhere in the diary," writes Jacques Dupuis, who recounts Abhishiktananda experiencing an "ocean of anguish wherever I turn." Dupuis further quotes the agonized words of the Hindu-Christian monk, "I cannot be a Hindu and Christian at the same time nor can I be either simply a Hindu or simply a Christian."[7] To be a Hindu and a Christian at the same time! This Monchanin could not accept. Much later the Dalai Lama spoke humorously of putting a sheep's head on a yak's body. Was Abhishiktananda trying to do just this? Such an enterprise could only cause heart-rending anguish.

Furthermore, Abhishiktananda's sad limitations as a theologian appear in an essay written shortly before his death. Asked to speak about advaitic or Upanishadic prayer he says:

> First, truly speaking, there is no such thing as advaitic *prayer.* Advaita is the central teaching of the Upanishads, and no prayer remains possible for him who has realized the truth of the Upanishads . . . for the duality which makes it possible for man to think of himself as standing in front of God has disappeared in the burning encounter with the Real, *sat.*[8]

That no prayer remains possible for one who has realized the truth of the Upanishads is very questionable. Great Hindus like Ramakrishna, Gandhi, Tagore and Aurobindo were quite capable of prayer to God. For at the heart of all prayer is a great paradox—we are one with God and we are not one with God. In "the burning encounter with the Real, *sat*" we are one with God but paradoxically we can still cry out to God in prayer. At the summit of the mystical life the Christian becomes God "by participation," yet he or she can still call out, "Abba, Father!"

Equally questionable is Abhishiktananda's talk of the "duality" of man standing in front of God. The Christian mystical tradition states unequivocally that the stance of the human person before God is not dualistic but relational. The person who prays is not dualistically separated from God but is closely united with God in a love that is always moving toward oneness. Indeed, simple Christians often feel one with God while praying "Our Father . . . "—and in this they see no contradiction. For them it is a non-problem.

For all his adaptation to India, Abhishiktananda still belonged to a Western world that found it difficult to live with paradox. As Monchanin saw so well, he was educated in a theology that was little attuned to Asian thinking. Accustomed to reasoning in terms of black and white, he anguished unduly over the reconciliation of opposites. Yet his noble anguish speaks powerfully to a world that is struggling with interreligious dialogue. This Hindu-Christian sannyasi was surely a prophetic voice crying in the wilderness of the twentieth century.

But it is now time to consider yet another prophet. The third sannyasi is Bede Griffiths.

BEYOND THE SIGNS

Bede Griffiths came to Shantivanam in 1968 and died there in 1993. His aim was "to establish a form of contemplative life based alike on the traditions of Christian monasticism and Hindu 'sannyasa.'"[9] Following the tradition of Monchanin and Abhishiktananda, his little community lived a life of great poverty, warmly welcoming all who came their way. Yet the central thing was not the service of people but the life of prayer and the search for Ultimate Reality. In this they were true to sannyasa.

Griffiths's theology of dialogue developed from a *theology of fulfillment,* which saw the gospel of Jesus Christ as the fulfillment or completion of Hinduism to a *theology of complementarity,* which saw the great religions as complementing one another. "I did once hold the view of 'fulfillment,'" he said at the end of his life. "But for many years now I have accepted 'complementarity.' This means that each tradition is unique in its own way."[10] Yet with characteristic second thoughts he adds, "I would say honestly that to me there is a fullness and finality in Christ which I don't find in others. But I wouldn't press that on the Hindus obviously. I would rather simply emphasize the distinctive character of the Christian revelation and of Christ."[11] And he explains:

> We need to bring out what is unique in the Mystery of Christ, the Trinity, the incarnation, redemption and certain concepts

that are quite distinct in Christianity. We do not say that they are better or anything else. But they are the unique Christian revelation and we respect the Hindu and Buddhist revelations.[12]

He was spared the anguish of Abhishiktananda. This was partly due to his English sense of humor, his Anglican background and his great ability to live with paradox. But it was also due to his unambiguous commitment to his vocation as a Christian monk. He would never accept initiation into sannyasa from a Hindu guru as Abhishiktananda had done:

> I would not be in favor of taking sannyasa from a Hindu sannyasin. I would think that would not be good. Sannyasa is a particular way of experience which is not specifically Christian. Abhishiktananda went to Thirukkovilur to Swami Gnananda and he thought he had a sort of initiation then. But that is a form of diksa which I would not be happy to accept.[13]

He goes on to say that his primary commitment is his solemn profession as a monk. Yet his ideal of dialogue is surely challenging:

> I do try to share the Hindu experience of God . . . The experience of God in the Upanishads and the Bhagavad Gita is distinct from that of the Christian and yet not opposed to it. We seek to assimilate the Hindu experience of God and bring it into our experience of God in Christ . . . We fully accept the Hindu experience of God.[14]

When speaking about the path of the sannyasin, Bede verges on the poetic. The world we see around us is a world of signs. The world of economics and politics and sociology, the world of art and music and poetry, the world of television and Internet and fax—this world seems very real, but in fact it has no reality whatever apart from the Ultimate Reality toward which it points. Even the world of religion—the dogmas, the doctrines and the sacraments are signs. The church, too, is "a kind of sacrament or sign."[15] Even God, *insofar as God can be named,* is a sign, a name for the Ultimate Truth that cannot be named. "Thus the Sannyasin is called to go beyond all religion, beyond every human institution, to go beyond every scripture and creed, till he comes to that which every religion and scripture and ritual signifies but can never name."[16]

To go beyond the sign, it must be remembered, is not to reject the sign but to reach the thing signified. "I have not felt called to reject anything that I have learned of God or of Christ or of the Church," writes Griffiths.[17] In the terminology of St. Thomas Aquinas he is passing from the *sacramentum* to the *res*. Yet the signs are completely necessary. Indeed, the modern world will perish if it does not rediscover and recognize the signs, the myths and the symbols that lead to Ultimate Truth.

A wide gulf, however, separates the Hindu sannyasin from the Christian monk. Whereas the Hindu leads a wandering, solitary life deprived of all security, whereas even those who live in groups put little stress on community, does not Christian monasticism put community and, above all, the celebration of the liturgy at the center of everything? And does not community life, particularly the highly institutionalized community life that now exists in Christian monasticism—does not this give the Christian monk a security that the Hindu does not have?

Asked about this Griffiths replied that the monastic tradition that came to the West with St. Benedict centers around community—and this community undoubtedly gives the monks great security. However, if one goes further back, to the desert fathers, one finds monks who were much less secure, wandering monks who went out into the desert to pray in solitude and in silence. This tradition died out, but, Griffiths believes, it could be revived, especially in India. He sees the Camaldolese order as a possible place for such experimentation.

As for liturgy, Christianity, Bede maintains, differs from Hinduism in the value it attributes to this form of worship. This must be taken into account. If the Christian sannyasi transcends all signs and sacraments to encounter the Transcendent Reality, this does not mean that he dismisses them but that *"he relates to them in a new way . . .* He is gone beyond. But then he sees how the Infinite, the Eternal is mirrored, reflected and manifested in the sacraments and rites. And so I don't feel any opposition."[18] In the Eastern church the mature monk can go beyond the liturgy, like Seraphim of Sarov, who lived in solitude. "The liturgy is now within him. So he doesn't need to share with the celebration. That is exceptional. But it shows that there could be a certain freedom from the sacraments. We shouldn't feel bound by them."[19] Griffiths then goes on to say that in India and in his ashram personal prayer is primary.

Bede Griffiths was a pioneer and a searcher. He knew he had no definitive answers. Yet with confidence and humor he walked the way of Christ in a new culture and in dialogue with another religion.

THE SAME AND DIFFERENT

In going beyond all signs to witness to Ultimate Reality the sannyasin finds himself closely united with his Buddhist, Hebrew, Muslim and Christian counterparts. In all religions we find men and women who renounce everything in search of the Great Mystery that cannot be named.

This raises a question that has been asked again and again since the time of the good and pious Friedrich Schleiermacher (1768-1834)—Is there a universal religious experience common to all religions? This question becomes all the more challenging in the area of mysticism, where the search for supreme wisdom carries one beyond all reasoning and thinking, beyond all words and signs into the silence of a cloud of unknowing. Is the silent, wordless, imageless wisdom of the sannyasi and the bodhisattva and the Christian mystic the same? Do they finally have the same enlightenment?

Take the bodhisattva.[20] Like the sannyasin, he or she is acutely aware of the transience of all things. This phenomenal world that we see around us is passing and we are passing with it. This is the truth of impermanence expressed in the much quoted Buddhist axiom *shogyō mujō*,

諸行無常

All things are passing. Just as the sannyasin sees all things as signs, so the bodhisattva sees all things as fingers pointing to the moon. One who would walk the way of the Buddha becomes detached from these fingers in order to look at the reality toward which they point. With this detachment comes a great emptiness, which is also a great compassion. Clearly such a way has much in common with sannyasa, but bodhisattva and sannyasin would agree that their paths are not the same. They are the same and different.

Then there is the Christian mystic. One who climbs Mount Carmel realizes, like the sannyasin and the bodhisattva, that "we have not here a lasting city" (Heb 13:14). Like her Hindu and Buddhist counterparts, the bride clings to nothing. "Nothing, nothing, nothing—and even on the mountain nothing." Filled with a burning love she moves toward union with the beloved. Her way has much in common with the way of the sannyasin and the bodhisattva, but all would agree that their paths are not the same. They are the same and different.

Granted that the ways differ, one might ask about the Great Reality they all seek, the Great Mystery that surrounds us—is not this the same? And is not the final wordless, imageless, experience—whether this life or beyond the grave—is it not the same?

That the Great Mystery is the same no one will deny. But what an incomprehensible mystery it is! The final grasp of this mystery is beyond all human comprehension, as Paul knows so well when he says that "no eye has seen, nor ear heard, nor the human heart conceived, what God has prepared for those who love him" (1 Cor 2:9). Consequently, can we not say that the sannyasin, the bodhisattva and the Christian mystic each has a very tiny, yet unique grasp of a Mystery that transcends all human understanding?

I say this also from a consideration of the important Chinese character pronounced *tao* in Chinese and *dō* in Japanese and usually translated into English as "way."

道

In Western languages we speak of a "way to," but in Chinese and Japanese one more commonly speaks of a "way of." Thus there is a way of tea, a way of the bow, a way of the flower and so on. In other words, *tao* or *dō* is a way of life rather than a way that leads somewhere.

Now the religions are ways; that is, ways of life. The way is not a means. The way is not like a ladder that one kicks away after climbing in through the window. It is not dualistically separated from the goal. The way is contained in the final mystical experience. That is why Griffiths can say so well that we never cease to relate to the signs, even when we transcend them. If our way is Christian, the whole gospel is contained supraconceptually in the highest enlightenment. And the same holds true for the Vedas, the Upanishads and the Buddhist Sutras: the enlightened person does not discard the scriptures but grasps them in a supraconceptual way. In short, *the way is the enlightenment.* As we seek unity in diversity, so we realize that our ways are the same and different and that our enlightenments are also the same and different.

The great mystic Thérèse of Lisieux (1873-97), now a doctor of the church, explains in her deceptively simple way the wonderful variety that exists even among the blessed who have entered into glory:

> He set before me the book of Nature: and I understood how all
> the flowers created by Him are beautiful, how the splendor of
> the rose and the whiteness of the lily do not lessen the perfume

of the little violet or the delightful simplicity of the daisy. I understood that if all flowers wanted to be roses, Nature would lose her springtime beauty, and the fields would no longer be decked out with little wild flowers . . . It is the same in the world of souls, Our Lord's living garden.[21]

The universe is God's living garden, and unity in diversity is its basic law. Even in the most sublime mystical experiences—experiences that reach fruition only after death—there is variety; yet there is also unity since all are pointing toward, or sharing in the life of, the same Ultimate Reality.

The Greeks saw that there was a baffling paradox at the heart of existence, and they spoke of "the problem of the one and the many." How can there be one thing and many things? The philosophical solution of Aristotle and Aquinas need not concern us here. Enough to say that a lot of people cannot endure paradox. Either they live in the busy and anxious world of the many, denying the one, or they aspire to a lofty unity, denying the many. As we enter the third millennium, the great challenge is to accept that there are many religions and many religious experiences while recognizing that there is one origin and one goal. We must live with paradox if we want to survive.

DANGERS OF SANNYASA

In a world of violence and greed, a world that believes above all in the power of money, men and women who renounce everything to search for, and witness to, Ultimate Reality make a profound impression. The sannyasin, the bodhisattva and the Christian mystic give hope and life to a despairing generation. They are the salt of the earth and the light of the world. "Let your light shine before others, so that they may see your good works and give glory to your Father who is in heaven" (Mt 5:16). In religious cultures where spiritual values are still esteemed, the man or woman of God is greeted with special reverence, love and respect.

And here precisely is the danger. Honor and respect can destroy human beings, making them forget that they are wretched, pitiable, poor, blind and naked. It can make them pretenders, acting a part that does not correspond with their inner frailty. They can come to God like that man in the gospel who said that he was not like the sinful tax collector. Alas, the salt can all too easily lose its taste. Then it is no longer good for anything but is thrown out and trampled underfoot.

Bede Griffiths warns of hypocrisy among the so-called sannyasins of Tamil Nadu. And what a dangerous and subtle temptation is hypocrisy!

"When you pray, do not be like the hypocrites; for they love to stand and pray in the synagogues and at the street corners, so that they may be seen by others" (Mt 6:5). And then there is that terrible condemnation of religious hypocrites who are like whited sepulchers—beautiful on the outside but inwardly full of bones and all kinds of filth.

Yet even more dangerous than hypocrisy is pride, the sin of Lucifer himself. When the seventy return with joy, boasting that even the demons submitted to them, Jesus greets them with a stern and extraordinary warning, "I watched Satan fall from heaven like a flash of lightning" (Lk 10:18). He goes on to thank his Father who has hidden these things from the wise and intelligent and revealed them to little ones.

It is hardly surprising, then, that the Christian tradition is at one with the traditions of other religions in putting humility—the recognition of one's nothingness—at the very basis of the spiritual journey. "Humility! Humility! Humility!" writes Teresa of Avila. And the First Week of the Ignatian Exercises, after proposing a meditation on the sin of the angels, tells us to meditate on the temptation of our first parents—"You will be like God" (Gn 3:5). Likewise, Zen Buddhism insists that the first and last stage in the journey is to realize one's nothingness. The great temptation is to build up the ego, which ought to die.

In short, the mystical journey begins and ends with humility.

HUMILITY AND POWERLESSNESS

In today's world the word *humility* has lost its appeal. Yet one of the great spiritual movements of the twentieth century speaks graphically about humility in other terms. Alcoholics Anonymous, commonly known as A.A., makes "powerlessness" the first and most basic of its twelve steps on the road to wholeness.[22]

A.A., it should be noted, is not affiliated with any religion. It is a community that welcomes any person of any religion (or of no religion) who wants to be liberated from his or her addiction. Founded by recovered alcoholics, it gradually became clear that the twelve steps could liberate people addicted to drugs, to gambling, to sex, to almost anything. For we now know that few human beings are without addictions. People can be addicted to power, to honor and glory, to making money, to writing books, to reading comics, to drinking coffee, to eating chocolate, to a relationship, to sex, to travel, to tobacco, to computers and even to religious experience. The sannyasin, the bodhisattva and the Christian mystic are no exceptions. Like other people, they have their addictions, often more dangerous because more subtle and more spiritual.

The first step is the admission of one's powerlessness. "Vis-à-vis alcohol (or whatever the addiction may be) I am powerless. My life has become unmanageable." A.A. wisely avoids religious words like *humility, sin* or *guilt,* and the word *God* only comes later in the process, while *meditation* and *prayer* appear at the very end. At the beginning the important word is *powerlessness.*

Now for human beings to admit that they are powerless and that their life has become unmanageable is very, very difficult. For the sannyasin, the bodhisattva and the Christian mystic it is particularly difficult. It is a death, a total loss. Often people can only make this admission when they are lying in the gutter or groveling in the dust. Such people know that addiction is demonic. It is like possession by an unclean spirit. One is helpless. Human effort is of no avail. "I will" or "I will not" may even be counter-productive. What is one to do?

The second step of A.A. is belief that a power greater than oneself can restore one to sanity, and in the third step one appeals to this higher power. Put in religious terms, the answer of A.A. is humble prayer to God as one understands God.

In the gospel of St. Mark we read of a father who brought to Jesus his son who had all the symptoms of demonic affliction. "Teacher," he said, "I brought you my son; he has a spirit that makes him unable to speak; and whenever it seizes him, it dashes him down; and he foams and grinds his teeth and becomes rigid; and I asked your disciples to cast it out, but they could not do so" (Mk 9:17, 18). When Jesus had cast out the demon in a dramatic way, the disciples ask why they were unable to cast it out. And Jesus answered, "This kind can come out only through prayer" (Mk 9:29).

This is the enlightened discovery of A.A. Addictions are not cast out by counseling or by psychotherapy nor by moral instruction or by imposition of rules or by threat of imprisonment. Only acknowledgment of one's powerlessness and humble prayer to a higher power will exorcise the demon of addiction.

One mystic who, recognizing his own powerlessness, called out to a higher power was St. Paul.

PAUL THE MYSTIC

Paul writes to the Romans about his own powerlessness, telling them that his life has become unmanageable. "I do not understand my own actions. For I do not do what I want but I do the very thing I hate" (Rom 7:15). As if to emphasize this sense of utter powerlessness, he repeats, "I can will what is right, but I cannot do it. For I do not do the good I want, but the evil I do not want is what I do" (Rom 7:19). Poor Paul! What had happened? Yet anyone familiar with A.A. will understand.

Within Paul there rages a conflict between an inmost self, a true self that delights in the law of God, and a small self, an ego that is torn this way and that, holding him captive. "For I delight in the law of God in my inmost self, but I see in my members another law at war with the law of my mind, making me captive to the law of sin that dwells in my members" (Rom 7:22). And so he cries out for help, "Wretched man that I am! Who will rescue me from this body of death?" (Rom 7:24). With this poignant cry to a higher power comes the overwhelming joy of enlightenment,

> Thanks be to God through Jesus Christ our Lord! (Rom 7:25)

Jesus is the higher power! Jesus is Savior! Jesus is Lord! Paul is liberated. But his troubles are not over, as is clear from his second letter to the Corinthians.

Paul describes his suffering vividly—his imprisonments, his countless floggings, his sleepless nights, his hunger and thirst, his cold and nakedness, his anxiety about the churches. "Three times I was beaten with rods. Once I received a stoning. Three times I was shipwrecked; for a night and a day I was adrift at sea" (2 Cor 11:25). His was a life full of danger and closeness to death. "On frequent journeys, in danger from rivers, danger from bandits, danger from my own people, danger from Gentiles, danger in the city, danger in the wilderness, danger at sea, danger from false brothers and sisters" (2 Cor 11:26). What a graphic description of kenosis!

When Paul had hit rock bottom, when he had lost everything, when he had become nothing, when his humiliation was complete, only then did he rise dramatically to the heights of ecstasy. His visions and revelations of the Lord are as remarkable as his sufferings:

> I know a person in Christ who fourteen years ago was caught
> up to the third heaven—whether in the body or out of the body
> I do not know; God knows. And I know that such a person . . .
> was caught up into Paradise and heard things that are not to be
> told, that no mortal is permitted to repeat. (2 Cor 12:2-4)

Just as Jesus became obedient unto death, even death on a cross, and was then raised to the highest glory, so Paul was totally emptied of self and then caught up into Paradise, where he heard things that no mortal is permitted to repeat. Some of the old mystical theologians (including

St. John of the Cross) claimed that Paul, caught up into Paradise, attained to the vision of God ordinarily reserved to the blessed. Modern theologians, however, while agreeing that Paul had sublime mystical experience, see no evidence for such a claim. It is enough to say that Paul is one of the greatest Christian mystics.[23]

Yet even the consummate mystic struggles with temptations and addictions. "Therefore, to keep me from being too elated, a thorn was given me in the flesh, a messenger of Satan to torment me" (2 Cor 12:7). Paul repeats "to keep me from being too elated," as if to make it clear that this thorn was given to keep him humble.

What was this thorn in the flesh? What was this messenger of Satan? The old authors maintained that it was a sexual temptation. St. John of the Cross refers his readers to this passage when speaking of the upheaval that takes place in the night of the senses when the mystic is buffeted by "an angel of Satan which is the spirit of fornication."[24] Most modern exegetes, however, do not accept this, and many interpretations of the Pauline thorn in the flesh have been given.

Whatever it was, this thorn in the flesh did not go away, in spite of Paul's repeated prayer. Instead, he got the answer, "My grace is sufficient for you, for power is made perfect in weakness" (2 Cor 12:9).

Here it is useful to remember the A.A. insistence that an addiction does not go away. It remains for life. What happens is that a tendency or inclination that was once compulsive ceases to be so. It no longer dominates and destroys one's life. Indeed, this tendency now shapes one's personality in a noble way, so that the recovered addict has beautiful qualities that the person without this addiction cannot have. In short, the very weakness is extremely powerful.

So it is with Paul. The thorn in the flesh, the messenger of Satan, does not go away, but his very weakness becomes his strength. "So I will boast all the more gladly of my weakness, so that the power of Christ may dwell in me . . . for when I am weak, then I am strong" (2 Cor 12:9).

Here we are at the heart of Pauline mysticism—or of any mysticism. Paul never denies his weakness. He does not cover up, pretending that he is a saint. He glories in a weakness that leads him to recognize his total dependence on God. Here is a message for the sannyasin, the bodhisattva, the mystic of any persuasion.

MYSTICISM IN THE INSTITUTION

Ordinarily, though not invariably, the sannyasin, the bodhisattva and the mystic are prophetic people who live on the fringe of the institution.

But what, one might ask, about the institutional people? What about the administrators, the procurators, the lawyers, the zealous people whose duty is to maintain discipline, to see that orthodox doctrine is taught, that rules are obeyed, that the reputation of the religion remains unsullied? Are they also called to total renunciation and to the heights of sanctity? Can they also undergo the *kenosis* whereby they lose all to find all?

The Second Vatican Council spoke in glowing terms of the holiness of the church, making just a few references to the peccadillos of the people of God. Only after a few decades did the world begin to learn of the real sinfulness of this holy institution. As the triumphalism, the hypocrisy, the cult of prestige, the grasping for money and power, the failures in celibacy and the abuse of children appeared in the media, the institutional church was faced with devastating humiliation. Yet this was an hour of opportunity. Was not this a glorious time when church leaders could fall prostrate before God and say: "We are sinners. Our life has become unmanageable and we humbly appeal to a higher power"? This utter humiliation could lead to what Ignatius called "the third degree of humility." It could be the basis of a wonderful institutional mysticism.

That institutional sanctity is possible and is indeed a reality has been proved to the world by the saintly life and death of the heroic cardinal archbishop of Chicago. Joseph Bernardin (1928-96) writes of his spirituality of self-emptying. Never far from his mind is the Pauline text that speaks of Jesus emptying himself and taking the form of a slave. And then came the call to a total self-emptying like that of Jesus: the false accusation of sexual abuse leveled against him by a former seminarian. "I thought of my sincere prayer to learn to let go and empty myself. Was God's answer hidden in this lawsuit through which faceless accusers threatened to brand me indelibly as a sex abuser?"[25]

It is not necessary to speak here of his simple fidelity to truth, his deep peace in the agonizing loneliness, his boundless trust in God. Enough to say that after his innocence was proved, he not only forgave but was reconciled with his accuser. Together they celebrated the eucharist and remained close friends until the parting of death.

As he was dying of cancer, he could write that he had always cared for people, had always tried to reconcile people, had always tried to be the instrument of God's healing love. This is what people expect from their priests. "They don't want us to be politicians or business managers; they are not interested in the petty conflicts that may show up in parish or diocesan life."[26] Though he was a cardinal, administrative work was very secondary:

I understand that organization is important. The Church as a human institution needs a certain amount of administration. But structures can take on a life of their own and obscure the real work with people that priests should be doing.[27]

And so his last months were spent in compassionate union with cancer patients throughout the world, writing and speaking and encouraging, helping people to befriend death. A few weeks before the end he wrote simply that God was calling him home, and he adds: "What I would like to leave behind is a simple prayer that each of you may find what I have found—God's special gift to us all: the gift of peace."[28] As his life had been one of forgiveness, reconciliation and peace, so his last prayer was that these gifts of forgiveness, reconciliation and peace might be granted to a Catholic church that was deeply polarized. Yet his life and death speak magnificently to people of any religion in any part of the world.

Let me conclude.

It becomes clearer day by day that Christianity has a great future in Asia. The third millennium will witness the rise of a new mystical Christianity that, in fidelity to the gospel and tradition, will humbly learn from the sannyasin, the bodhisattva and the spiritual giants of Asia. Above all, Asian Christianity will learn from the *kenosis* of Jesus, who emptied himself, taking the form of a slave; it will celebrate his death and resurrection in its own eucharistic liturgy. Asian Christianity will ask for institutional leaders of great compassion—men and women who can transcend words and letters to enter the cloud of unknowing, men and women who can transcend petty politics to speak of pardon and peace and reconciliation to a suffering world.

ELEVEN

"That Ultimate and Unutterable Mystery"

QUESTIONS, QUESTIONS, QUESTIONS

What do the great religions have in common?

The Second Vatican Council tells us that throughout history men and women have approached religion with the same questions. What is a human being? What is the meaning and purpose of life? What is goodness, and what is sin? Why must we suffer? Where lies the path of true happiness? What is the truth about death? "And what, finally, is that ultimate and unutterable mystery which engulfs our being, and whence we take our rise, and whither our journey leads us?"[1] These questions have always stirred the human mind and heart. And people look to the great religions for an answer.

With the advance of science we ask these questions with even greater urgency. Whence these trillions of stars? What was the Big Bang that started the whole thing? Where is humanity going? What is it all about? And with the approach of death the riddle of existence becomes even more acute. To be or not to be—that is the question. What indeed is "that ultimate and unutterable mystery which engulfs our being and whence we take our rise, and whither our journey leads us"?

Humanity has never failed to find an answer, however obscure that answer may be. "From ancient times down to the present, there has existed among diverse peoples a certain perception of the hidden power which hovers over the course of things and over the events of human life."[2] This perception of the hidden power that hovers over the course of things seems to be the basic religious experience of humanity. Did not Hamlet have such an experience when he mused thoughtfully—"There is a divinity that shapes our ends, rough hew them how we will"? Do not

136

thousands, even millions, of people today have this sense of a hidden power when they meditate, silently present to the ultimate and unutterable mystery? Here is a religious experience that is the monopoly of no one religion but is just human, an experience that imbues human beings with a profound religious sense that the most ruthless persecution cannot crush.

Religions bound up with cultural advancement have struggled to reply to these basic questions and to speak about the ultimate mystery with more refined concepts and in highly developed language. Now we realize that no one religion has all the answers. Each religion has its unique message. We learn from one another. We enter into a mutually enriching dialogue. Indeed, as we enter the third millennium, we at last realize that we *need* one another.

Let us not forget that since its very foundation, Christianity has been open to learn from the culture and philosophy of the surrounding world. In a remarkable section of *Gaudium et Spes* entitled "The Help Which the Church Receives from the Modern World" the Second Vatican Council speaks of how richly the church has profited from the wisdom of philosophers and from the history and development of humanity, how it has profited from the experience of past ages, the progress of the sciences, and the treasures hidden in the various forms of human culture.[3] Now we enter a new age when this same church, ever faithful to Jesus Christ and the gospel, will learn from the Vedas and the Upanishads, from the Tao Te Ching and the I Ching, from the Buddhist Sutras and the Islamic teachings. As Christianity learned from Greece, so it will now learn from Asia. What a new and powerfully enriched Christianity will come to birth in the third millennium!

We must ask more explicitly what Christianity will learn from Asia.

ASIAN MYSTICISM

The Second Vatican Council, with admiration and respect, turned its attention to Hinduism:

> In Hinduism men and women contemplate the divine mystery and express it through an unspent fruitfulness of myths and through philosophical inquiry. They seek release from the anguish of our condition through ascetical practices or deep meditation or a loving, trusting flight toward God.[4]

This may sound like a simplistic assessment of an ancient and rich religion. Nevertheless, the council puts its finger on the central message of

Hinduism—contemplation of the divine mystery and a wealth of myth. Practically speaking, the council recognizes that Hinduism is a mystical religion—and the same can be said of Buddhism and Taoism. That is to say, these religions go beyond the rational consciousness, with its reasoning and imagining and dualistic thinking, to enter the cloud of unknowing, where dwells the mystery of mysteries. This is precisely what the Western churches must learn from Asia if they are to survive. They must learn to go beyond the rational to the mystical; they must relearn the language of myth.

Assuredly, Western Christianity has a rich mystical tradition. But how often were the mystics ignored or marginalized or persecuted by an establishment that put its emphasis on words and letters, on doctrines and dogmas, on the strict observance of church law?! The establishment insisted that religious people either use the right words and subscribe to the correct formulas or be burned at the stake, excommunicated or reduced to silence. The tragedy of Western Christianity is that there were, and are, so few mystics in the establishment.

This is not to say that doctrines and dogmas are false or unnecessary. It is to say that they are always inadequate to express the reality. The ultimate and unutterable mystery can never be encapsulated in words. No one has ever seen God. This is the lesson that Western Christianity must relearn from the religions of Asia.

PHILOSOPHERS AND MYSTICS

Here it may be of interest to consider briefly three Asian philosophers who throw light on the ultimate and unutterable mystery. Their doctrine can only be understood in the light of their mysticism.

The first is the great master Sankara, who lived in South India in the ninth century of our era and has been called the Aquinas of Hinduism. He was primarily influenced by the Upanishads, wherein the seers' experience of ultimate mystery is summed up in the word *saccidananda*, meaning being-consciousness-bliss.

Sat—Being
Chit—Consciousness
Ananda—Bliss

It is significant that *saccidananda* signifies not only Ultimate Reality but also *the experience of Ultimate Reality*. The reality and the experience are identical.

Saccidananda, then, is an experience of blissful joy that is found when consciousness and being are one. That is to say, when one has gone beyond subject and object, when being is not "out there" but is one with the consciousness of the knower. Now one discovers total unity with great joy. Such an experience is found in the mystics of all religions.

This experience of *saccidananda* is at the core of Sankara's famous doctrine of *advaita* or non-dualism, which asserts that there is no duality between God and the world. This has been interpreted as pantheism or monism. Some scholars, both Oriental and Occidental, interpret Sankara more or less as follows: The world we see with our senses is no more than illusion *(maya)*. Ultimate reality is beyond all distinctions and differences. While we are in our present state of consciousness, it is true, we see a difference between ourselves and the fish and the animals and the landscape and other persons. But when we awaken to reality there are no distinctions. All is one.

Bede Griffiths, however, questions this monistic interpretation of Sankara. Referring to eminent scholars, he claims that Sankara is much more subtle than is often realized. For Sankara the world is neither being nor nonbeing. It is becoming. It has a purely relative existence. Griffiths goes on to ask if there can be a Christian *advaita* and, quoting the Greek fathers, he answers in the affirmative. The world depends totally on God. Without God the world would be nothing. This is traditional Christian theology. And Sankara, Griffiths claims, can be interpreted in this way.[5]

Quite certainly this great mystic and philosopher throws light on that ultimate and unutterable mystery that Christians call God. And yet I am wary of the terminology "Christian *advaita*," since the interpersonal dimension of Christianity—as in the Blessed Trinity—must always be stressed. Would not both Hinduism and Christianity be more enriched by dialogue between Hindu *advaita* and Christian *communion*?

Perhaps Bede Griffiths was of this opinion at the end of his life. In his last book he stresses that in the Christian mystical experience "the human person is not lost in the divine but enjoys perfect oneness in love." Making a mild criticism of Hinduism and Buddhism he writes:

> Again and again the tendency is to lose the person in the Ultimate. In both Hinduism and Buddhism this tendency is always at work, so that ultimately there is no individual left and everything dissolves in the pure oneness of being.[6]

He goes on to speak of the fundamental difference, saying that at the heart of Christian mysticism is *a mystery of love*, whereas both in Hinduism and Buddhism it is primarily *a transformation of consciousness*. By loving we become persons. It is all a matter of interpersonal relationship.

About Christian non-dualism I will speak later in this book. Now it is time to speak about a second philosopher who was also a mystic.

Nagarjuna, who flourished in South India in the second or third century of our era, is honored not only as a great Buddhist philosopher but also as a great Buddhist saint. Associated with the Madhyamika School of Mahayana, a school that teaches the Middle Way, Nagarjuna is chiefly remembered as "a teacher of emptiness." The word *emptiness* is a translation of the Sanskrit *sunyata,* which was translated into Chinese by the famous translator Kumarajiva with the character

$$空$$

This character, pronounced *k'ung* in Chinese and *kū* in Japanese, also means "sky." The vast, cloudless sky is totally empty.

Now if I begin to reason philosophically about emptiness, if I assert that all the things surrounding me are empty, it may seem that I am talking nonsense. However, if I sit cross-legged with my back straight and my eyes open, just breathing in and breathing out, I may *experience existentially* first my own emptiness and then the emptiness of all things. I may come to the conviction that Nagarjuna was correct and that all things really are empty.

But what about the ultimate and unutterable mystery? Is it also emptiness?

As I sit in wordless meditation the total emptiness of everything may rise up before me in a moment of enlightenment. I may feel like Avalokiteshvara of the *Heart Sutra*—a Sutra that was deeply influenced by Nagarjuna—who says that "form is emptiness and emptiness is form." All is emptiness!

Is this completely different from anything Western?

In fact, we find a somewhat similar theology in St. John of the Cross, who also saw the emptiness and nothingness of all things. As for God, St. John of the Cross distinguishes between God and *our experience of God*. God is all in himself but nothing to us. God is fullness in himself but emptiness to us. God is light in himself but darkness to us. And St. John of the Cross, while talking out of his own experience, follows an apophatic tradition that may in its origins have had Indian influence.

At the same time there is one important difference between St. John of the Cross and Nagarjuna. Emptiness in St. John of the Cross can never be separated from the cross of Jesus, who "emptied himself taking the form of a slave" to be raised and to have a name above all names.

The nothingness of St. John of the Cross is always rooted in the crucified Jesus of Nazareth.

Yet Nargarjuna has a mystical message for Christians and for the world, reminding us that the ultimate and unutterable mystery can be experienced as emptiness. He speaks of the mystical dimension of religion, and his life shows us that philosophy cannot be separated from spirituality.[7]

The third philosopher, who is also a mystic, is Lao Tzu, who flourished in China somewhere between the fourth and the sixth centuries B.C. To him is attributed the Tao Te Ching (The Book of the Way and the Virtue), which was originally given the title Lao Tzu. That the author was a mystic is clear from the opening:

> The Tao that can be told is not the eternal Tao.
> The name that can be named is not the eternal name.

The author is speaking of a mystery that cannot be described or named or told or expressed in human language. It is an eternal truth that can only be grasped by one who has gone beyond reasoning and thinking and conceptualization to enter the formless region of the cloud of unknowing. Lao Tzu urges us to enter into the emptiness. He calls the Tao dark and unknowable. Such is the ultimate and unutterable mystery.

The basic question of the Second Vatican Council, it will be remembered, was about "that ultimate and unutterable mystery which engulfs our being, *and whence we take our rise, and whither our journey leads us.*" The Tao Te Ching addresses itself, also, to this fundamental question, telling us about the origin and goal of all things: "Tao gives birth to one. One gives birth to two. Two gives birth to three. Three gives birth to ten thousand things" (Tao sheng i; i sheng erh; erh sheng san; san sheng wan wu).

道 生 一

一 生 二

二 生 三

三 生 萬 物

Since "ten thousand things" means all things, Tao is the source of every-thing in existence. Some scholars claim that this text speaks of a tran-scendent Tao. Others hold that the "one, two, three" indicates a trinitarian approach to reality. But as there are hundreds of commentar-ies on the Tao Te Ching and numerous interpretations of its mystical sentences, it is not likely that scholars will ever agree on these points.

So much for the origin of all things. But what about the goal? What about the destiny of the universe and of the human race?

The French Jesuit Yves Raguin (1912-98), claiming that a great num-ber of religions and philosophical systems speak of "the return" and reminding us that all things come from God and return to God, tells us that all things come from the Tao, which is the absolute Way, and all things must return to the Tao. Lao Tzu speaks of returning to the root. Raguin comments: "This root is seen by Lao Tzu as the mother of all creatures. The return to the root is the natural return of children to their mother."[8] One is reminded of Job: "Naked I came from my mother's womb and naked shall I return there" (Jb 1:21).

Sankara, Nagarjuna and Lao Tzu have had immense influence all over Asia. Their philosophy and their mysticism will continue to penetrate the lives of Asian people and form their culture. They will speak also to other religions, and the world will benefit from their profound wisdom.

Next I will speak of a Jewish poet who faced the question of Judaism and emptiness.

THE JEW IN THE LOTUS

In 1990 Rodger Kamenetz, a Jewish poet and professor, traveled to Dharmsala with a group of Jewish delegates to meet the Dalai Lama and to dialogue with Tibetan Buddhism. Kamenetz, like many of his co-reli-gionists, was perturbed by the vast number of Jews who had abandoned their ancestral religion to become teachers of Buddhism in America. At the same time he was willing to learn, and he wanted to work for recon-ciliation between the Jewish Buddhists (JUBUs he calls them) and reli-gious Jews who were faithful to tradition. While Orthodox Judaism has never been open to explicit dialogue with other religions, Kamenetz was encouraged by Martin Buber, who was committed to dialogue and even flirted with Buddhism in his youth. Kamenetz felt that the spirit of Buber was hovering over this dialogue with the Dalai Lama.

The two groups found that Jews and Tibetans have much in common. Both have suffered cruel persecution. Both have faced the question of survival. One of the visiting rabbis admitted that he was impressed by the Buddhist commitment to nonviolence but maintained that neither Buddhists nor Jews could afford to be pacifists if their survival was at stake. To this a Tibetan Buddhist nun, who had formerly been an American Jewish housewife, responded that if Tibetans became terrorists they might win back Tibet, but Buddhism would be destroyed by such an attitude.

Some common ground was found in discussions about reincarnation, about angels and devas, about feminism, about sexuality and religion, about meditation. But most important was the question of God. What about the God of Abraham and Isaac and Jacob?

To this the Dalai Lama responded: "Of course, you know, Buddhism does not accept a creator. God as an almighty or as a creator . . . we do not accept. But at the same time, if God means truth or ultimate reality, then there is a point of similarity to *sunyata* or emptiness."[9]

Rodger Kamenetz was impressed by this comment of the Dalai Lama. It corrected a simplistic notion—common even among Western Buddhists—of God as an autocrat, an all-powerful commandant. In short, it corrected an anthropomorphic notion of God. In the Jewish mysticism of the kabbala God is described in terms of emptiness and nothingness:

> The name the kabbalists use for God . . . is *ain sof*. This literally means no limit or infinite. Yet in some interpretations, *ain sof* is translated as *ayin*—nothing.[10]

He goes on to say that in some of the kabbalists the primordial being is called *ayin*, which means "nothing." If one asks, "What is it?" the answer is *"Ayin"*—that is to say, no one can understand anything about it. Kamenetz further claims that the kabbala or Jewish mystical tradition draws its inspiration from canonical texts, mainly Genesis, the Song of Songs and Ezekiel.

Kamenetz is careful to say, however, that the kabbalistic *ain sof* and the Buddhist *sunyata* are not exactly the same. The kabbalists affirm an absolute existence, even if ineffable; Buddhists claim that all existence has no absolute reality in itself. Nevertheless, he felt a tremendous excitement at the real meeting of two traditions. *Sunyata had met ain sof.* The gap was narrowed. "I felt the sparks leaping across the empty space."[11] Later he comments enthusiastically, "Maybe where sunyata meets *ain sof* I would find the high place where Jews and JUBU's and Buddhists could dance together again."[12]

The conclusions of Rodger Kamenetz and his Jewish companions are of the utmost significance for the monotheistic religions. They remind us that the two approaches to ultimate reality—God as Father and God as emptiness—are compatible and even complementary. Kamenetz ends his book with an appeal for religious renewal in Judaism, a renewal based on prayer, meditation and mysticism.

"I AM WHO I AM . . . "

The great religions, then, are at one in asking the vital question: What is that ultimate and unutterable mystery which engulfs our being?

And in answering this questions the Hebrew scriptures make their unique and earth-shaking contribution. For they tell us that the ultimate and unutterable mystery has a name. "God said to Moses, 'I AM WHO I AM.' He said further, 'Thus you shall say to the Israelites, I AM has sent me to you'" (Ex 3:14). I AM is the name of God.

When Rodger Kamenetz and his companions visited Dharmsala they were aware that dialogue is a two-way process. They went to learn from the Dalai Lama, but they also went to share. They claimed that, as a result of the sharing, the Dalai Lama's understanding of monotheism changed. This does not mean that the Dalai Lama came to believe in the God of Abraham and Isaac and Jacob. But he was made to think. He gave a sympathetic ear to the biblical message that the Great Mystery has a name. The Great Mystery can say, "I have loved you with an everlasting love" (Jer 31:3). Surely the meeting of Moses with God is one of the great breakthroughs in the history of humanity. Never will this mystical encounter fall into oblivion.

The precise meaning of I AM WHO I AM is not clear. How could a mystery be clear? The baffled exegetes of today must humbly concede that only the enlightened mystic has a tiny glimmer of what the sacred author was trying to say. As the story of Moses at the burning bush entered the Western mystical tradition, Gregory of Nyssa and Dionysius the Areopagite gave their own interpretations of the Book of Exodus. They gave graphic descriptions of Moses climbing to the summit of the mountain where he entered the darkness, the emptiness and the nothingness of the cloud of unknowing. Yet this same Moses (paradox of paradoxes) met a personal God who spoke to him face to face as one might speak to a friend.

The mystics had no difficulty in reconciling the Moses who entered the emptiness of the cloud of unknowing with the Moses who spoke to a personal and loving God. This was because they spoke out of their own experience and spent little time in libraries. They knew that the darkness was brightened by flashes of lightning, that the silence was interrupted by peals of thunder. They reconciled a theology of negation with a theology of affirmation. Moses the mystic was Moses the law-giver.

Thomas Aquinas in the thirteenth century inherits the same tradition, though he has his own distinctive characteristics. Deeply influenced by Aristotelian metaphysics, he sees God as the First Cause, the Unmoved Mover, the Final Cause, the Exemplary Cause. But metaphysics is the science of being (*scientia entis,* said the scholastics), and when Thomas comes to the primary name of God he speaks in terms of existence. God is Being. God is the One Who Is.

Now it is interesting and significant to note that when he comes to prove that God is primarily Being, Thomas quotes the Book of Exodus—I AM WHO I AM. And he concludes, "Therefore this name HE WHO IS, most properly belongs to God."[13] In short, in the *Summa Theologica* God is Being not because of Aristotelian metaphysics but because of the mystic revelation to Moses at Horeb, the mountain of God.

Let us not forget that Aquinas was at the same time metaphysician and mystic. As metaphysician he saw God as the Supreme Being in whom essence and existence are one. As mystic he saw God as the ultimate and unutterable mystery who called to Moses out of the burning bush, "Come no closer! Remove the sandals from your feet, for the place on which you are standing is holy ground" (Ex 3:5). And Moses the mystic hid his face, for he was afraid to look at God.

For Aquinas metaphysics and mysticism were complementary.

"GOD IS DEAD . . . "

Aquinas, I have said, was at the same time metaphysician and mystic. Not so his successors. A decadent scholasticism separated metaphysics from mysticism and even from religious experience. Seminarians were taught to *prove* the existence of God from the so-called five ways of Aquinas and to assert from "the light of pure reason" that God is Being. No mention was made of Moses or I AM WHO I AM. After all, it was said, metaphysics must not be confused with scriptural exegesis wherein Thomas had no competence. The God of philosophy was different from the God of Abraham and Isaac and Jacob.

And this God of the philosophers entered into the Western intellectual tradition. Incompetent teachers, contrary to the mind of Aquinas, spoke of God as one more being, the Greatest Being among other lesser beings. The *mystery of God* was forgotten. Small wonder if Nietzsche's mad cry that God is dead echoed through the Western world. Feuerbach and Marx had no difficulty in finding sympathizers. God was dead. God-talk was out of place.

But what God was dead? Not the God who spoke to Moses. Not the God before whom David danced. Not the Ultimate and Unutterable Mystery that communicates with all human beings. Rather, it was the impoverished god of an impoverished metaphysics, whom Martin Heidegger was to describe poetically:

> Man can neither pray nor sacrifice to this god . . . can neither fall to his knees in awe nor can he play music and dance before this god.[14]

Heidegger rejected not only the God of metaphysics but all metaphysics. He called for "the overcoming of metaphysics."

His influence was immense, as was that of the so-called deconstructionists led by Jacques Derrida. It looked as though metaphysics, which had been the core of Western philosophy for two millennia, had collapsed.

To reject God as Being and to "overcome metaphysics" seemed shocking to some orthodox theologians. Yet some theologians of note took Heidegger seriously. They began to look for ways of speaking about God that would be acceptable to contemporary intellectuals, ways that would not be contemptuously labeled as "God-talk."

One such theologian is the French Jean-Luc Marion, who in *God without Being*[15] argues that we must push beyond metaphysics, beyond all concepts, *beyond the language of being* to discover that the primary name of God is Love. Marion writes about the icon as a window through which one can see God. The face of the icon is a personal invitation to eternal life with God.

The German Walter Kasper in *The God of Jesus Christ* also stresses love and interpersonal relationship: "Seen in the horizon of the person, the meaning of being is love . . . To call God a person is to say that God is the subsistent being which is freedom in love. Thus the definition of God's essence brings us back to the biblical statement: 'God is love.'"[16]

Most challenging and provocative is the work of a theologian who is also a Buddhologist. John P. Keenan in *The Meaning of Christ: A Mahayana Theology*[17] argues that Hellenistic metaphysics no longer provides a basis for a Christian theology that is fast becoming irrelevant. Only the wisdom and insights of Mahayana, he claims, can save Christian theology and help it develop the contemplative dimension that today's world demands. Mahayana thought could revive the contemplative or mystical dimension of theology, enabling us to experience the emptiness or nothingness of God in the cloud of unknowing.

BEING-IN-LOVE

While it may be true that we need a new way of speaking about God, and while it may be equally true that we must stress the biblical teaching that God is love, I have grave reservations about the wisdom of rejecting metaphysics.

Christianity would be greatly impoverished if we were to abandon the metaphysics of Aquinas with its link to mystical experience. Thomas could have quoted the Johannine epistle that God is Love but he preferred I AM WHO I AM because he saw that "being" is the richest of notions (it cannot be called a concept, for a concept is necessarily limited) and contains all. Being is all-embracing. The author of *The Cloud of Unknowing* says clearly that all names and all feelings are contained in the little word *is*:

> For if thou say: "Good" or "Fair Lord" or "Sweet," "Merciful" or "Righteous," "Wise" or "All-witting," "Mighty" or "Almighty," "Wit" or "Wisdom" or "Strength," "Love" or "Charity," or whatever such thing that thou say of God: all it is hid and enstored in this little word *is*.[18]

In short, when we say that God is, we have said everything. After having said that God is "Being," there is no more to say.

What a grasp of Thomism this author had! He makes the thought of Thomas the basis for a mystical prayer of emptiness. He tells his disciple just to be—to apply his blind being to the blind being of God without thinking or reasoning or reflecting on the goodness and mercy of God. Prayer of thanksgiving and petition and trust and love—all are contained in the existential prayer of being. In short, the Being of whom the author of *The Cloud* speaks is a Being to whom *(pace,* Heidegger) people can pray and sacrifice and fall on their knees in awe and play music and dance. It is the Being before whom Moses hid his face, for he was afraid to look at God.

Furthermore, Aquinas saw that to abandon the notion of God as Being could lead to serious error. Dionysius the Areopagite had extolled transcendence to such an extent that he spoke of a God beyond being. Thomas did not accept this. If God is not Being we cannot even say that

God is, much less can we say that God is Love. If we were to reject God as Being, how would we differ from atheists or agnostics?

The fact is that Aquinas consummated in his own heart an ecstatic marriage between metaphysics and mysticism; the child of that marriage was the *Summa Theologica*. A decadent scholasticism, however, ignored Thomas's mysticism and had only an imperfect understanding of his metaphysics, while Heidegger and the desconstructionists were familiar with neither his metaphysics nor his mysticism. It is not surprising, then, that the notion of God as Being was ridiculed and rejected in the West.[19]

But the answer to this urgent problem is not simply to revive authentic Thomism. Rather is it to build on Thomism in the light of what has happened in recent times and in the light of the biblical teaching that God is love. To do this I find useful the method of Bernard Lonergan.

It will be remembered that Lonergan's method reaches a climax with love. After intellectual and ethical conversion there comes a religious conversion wherein my being becomes being-in-love. Then I have a love that radiates to everyone, friend or foe, good or evil, man or woman, capitalist or worker, a love that radiates to everything, fish and animals, trees and plants, oceans and stars. Nor is this love the fruit of human effort. It is the gift of God, with whom I am most deeply united. And this God is BEING-IN-LOVE. This is God who radiates love upon the whole universe. This is the Trinitarian God wherein the Father loves the Son in the Holy Spirit.

In the interreligious dialogue the peculiarly Christian contribution can be the belief that the Ultimate and Unutterable Mystery is BEING-IN-LOVE.

TWELVE

Incarnation

DESCENT

From the dawn of history people in various lands have spoken of spirits or souls or deities taking physical shape and becoming incarnate in the phenomenal world. Among the Tibetans the Dalai Lama is revered as an incarnation of the bodhisattva Avalokiteshvara. The emperor of prewar Japan was honored as a god who manifested himself in human form.[1] In the New Testament we read that King Herod was worried when he heard about the miracles of Jesus. "Some were saying, 'John the baptizer has been raised from the dead, and for that reason these powers are at work in him.' But others said, 'It is Elijah.' And others said, 'It is a prophet, like one of the prophets of old'" (Mk 6:14, 15). These cases witness to a belief that spirits from the invisible world can enter the phenomenal world of human beings. Scholars of religions call this *incarnation* in the broad sense of the word.

Hinduism speaks of the *avatāra*, the physical manifestation of a deity who "descends" from heaven to earth. Of special importance is the god Vishnu, who out of great love for the universe has again and again embodied himself wholly or partially in the phenomenal world. The Bhagavad Gita tells us that Vishnu, who becomes incarnate in Krishna, can manifest himself also in other bodily forms, whether of animals or humans. The reasons for his incarnation are stated clearly:

> Whenever the law of righteousness withers, I come into being age after age to protect the good, to destroy evildoers, and to establish the law of righteousness.[2]

149

The *avatāra*, then, appears to restore cosmic order. Once this task is performed, the *avatāra* disappears or merges back into God.

Primitive Buddhism was preoccupied principally with the historical Buddha, Shakyamuni the Enlightened One. However, as Mahayana developed, some Buddhist sects paid more and more attention to the Eternal Buddha, absolute and infinite. This essential or cosmic Buddha, called the *dharmakaya* or "body of the law," is the ultimate reality, transcendent and immanent in the universe. The Eternal Buddha, out of compassion for suffering humanity, has become manifest in Gautama as the *nirmanakaya* or "body of transformation."[3]

From this it will be clear that belief in incarnation of some kind has always been widespread in the human race. Aquinas claims that the Incarnation, as understood in the Christian tradition, is fitting *(conveniens)*. He quotes St. Paul to the effect that through visible things the invisible is made known:

> It would seem most fitting that by visible things the invisible things of God should be made known; for to this end was the whole world made, as is clear from the word of the Apostle (Rom. 1.20): For the invisible things of God . . . are clearly seen, being understood by the things that are made. And, as Damascene says *(De Fide Orthod., 3.1)*, by the mystery of the Incarnation are made known at once the goodness, the wisdom, the justice, and the power or might of God.[4]

At first sight it might seem fantastic and even far-fetched to say that the Ultimate and Unutterable Mystery should become visible and enter into human history. Yet the thesis of Aquinas may well have come from his deep mystical experience. Certainly it is corroborated by the experience of many prayerful Christians who, sitting in silent contemplation before the mystery, realize in a flash that "the Word was made flesh and dwelt amongst us" (Jn 1:14). Then they come to accept with joy the Johannine teaching that God so loved the world as to give his only Son.

THE EVENT

The distinctive feature of Christianity is its claim that the Incarnation was a historical event that took place once for all. "But when the fullness of time had come, God sent his Son, born of a woman, born under the law" (Gal 4:4). The poet T. S. Eliot describes this event in a masterly phrase, speaking of "the intersection of the timeless with time." There came an earthshaking moment when the timeless reality cut across the historical process and the Word became flesh.

Toward the end of his life Bede Griffiths, who had always stressed the unity of religions, spoke of the distinctive characteristic of Christianity:

> The unique value of Christianity is its profoundly historic structure. That to me is a key point. Christ is not an *avatāra*. The Incarnation is a unique historic event and Jesus a unique historic person.[5]

In India, Griffiths had often heard the comment, "Christ in Christianity; Krishna in Hinduism." He wanted to stress that, while we are closely united, each religion has its own peculiar characteristics and that these characteristics may constitute its very identity. The *avatāra* in Hinduism, he insisted, is not the same as the incarnate Word in Christianity, nor is Krishna the same as Jesus. Clearly influenced by Teilhard de Chardin, he goes on to speak of the implications of this historic event:

> In gathering all things, all matter into one in himself, he (Christ) transforms the world, bringing the cosmos, its matter and its processes, back to its source in the transcendent Reality whom he calls Abba, Father. This is unique.[6]

Here we are reminded of the Epistle to the Ephesians, which tells us of the mystery of Christ and of the Father's plan "for the fullness of time, to gather up all things in him, things in heaven and things on earth" (Eph 1:10).

Such is the Christ event.

But the memory of this event must not fade. It must be transmitted from age to age down through the centuries until the end of time. This was the wish of Jesus, who took bread and blessed and broke and gave to the disciples saying "This is my body which will be given up for you." And he added the momentous words:

> Do this in memory of me.

From that time until now the disciples of Jesus have done this in memory of him. By the breaking of the bread they have transmitted the memory of the death and resurrection of Jesus from generation to generation. Just as the Hebrews passed on the memory of their flight from Egypt by celebrating the paschal meal, so the disciples of Jesus celebrated, and continue to celebrate, the memory of their liberation from the captivity of sin by celebrating the eucharistic meal. "Let us proclaim the mystery of faith," cries the celebrant; and all respond:

> Christ has died,
> Christ is risen,
> Christ will come again.

and:

> Dying you destroyed our death,
> Rising you restored our life,
> Lord Jesus, come in glory.

If we are looking for mystical experience can we not find it in this cry of the faithful who enter into the death and resurrection of Jesus?

But why did the Son take on human flesh? This question has been asked again and again. *Cur Deus homo?* "Why did God become human?" asked Anselm of Canterbury in the eleventh century.

SPIRITUAL MARRIAGE

The Flemish mystic John Ruusbroec (1293-1381) speaks of the Incarnation in terms of spiritual marriage. "See, the bridegroom is coming. Go out to meet him" (Mt 25:6). These words are spoken to each one of us and to the whole of humanity. We are all called to meet the bridegroom, who is Jesus Christ. Ruusbroec tells a charming story.

In the beginning God placed his bride in the most beautiful, noble, rich and luxuriant place on earth. She was to love him and be faithful to him. But then came the hellish fiend in the form of a serpent. He seduced the woman and the man, and human nature, God's bride, was banished to a strange land.

But when the right time came, God took pity on his beloved bride, who was suffering so much. Ruusbroec goes on:

> God sent his only-begotten Son to earth into a magnificent palace and a glorious temple, that is, into the body of the glorious Virgin Mary. There the Son wedded this bride, our nature, and united her with his own person through the purest blood of the noble Virgin. The priest who witnessed the bride's marriage was the Holy Spirit. The angel Gabriel brought the message. The glorious Virgin gave her consent.

> Thus did Christ, our faithful Bridegroom, unite our nature
> with himself.[7]

In this way Christ, our faithful Bridegroom, broke open the bars of our prison, vanquished our death and redeemed us through his blood.

For Ruusbroec, then, the Incarnation is a marriage between the Son of God and the Virgin Mary, who symbolizes the human race. The consequences of this marriage are enormous. Not only is human nature liberated and redeemed, *human nature is divinized*. Later St. John of the Cross comes up with a similar doctrine. Speaking of the spiritual marriage as a total transformation in the Beloved he writes: "The soul thereby becomes divine, becomes God through participation, insofar as is possible in this life."[8]

This doctrine of the divinization or deification of humanity through grace is highlighted in the mystics, who frequently quote the Second Letter of Peter with its prayer that the faithful "may become participants of the divine nature" (2 Pt 1:4). Indeed, the Second Vatican Council refers to this text, reminding us that "the Son of God walked the ways of a true Incarnation that he might make us sharers in the divine nature."[9] The doctrine of divinization is particularly important in the East, where mystical theology, the center of all theology, speaks constantly of *theosis,*

θέωσις

Vladimir Lossky, the great mystical theologian of Orthodoxy, stresses the doctrine of the deification of the human person through grace. Claiming that fascinated by the "holy fault" of our first parents and our redemption from sin, we might easily forget the teaching of the church fathers that God became human in order that humanity might become divine, he writes:

> Fascinated by the *felix culpa*, we often forget that in breaking
> the tyranny of sin, our Savior opens to us anew the way of
> deification, which is the final end of man. The work of Christ
> calls out to the work of the Holy Spirit (Lk 12:49).[10]

The deification of humanity! Some mystics, it is true, got into trouble for not making the necessary distinction between "becoming God by participation" and "becoming the essence of God." But main line theology, East and West, was careful to make the necessary distinctions and to avoid all taint of pantheism. Here is an area in which Christians can enter into meaningful dialogue with Hindus, sharing our belief in deification and learning humbly about *advaita*.

DIVINIZATION

The mystics have always taught that the divinization of the individual person and of the human family is the result and the reward of a long process of purification and purgation in this life and in the next life, reaching a climax with the vision of God in eternity. St. John of the Cross teaches that the spiritual marriage in this life is no more than a prelude to the marriage in glory that takes place after death. At the same time we must not think that divinization is the monopoly of mystics or of Christians. The whole human race is called to divinization, as the Second Vatican Council makes clear. After speaking of the great gifts of God, the council goes on to say that these gifts are given not only to Christians but to all people of good will in whose hearts grace works in an unseen way. "The Holy Spirit in a manner known only to God offers to everyone the possibility of being associated with this paschal mystery."[11]

For Christians divinization comes through union with Christ in prayer and in a life of love. Of special importance is the eucharist, of which St. Leo the Great in the fifth century could say—"the partaking of the Body and Blood of Christ does nothing other than transform us into that which we consume."[12] And Augustine in *The Confessions* tells us that he heard a voice from on high saying:

> I am the food of grown people. Grow, and you shall feed upon me. You will not change me into yourself, as you change food into your flesh, but you will be changed into me.[13]

What voice does Augustine hear? Surely the voice of the risen Jesus who has entered into his glory, the Jesus whom we call the cosmic Christ. That the eucharist is the mysterious, glorified body of Jesus is made clear by the Council when it speaks of "that sacrament of faith where natural elements refined by humans are changed into His glorified Body and Blood."[14] Indeed, contemplation of the glorified or cosmic Jesus is the key to the understanding of the eucharist and the divinization that the eucharist brings.

I recall how, as a seminarian, I wrote a dissertation saying that by grace the Christian becomes "another Christ." My mentor, a distinguished

Hungarian theologian, corrected me. "Not *another* Christ," he said, "but Christ." He was following the Pauline doctrine—"Now you are the body of Christ and individually members of it" (1 Cor 12:27). And so we become members of the body of which Christ, not the historical Jesus but the glorified Jesus, is the head. Yet it would be more faithful to Paul to say that through baptism we *are* members of the body of Christ and that Christian enlightenment is a growing understanding of who we are.

The final stage of divinization comes when, one with Christ, we cry out, "Abba, Father" in the Spirit. That is to say, the final stage is reached when the human person and the human race, united with the Son, enter into the blessed Trinity.

THE GREEK COUNCILS

As time went on, the praying church became more and more conscious of the meaning of the Incarnation. In prayer Christians ruminated on the great question of Jesus, "Who do the people say that I am?" (Mk 8:27); under the guidance of the promised Holy Spirit they entered more and more deeply into the mystery. They found it necessary to respond both to those who questioned the divinity of Jesus and those who questioned his humanity. And they did so in the language of the Greek world in which Christianity was fast becoming inculturated.

The Council of Nicaea (A.D. 325), which gave us the Nicene Creed, affirmed unequivocally the divinity of Jesus and spoke clearly about the Christ event—that Jesus was born of the Virgin Mary, suffered under Pontius Pilate, was crucified and rose from the dead. The Council of Ephesus (A.D. 431) defined that Jesus Christ was both God and man but one divine Person, with divine and human natures joined in what was called the hypostatic union. It further deposed Nestorius, patriarch of Constantinople, who held that God merely dwelt in the human nature of Christ. The council made its point clear by proclaiming that Mary was not just the mother of the man Jesus but was the mother of God. The title Mother of God (theotokos) was central to all subsequent Christology.

Θεοτόκος

The Council of Chalcedon (A.D. 451) defined that Jesus was perfect God and perfect man in two natures without confusion, without change, without separation, without division, both natures being united in one person and one hypostasis. This was against the so-called monophysites who held that there was one nature in Jesus Christ.

All this theology, formulated before the Great Schism, was accepted by both Eastern and Western Christianity. To people of the West it sounds abstract and unreal. Not so in the East. For the Eastern church has always had a very human grasp of its practical significance, always associating *our* divinization with the divinity of Jesus. Vladimir Lossky claims that the christological arguments of the Greek fathers against their adversaries "refer particularly to the fullness of our union, our deification, which becomes impossible if one separates the two natures of Christ, as Nestorius did, or if one only ascribes to Him one divine nature like the Monophysites." Then Lossky distinguishes our deification from the deification of Jesus:

> What is deified in Christ is His human nature assumed in its fullness by the divine person. What must be deified in us is our entire nature, belonging to our person which must enter into union with God, and become a person created in two natures: a human nature which is deified, and a nature or, rather, divine energy, that deifies.[15]

Following the Orthodox tradition Lossky sees that theology—and particularly Christology—is not some abstract speculation but the very basis of Christian spirituality. In understanding Christ we understand ourselves.

IMAGE AND ICON

In the Eastern tradition the truths of revelation have been handed on by word and by image. Leonid Ouspensky in his classical work on the theology of the icon writes that the icon corresponds entirely to the *word* of scripture. He continues:

> "That which the word communicates by sound, the painting shows silently by representation" says St. Basil the Great. And the Fathers of the Seventh Ecumenical Council repeat these words and specify that "through these two mediums which accompany each other . . . we acquire the knowledge of the same realities."[16]

The icon, then, is "theology in image." Study of the icon is parallel to study of sacred scripture. Just as there is a presence of God in sacred scripture, so there is a presence of God in the holy image.

At the center of iconology is the Incarnation. "The Church declares," writes Ouspensky, "that the icon is an outcome of the Incarnation; that it is based upon the Incarnation and therefore belongs to the very essence of Christianity."[17] The task of the iconographer is to portray "as faithfully and completely as possible the truth of the divine Incarnation, insofar as this can be done by art."[18] Indeed, the Orthodox tradition, Ouspensky tells us, declares that the first icon of Christ appeared during his life on earth. This is the icon of "The Holy Face," called in the Orthodox church "the icon not made with human hands." Ouspensky further tells us that Orthodox tradition attributes the first icon of the Virgin Mary to St. Luke.

From all this it is clear that the icon is central to the theology, the liturgy, the prayer and the mysticism of Eastern Christianity. Yet this holy icon has been the center of bitter and even violent controversy from the beginning of Christianity to this very day. The early church, fearful of idolatry and influenced by the Old Testament, was wary about venerating pictures or statues of Jesus and the saints. Yet the icon continued to grow in popularity until the eighth century when the Byzantine emperor, Leo III, for reasons that were both political and theological, forbade all veneration of icons, thus provoking the tumultuous upheaval that we call iconoclasm. The imperial condemnation was followed by a massive destruction of icons. Monasteries were sacked and burned. Monks were imprisoned, tortured and mutilated. The Christian world was in turmoil.

In 787, however, the Empress Irene convoked a council at Nicaea in which iconoclasm was condemned and the veneration of images was reestablished. From that time the icon flowered throughout the Eastern world, becoming particularly important for the prayer and spirituality of Russia. But the Protestant Reformation of the sixteenth century brought a renewal of iconoclasm, which was particularly vehement among the Puritans in England. How account for this opposition to something so holy?

Following the Orthodox tradition, Leonid Ouspensky claims that the icon can only be understood in the context of the Incarnation. Without the Incarnation veneration of icons would be idolatry:

> If, in the Old Testament, the direct revelation of God was made manifest only by word, in the New Testament it is made manifest both by word and by image. The Invisible became

visible, the Nonrepresentable became representable. Now God does not address man only by word and through the prophets. He shows Himself in the person of the Incarnate Word.[19]

The Incarnation! There are no icons of God the Father. Icons portray Jesus or Mary or the saints.

Ignatius of Loyola reminds us that in the gospel there are times, as in Gethsemane, when "the divinity hides itself"; and there are other times, as on Mount Tabor, when "the divinity shines forth." Icons, even those of the crucifixion, portray Jesus in whom the divinity shines forth. They portray Jesus who has entered into his glory. Think of the magnificent icon of the Pantocrator, with the letters Alpha and Omega on either side of the image of Christ. Here we see Jesus the man as Son of God.

As for the Marian icons, they also show us the transfigured Mary, always with her Son. Ouspensky tells us that they represent the first human being to realize the goal of the Incarnation, which is deification. The Virgin Mary was "the first of all humanity to have attained, through the complete transfiguration of her being, that to which every creature is summoned."[20]

MYSTICISM AND IMAGE

Mystical experience, everyone knows, goes beyond words and images into the silence and emptiness and nothingness of the cloud of unknowing. This is particularly true of the so-called apophatic mysticism, which forbids all clinging to pictures or to sensible reality. What, then, about the icon? Does it have a place in the void? Or is it the very enemy of imageless, mystical prayer?

First, it should be noted that the icon is the fruit of the religious experience of the artist, who fasts and prays and is guided by the Holy Spirit. We know that many of the great iconographers were mystics, trying to express the inexpressible, knowing full well that their icons were inadequate to portray what they had seen. Furthermore, ideally speaking, the person who contemplates the icon is drawn beyond the image into the religious experience that inspired the artist.

In the 1990s I conducted several meditation sessions for Lutherans and Catholics in Sweden. For many hours each day we sat silently before a great icon of the transfiguration of Jesus. We did not *think about* the icon. Perhaps some of the meditators did not even look at it. We were simply present to the mystery, quietly repeating the Jesus prayer or remaining in wordless silence. We realized in our very bodies that the icon, unlike the idol, is a window to the divine. It leads to deep and imageless contemplative experience.

The icon, I have said, portrayed the transfiguration of Jesus. This is important. In this scene, so dear to the hearts of Eastern Christians, Jesus becomes the light of the world. And then something remarkable happens. "A cloud came and overshadowed them; and they were terrified as they entered the cloud" (Lk 9:34). This was the cloud of unknowing. This was the void, into which they entered with great fear. Jesus was present. But they did not see him. They only heard the voice, "This is my Son, my Chosen; listen to him!" (Lk 9:35).

The icon, then, is a symbol that points beyond itself. Just as the repetition of the Jesus prayer leads to silence and emptiness, so contemplation of the icon leads to the rich nothingness of the apophatic mystics. Let me go one step further and say that the word and the image are completely necessary for one who would enter the divine silence. There is no mystical experience without symbolism. Words and letters, it is true, are no more than a finger pointing to the moon, but without that finger who will see the moon?

A final word about Buddhism.

Those of us who engage in interreligious dialogue are quick to note that the icon has much in common with the exquisite statues of the Buddha that create an atmosphere of mysticism throughout Asia. One who sits silently in the lotus posture before such a statue does not pray to a Buddha who is "out there." One is present to the mystery enshrined in the statue. Or one "becomes" a Buddha. Or one realizes that "I myself am a Buddha." Furthermore, the sculptor who creates an authentic statue of the Buddha is deeply enlightened, in such wise that the statue is an expression of his or her profound wisdom. An experienced Zen master can at a glance judge the degree of enlightenment of the artist.

And one more meeting point between Buddhism and iconography. Statues of the Buddha do not depict the historical Shakyamuni, nor do they claim to portray realistically the anguishing struggles of human life. They are images of the Enlightened One.

MATTER AND MYSTICISM

The Incarnation, then, affects not only the historical Jesus Christ but the whole human race and the whole material cosmos. One who truly believes in the Incarnation will have a deep sense of the dignity of the human body and a loving appreciation of the material world that is our home. The early Christians fought bravely against gnostics, who despised the body, as we already see in the First Epistle to Timothy, which warns readers against those who "forbid marriage and demand abstinence from foods, which God created to be received with thanksgiving" (1 Tm 4:3). In subsequent centuries devout Christians venerated the body of Christ *(corpus Christi)*, composing exquisite hymns to the bread of angels that becomes the bread of humans, while saints like the ecstatic Francis, lovers of nature and lovers of God, sang the praises of Brother Sun, Sister Moon and all the twinkling stars.

Nevertheless, from its very beginnings Christian mysticism was affected by (some might say contaminated by) a neoplatonic dualism that spoke of the flight from matter to a realm of pure spirit. Plotinus saw contemplation as "the flight of the alone to the alone." For people of a certain temperament this is a fascinating ideal. To what extent it squares with the gospel of Jesus Christ is another matter.

Yet a neoplatonic trend is found even in Augustine. Think of the mystical experience of Augustine and Monica at Ostia, when mother and son were carried beyond the heavens and beyond all created things to the realm where "God alone speaks, not through such things but through himself."[21] Beautiful and by no means un-Christian, but also neoplatonic. And scholars find less attractive neoplatonic influences in the saintly bishop of Hippo.

But neoplatonism is most evident in the Greek fathers. In the third century there is Origen, whose commentary on the Song of Songs is a flight from ordinary human sexuality to a sexuality of pure spirit. Then there is Gregory of Nyssa, called the father of Christian mysticism, who describes vividly a neoplatonic Moses climbing the mountain, entering the cloud, leaving the world and all material things to speak with God alone. But most influential was the fifth-century Syrian monk known as Pseudo-Dionysius, whose *Mystical Theology* inspired the great current of dark, apophatic mysticism that we find in Meister Eckhart, the author of *The Cloud of Unknowing*, St. John of the Cross and all mystical theology until the Second Vatican Council.

The emphasis was on flight. The mystic is above all unworldly. He or she must leave the world and cultivate the things of the spirit. Alone with the alone. And together with this comes a negative attitude toward the body and sexuality and a disproportionate glorification of the celibate life. Psychologists have found something unhealthy in the lifestyle of religious congregations that repressed human instincts in the search for spirituality.

The Protestant reformers of the sixteenth century refused to accept all this. Crying "back to the Bible," they rejected Greek influence (Martin Luther would have no truck with Dionysius) and the whole mystical tradition. They likewise rejected monastic life and celibacy and voluntary poverty. The Protestant ethic put great store on worldly success and skill in making money. Material prosperity, it taught, is a wonderful gift of God.

The Catholic church tried to remain unworldly. It kept the mysticism and nourished a rich monastic life that highly valued poverty and celibacy. But from the beginning of the twentieth century spiritual leaders saw that the neoplatonic flight from the world had entered too deeply into Catholic spirituality and was not in accordance with the gospel of Jesus Christ. This was a time when Christians were becoming more and more involved in social issues. They saw that they must feed the hungry, give drink to the thirsty, clothe the naked, harbor the harborless, visit the sick, visit the imprisoned and bury the dead. Later they came to see that they must work to change unjust structures that were oppressing the poor, making their life inhuman. And above all, they were beginning to realize that they must work with might and main for world peace. What help could they get from a mysticism of flight?

Furthermore, as the twentieth century progressed, it dawned on humanity that we had plundered the earth. Crazy for money we were polluting the air, destroying the fish and the forests, killing the insects and animals, endangering our very existence. We now see that this cannot continue. And we also see that politicians and scientists and economists alone cannot solve the problem. Humanity needs a deep conversion of heart that will lead it to love, nurture and protect the material earth that is our home. A mysticism that rejects matter! Will such a mysticism help us save the earth? Or is such mysticism irrelevant and useless?

Then came one of the most surprising events of the twentieth century. Certain leading scientists became interested in mysticism. With the discovery of quantum theory and relativity the Newtonian worldview had collapsed. The old way of thinking no longer seemed valid. Heisenberg and Niels Bohr felt that the rug had been pulled from under their feet. Einstein was perplexed. The vision of trillions of stars and the breathtaking beauty of the universe together with the wonders of the subatomic world were too much for them.

When scientists became interested in mysticism, they looked not to the West but to Asia. They asked about the Zen koan. Niels Bohr inscribed the yin-yang on his coat of arms. Others wondered if Hindu seers and Tibetan mystics might possess the wisdom they sought. The Jewish, Islamic and Christian mystics had little appeal.

Yet one scientist found in the Christian tradition the wisdom that he sought. Teilhard de Chardin (1881-1955), a son of Ignatius of Loyola, had a profound sense of the Incarnation and of the presence of God in matter. His writings point the way to a new mysticism for the third millennium.

A NEW MYSTICISM

That a new mysticism is necessary no one will deny. We need holistic mystics who will teach us to embrace both matter and spirit. We need a mysticism of the earth, a mysticism of the human body, a mysticism of sexuality, a mysticism of science. It may be a question of survival. What answer can Christians give to this momentous challenge?

It seems to me that in spite of its limitations we must by all means preserve and develop the apophatic mystical tradition. It transcends historical and cultural conditioning. The neoplatonic influence, however real, is finally superficial. The core of authentic Christian mysticism is the gospel of Jesus Christ and its message of incarnational love. Gregory of Nyssa, Eckhart, the author of *The Cloud of Unknowing*, St. John of the Cross and the rest were lovers. Their being was being-in-love. Their lives and their teachings were dominated by the gospel message that God is love and by its commandment to love God with our whole heart and soul and mind and strength and our neighbor as ourselves. "The love of God has been poured into our hearts by the Holy Spirit that has been given to us" (Rom 5:5).

At the same time this mysticism of darkness needs purification if it is to answer to the needs of the twenty-first century. How will purification come about?

First, the apophatic mysticism of darkness must join hands with the kataphatic mysticism of light, which has appealed to a large number of women. We already hear more and more of Catherine of Siena, Julian of Norwich, Teresa of Avila. Here the theology of negation is little in evidence; feminine mysticism, which emphasizes the earth, comes to the fore. This feminine dimension will more and more predominate as the century progresses.

Second, mystical theology must listen to Teilhard de Chardin. Whereas Augustine spoke of all things *pointing to God*, Ignatius of Loyola spoke of God *present in all things*. This inspired Teilhard. He found God not by flight from matter but by entering more and more deeply into matter.

With a profound faith in the historical Jesus of Nazareth he prayed to the cosmic Christ who vivifies our universe. Fascinated by the material universe, he listened to its glorious hymn of praise. Remarkable indeed is his vision of the cosmic dimension of the Incarnation, the Resurrection and the Parousia or Second Coming. Has he not written a brief history of a cosmos moving toward its point of convergence in Christ Omega? He saw, moreover, the cosmic dimension of the eucharist and loved to celebrate the Mass of a universe in process of being divinized by the Bread of Life. His vision complements, and never contradicts, *The Spiritual Canticle* of St. John of the Cross.

Third, a mystical theology that would appeal to the twenty-first century must listen to the masses of the people who are hungry and oppressed. It must listen to the voices of Mahatma Gandhi and Mother Teresa, to Martin Luther King Jr. and Dorothy Day. It must listen to liberation theology. This will bring it down from the neoplatonic heavens to the good earth and to the cross of Jesus Christ.

Finally, mystical theology needs the mystics of Asia.

Traditional Western philosophy, theology and science are incorrigibly dualistic. In recent times science, aware of the inadequacy of its dualistic foundations, has begun to look to the East for integration and unity. In the twenty-first century philosophy and theology will do likewise.

Wise men and women of the East have always had a vision of unity. They have experienced that *saccidananda* which is being-consciousness-bliss. They have spoken of *advaita* or non-dualism. Their talk of emptiness and nothingness and the like are stumbling attempts to describe a universe that as scientists now say, is a unified web of interconnected energies.

They also see the unity of the human person, and they teach us to experience that unity. The word *yoga* means "union." From the beginning of the twentieth century Westerners have practiced yoga in an effort to escape from their anguishing inner division and to find interior peace. The "ways" of China and Japan (the way of tea, the way of the bow, the way of Zen and so on) likewise lead to inner unity, in accordance with the well-known Zen saying that "mind and body are one" *(shinshin ichinyo)*.

The human person is unified by controlling the energy that flows through the meridians and by balancing the yin and the yang in the whole body.

Sexual energy is also integrated and harnessed in the search for wisdom. And, most important of all, one discovers that human energy is linked to cosmic energy. This, in turn, is joined to the Source of All Energy, the Ultimate Reality that Christians call God.

All this has something in common with the doctrine of Uncreated Energies expounded by mystical theologians of the Orthodox tradition. But I cannot discuss that here. Enough to say that Asian thought in dialogue with the Christian tradition will form the basis of a mystical theology of the future.

THIRTEEN

The Search for Jesus

SPIRITUAL SEARCH

From the dawn of Christianity men and women throughout the world have devoted their lives to the search for Jesus. The externals of his life they have learned from the four gospels and from the living tradition of the Christian community. But devout Christians have always wanted to know more than the externals. Through prayer in faith they have endeavored to understand the mind and heart of Jesus, to assimilate his message of love, and to penetrate the mystery of his existence. "Who do you say that I am?" Jesus asked (Mt 16:15). This question, which challenged his disciples, continues to challenge millions of people today. Who was Jesus?

Christian men and women pray to Jesus, who, they believe, was raised to heaven and sits at the right hand of the Father. But they also contemplate the historical Jesus, who walked by the Sea of Galilee and spoke to the multitude on the mountain. The aim of the Second Week of the Spiritual Exercises of Ignatius is "to know him more intimately, to love him more dearly and to follow him more closely." And while such meditation on the public life of the historical Jesus has always been basic to the Christian life, the great mystics have found even greater wisdom and consolation in contemplating the Jesus who sweated blood in Gethsemane and died on the cross. "Eloi, Eloi, lama Sabacthani?" (Mt 27:46). So deep was their love for the Crucified that mystics like Francis of Assisi and Padre Pio Forgione came to bear his wounds in their very flesh. Were they not following in the footsteps of one who cried: "I want to know Christ and the power of his resurrection and the sharing of his

165

sufferings by becoming like him in his death, if somehow I may attain the resurrection from the dead" (Phil 3:10, 11)?

When asked, then, "Who do you say that I am?" men and women of faith have always answered with Peter: "You are the Christ, the Son of the living God" (Mt 16:16). Or kneeling before Jesus, they have said with Thomas: "My Lord and my God!" (Jn 20:28). Or with Paul they have cried out: "Jesus Christ is Lord, to the glory of God the Father" (Phil 2:11).

SCIENTIFIC SEARCH

The early nineteenth century, however, saw the beginning of a new search for the historical Jesus. It all began in 1835 with *The Life of Jesus Critically Examined* by David Friedrich Strauss. Relying on the historical-critical method Strauss aimed at finding "the real Jesus" behind the gospel accounts and the writings of the early Christians. Whereas tradition saw the writers of the four gospels as saints inspired by God, holy people whose writings led the prayerful reader to profound religious experience, Strauss began to ask if these evangelists had embellished the facts for political reasons. Had they an axe to grind? Did they twist the facts to suit their message? Were they petty politicians, trying to prove a point? And then the early Christians! Whereas tradition claimed that "the praying community" *(ecclesia orans)* saw more and more deeply into the person and the message of Jesus Christ, scholars now began to ask if these early Christians had overlaid the facts with theological reflections and useless dogmas that falsified the picture of Jesus of Nazareth. Distinguishing between the Jesus of history and the Christ of faith, scholars now approached the gospels with what was subsequently called a hermeneutic of suspicion.

Thus began a century of intense scholarship and provocative controversy that continue in our day. The so-called Jesus Seminar has brought its message of skepticism to millions through books and magazines and even through the Internet.[1] While the question remains the same: Who was Jesus?, "Who do you say that I am?" is now situated in a scientific context. Can the historian get beyond these so-called myths and speak about Jesus with rigorously scientific objectivity? A leading scholar of the Jesus Seminar stated forthrightly that the scientifically minded men and women of the twenty-first century will only be satisfied with a scientific search for Jesus.

But what is a scientific search? And what is science? And is science really so objective? So dramatically has our understanding of science changed that it is necessary to say something about scientific method.

FIRST-PERSON SCIENCE

In his pioneering work *Perfect Symmetry: The Search for the Beginning of Time* physicist Heinz Pagels speaks of two approaches to the study of the cosmos: third-person science and first-person science. The aim of *third-person science*, exemplified by Isaac Newton, is to discover the objective laws of the universe, laws that are true at all times and in all places, laws that are meaningful for all men and women whatever their culture, education or temperament. The aim of *first-person science*, exemplified by Albert Einstein, is to provide "the personal thoughts of an individual in interpreting and responding to the reality of the world discovered by science."[2] In other words, first-person science puts great store by the subjective dispositions of the researcher—his or her education, culture, sensitivity and what is true to his or her personal experience, whereas third-person science stresses objectivity.

Pagels insists that both third-person science and first-person science are necessary and that they complement one another. In other words, we must pay attention both to the subjective dispositions of the researcher and the objectivity of truth.

All this fits with the method of Bernard Lonergan. Lamenting that the scholastics, in their preoccupation with objective truth, had neglected the subject, Lonergan stresses subjectivity. Human authenticity, he claims, is the key to any search for truth. And objectivity is "the fruit of authentic subjectivity." If I am authentic, I will be objective.[3] Lonergan's method attempts to unite first-person science and third-person science into a single process.

Now the writing of physicists like Pagels and theologians like Lonergan has made its impact on biblical studies. Scriptural exegetes now see the subjective dimension of their research. They speak of the "precomprehension" of the scholar. That is to say, they see that every scholar necessarily approaches the bible or history with a certain mindset, a certain culture, a certain education and sometimes with a certain faith. And this colors the whole enterprise.[4]

Furthermore, we all come to research as weak and unregenerate human beings in need of conversion. This we must humbly recognize. How often it happens that scholars who are conscious of the petty prejudices, the cultural conditioning and the political motivation of the writers of the New Testament are blissfully unaware of their own cultural conditioning, their own petty prejudices and their own political motivation. Lonergan makes us reflect on our own thought processes and our own need of conversion.

I have spoken at some length about the subjective dimension of all scientific inquiry and about the precomprehensions that necessarily underlie scholarly research. I have done so to examine the precomprehensions that underlie the search for the historical Jesus.

MODERN PAGANISM

The scholars who initiated the search for the historical Jesus were children of the Enlightenment. Quoting Peter Gay, Lonergan calls the Enlightenment "the rise of modern paganism" and describes it as "a far-flung attack on Christianity from almost every quarter and in almost every style." Lonergan goes on to say that the Enlightenment "was to replace the God of the Christians by the God of the *philosophes* and, eventually, the God of the *philosophes* by agnosticism and atheism. It . . . moved towards a materialist, mechanistic, determinist interpretation no less of man than of nature."[5] One of its most damaging aspects, Lonergan holds, was its rejection of tradition—"In effect it was out to destroy not only religious tradition but all tradition."[6]

The Enlightenment, which rejected tradition and attacked not only religious belief but all belief, formed the background and created the precomprehensions of those who initiated the search for the historical Jesus. Strauss denied the existence of a transcendent and personal God. There were no miracles. The miraculous stories of the gospel are unauthentic. The gospels were fictitious stories written to prove that Jesus was the Messiah. As for the Ascension—if Enoch and Elijah were taken up into heaven, then Jesus also had to ascend into heaven. And so it goes. Strauss was finally dismissed from his position at the seminary in Tübingen, but his influence on the theology of the nineteenth and twentieth centuries was immense.

Today the Enlightenment mentality continues to influence many scholars of the Jesus Seminar. Rejecting a religious tradition that inspired Irenaeus, Augustine, Bernard, Aquinas, Luther, Calvin and Melancthon these scholars "reconstruct" a Jesus based on personal research, claiming that the "real Jesus" was a social reformer, a political activist, a rebel against the Romans. That Jesus was sent by the Father, that he was the Messiah and the Savior of the world, that he rose from the dead—these, it is said, are later theological accretions obscuring the real Jesus.

Raymond Brown questions the scholarly credentials of those who would discredit the gospels "as totally the product of Christian imagination, with little or no foundation in fact." With unwonted severity he writes:

> Under the mantle of scholarly objectivity, advocates assert firmly but without proof that the early Christians knew little about how Jesus died and simply invented their narratives on the basis of Old Testament imagery. Indeed some scholars (of Christian upbringing) would paint them as creating lies precisely to vilify the Jews.[7]

Yet the scientific search for Jesus will go on. It will only bear fruit, however, when the scientific and the spiritual come together. It will only bear fruit when the scientist and the mystic walk hand in had. And this day will surely come when the gospel takes root in Asia.

DEAD END

I have spoken of the search for the historical Jesus insofar as it is rooted in the Enlightenment and is part of what Lonergan calls the rise of modern paganism. It is not my intention, however, to belittle the efforts of serious and competent scholars who search for the historical Jesus, giving us new insights into the mentality of those who wrote the gospels.

Of primary importance is the towering figure of Rudolf Bultmann (1884-1976) who came to the conclusion that the gospels contain almost no authentic information about Jesus and that the scholarly search for the historical Jesus is a useless enterprise. He preferred to fix his eyes on the Christ of the *kerygma*, saying that "the real Christ is the Christ preached."

Yet others, including some disciples of Bultmann, refusing to accept such radical skepticism, claimed that the gospels contain reliable historical information about Jesus. Joachim Jeremias (1900-1979), one of the great biblical scholars of the twentieth century, wrote about the prayer of the historical Jesus. The Anglican C. H. Dodd (1884-1973) wrote a life of the founder of Christianity. Other competent scholars today maintain that there is much more history in the gospels than Bultmann was willing to admit.

Of special importance is the Catholic scholar John Meier, who writes about Jesus, the marginal Jew. "I will try my best to bracket what I hold by faith," he writes, "and examine only what can be shown to be certain or probable by historical research and logical language."⁸ Could a Catholic, a Protestant, a Jew and an agnostic, all honest historians, come to any consensus about Jesus of Nazareth? Meier thinks they could. Many of his conclusions are tentative and open to revision, but he writes an impressive book about this marginal Jew.

Nevertheless, it becomes more and more clear that scholarship alone tells us little about the Jesus of history. Kenneth Woodward, giving a summary of recent literature on the subject, concludes:

> After 150 years of scholarly search, there are signs that the quest for the "historical" Jesus has reached a dead end. There has been no new data on the person of Jesus since the Gospels were written.⁹

This does not mean that we should abandon the scholarly search. It means that we must find a new methodology. I recall remarking to a friend of mine who practices Zen: "These scholars of the Jesus Seminar know how to study and how to think, but they don't know how to breathe!" From Asia we must learn to breathe and to meditate. From Asia we must learn to esteem our oral tradition. Then our scholarly study of the gospels will be extremely enriching. For this reason I will make a digression to speak about the wisdom of Buddhism.

THE WISDOM OF ASIA

My friend and colleague Hugo Enomiya-Lassalle, who had a great love and respect for Buddhism, told me of his visit to Thailand to meet a famous teacher called Buddhadasa. Boarding a rickety bus at Bangkok, Lassalle traveled in the stifling heat to the temple where Buddhadasa lived. When he arrived, however, the master was about to set out on a journey, so they had only a few minutes together. Buddhadasa made one short comment. "Christians would get enlightenment," he said, "if they knew how to read their own scriptures."

"If they knew how to read their own scriptures." What a long and arduous journey Lassalle made to hear these words of wisdom!

But how do Buddhists read their scriptures?

Buddhists of the twentieth century have not neglected scholarly study of the Sutras. Eminent professors in Asia and Europe and America have researched the *Lotus Sutra,* the *Heart Sutra,* the *Lankavatara Sutra,* learning the original languages, investigating the true meaning of the texts and finding what the writers really wanted to say. Their work is of great value. However, on one point Buddhist teachers are unanimous and clear: *Scholarship alone will not lead to enlightenment.*

We must distinguish between *knowledge,* which is conceptual, and *wisdom,* which is formless or supraconceptual. Knowledge comes from academic study. It is a poor thing if divorced from the gift of wisdom, which ordinarily comes from practice or *gyō.* That is to say, it is a poor thing if divorced from sitting in the lotus, breathing from the abdomen, chanting the sutras, repeating the sutras again and again—and *living the sutras.* Again, academic research is empty without great faith, faith that these books were written by enlightened people and will lead to enlightenment. In some sects of Buddhism the believers keep chanting "Honor to the Lotus Sutra" (Namu myō hō ren gekyō) with great faith and devotion. So great is their reverence for the holy books.

Furthermore, the holy books of Buddhism must be read within a certain context. One distinguished Tibetan Buddhist writes that some modern researchers have misinterpreted *The Tibetan Book of the Dead* because they were ignorant of the oral tradition that necessarily surrounds it:

> Because they have read and interpreted *The Tibetan Book of the Dead* without the benefit of the oral instructions and training that fully explain its sacred meaning they have oversimplified it and jumped to quick conclusions.[10]

So important is the living tradition handed down through the centuries. This is the necessary *comprehension,* without which the Buddhist scriptures may be miserably misunderstood.

From what has been said, then, it will be clear that tradition is the key to understanding the Buddhist search for wisdom. The Sutras do not stand alone. They are part of the *dharma.* That is to say, they are part of the totality of Buddhist teaching, to which the bodhisattva makes a total commitment; they are never separated from the *sangha,* which is the Buddhist community. One who would walk the path to enlightenment puts his or her faith in the Buddha, the *dharma,* and the *sangha.*

Now the *dharma* must be preserved. It must flow through the centuries, giving life and inspiration to successive generations. This happens through the process of transmission. While various Buddhist sects have their own lineage, all claim to go back through a series of enlightened patriarchs to the Buddha Shakyamuni, whose enlightenment beneath the bo tree in Varanasi set the whole process in motion. When people attain to enlightenment they sometimes cry out in gratitude to the patriarchs through whom they have received this wonderful gift that originates with the Buddha.

Of special importance is the process whereby the disciple comes to be recognized as an authentic teacher. This transmission is described in the beautiful Japanese term *ishin denshin*

以心伝心

These characters can be translated as "communion of mind with mind" or "immediate communication of wisdom from mind to mind." They are particularly important in Zen, which speaks of a special transmission outside the scriptures with "no dependence on words and letters." Here the key word is *dependence*. One needs words and letters; one needs the scriptures. But one does not *depend on them*. The important thing is the direct transmission of enlightenment from teacher to disciple, from mind to mind through the centuries.

From all this it will be clear that practicing Buddhists approach their scriptures with massive precomprehensions without which, they claim, their holy books will be misunderstood.

I have engaged in this long digression for a reason. I believe that Buddhadasa's comment to Enomiya-Lassalle is meaningful for those of us who would search for the Jesus of history. We Christians must relearn how to read our scriptures. While retaining great esteem for scholarship, we must realize that scholarship alone will not bring us to enlightenment. Scholarship alone will not bring us to an understanding of the evangelists. Scholarship alone will not bring us to an understanding of the words and actions of Jesus. For here *we are dealing with mystery*.

We can get a glimpse of wisdom (or, if you will, enlightenment) if we approach the gospel with faith in "the word of God" and with trust in the oral tradition from which it sprang. We need to meditate and pray with the gospel and to realize that its living message is not only written but is *transmitted* to us through the centuries.

What, then, of the Catholic search?

CATHOLIC SEARCH

The Catholic church of the eighteenth and early nineteenth centuries ignored the search for the historical Jesus. That was a church that would have no truck with liberal Protestants, much less with a movement that explicitly rejected faith, denied the inspiration of sacred scripture, abandoned tradition and was governed by arbitrary philosophical assumptions.

However, in 1943 the encyclical *Divino Afflante Spiritu* of Pius XII awakened Catholic scholars to the great value of the biblical criticism that was central to Protestant theology. From then on, Catholic scholars took their place side by side with their Protestant and agnostic colleagues in investigating the date of composition, authorship, literary character and theological purpose of the individual books of the Bible.

The Second Vatican Council, following in the footsteps of Pius XII, took a firm stand against fundamentalism, writing that "the interpreter of sacred scripture . . . should carefully investigate what meaning the sacred writers really intended, and what God wanted to manifest by means of their words."[11] It went on to speak of the various "literary forms," whether prophecy, poetry, history or whatever, and insisted that the exegete pay attention to the characteristic style of perceiving, speaking and narrating that prevailed at the time of the sacred writer. This rejection of a literal or fundamentalist approach to sacred scripture opened the Catholic world to new riches in the Bible.

However, while insisting that the Bible be read with faith, the council made some points that were peculiarly Catholic (though the Orthodox churches would willingly accept them) and remind us of Buddhadasa's advice to Enomiya-Lassalle. These points concern tradition.

Just as the Buddhist Sutras are part of the *dharma* outside of which they cannot be understood, so the council claimed that the scriptures cannot be understood apart from the oral tradition that gave them birth and that is still alive. "Sacred tradition and sacred Scripture," wrote the council, "form one sacred deposit of the word of God, which is committed to the Church." And it spoke of the close connection and communication between sacred tradition and sacred scripture.[12]

Following this tradition the council speaks of the historicity of the gospels. It tells us that "the apostles . . . by their oral preaching, by example and by ordinances, handed on what they had received from the lips of Christ, from living with Him, and from what He did, or what they had learned through the prompting of the Holy Spirit."[13] The gospels of Matthew, Mark, Luke and John are of apostolic origin; and the council continues with a statement that is of the utmost importance in the search for the Jesus of history:

> Holy Mother Church has firmly and with absolute confidence
> held, and continues to hold, that the four gospels just named,

whose historical character the Church unhesitatingly asserts, faithfully handed on what Jesus Christ, while living among men, really did and taught for their eternal salvation until the day He was taken up into Heaven (see Acts 1:1-2).[14]

Note that the council here appeals not to scholarship but to tradition—to what Holy Mother Church has always held and taught. It must also be noted that the words "historical character" refer to the notion of history that was current in the ancient Mediterranean world. Historians like Thucydides and Herodotus did not relate the actual words of the speakers, but they claimed that they were faithful to their ideas. To say, therefore, that many of the words in the gospel were not literally spoken by Jesus does not conflict with the Greco-Roman notion of history.

Be that as it may, belief in an oral tradition is the precomprehension with which Catholic and Orthodox scholars approach sacred scripture.

KNOWLEDGE AND WISDOM

Scholarship, I have said, does not lead to enlightenment. The bodhisattva chants the Sutras and meditates with great faith. Then enlightenment arises, sometimes unexpectedly, from the core of his or her being. Without practice, scholarship is a poor thing indeed.

In the same way scholarship, however profound, does not lead to the wisdom of the Bible. The Second Vatican Council, repeating the traditional teaching that God is the author of the scriptures and that the human authors were inspired by the Spirit, tells us that prayer in faith is necessary for one who would truly understand the sacred message:

> And let them remember that prayer should accompany the reading of sacred Scripture, so that God and man may talk together; for "we speak to Him when we pray; we hear Him when we read the divine sayings."[15]

Before and while reading the Bible, Christians have always opened their minds and hearts to the Spirit, who reveals the true meaning of the text. Profound enlightenment may come to children with no academic training; "I thank you, Father, Lord of heaven and earth, because you have hidden these things from the wise and intelligent and have revealed them to infants" (Mt 11:25).

There are many ways of praying that lead both scholars and infants to a deepening knowledge of the Jesus of the gospels.

One such way is the ancient "lectio divina." One reads the gospel very slowly, sentence by sentence, savoring the words and relishing the meaning. Sometimes one pauses with a single word or phrase, repeating it again and again. One may take, for example, the words of Jesus, "Dwell in my love" (Jn 15:9) and keep savoring this phrase until one enters the mystical silence where true wisdom resides.

Or again, parts of the gospel are as baffling as the Zen koan. Just as the rational intellect will never solve the koan, neither will it solve the paradoxes of the gospel. The message of the cross is foolishness, as Paul says. Yet to one who takes the cross into his or her *hara* and holds it tenaciously, the Crucified appears as the source of supreme wisdom.[16] Here is another way of meditating with the gospel.

In short, one who would know the Jesus of history must search not only for knowledge that comes from study but also for wisdom that comes from prayer. Many of the finest exegetes of today are men and women of prayer. Their ability to unite knowledge and wisdom explains the power of their message to the world.

TRANSMISSION

The transmission of the *dharma* from teacher to disciple through the ages, going back to the historical Shakyamuni—this, I have said, is one of the outstanding characteristics of Buddhism. Yet other religious traditions make a similar claim. The guru-disciple relationship is a key to the understanding of Hinduism. Moses tells the people of Israel: "Keep these words that I am commanding you today in your heart. Recite them to your children and talk about them when you are at home and when you are away, when you lie down and when you rise" (Dt 6:6). The living tradition is transmitted from generation to generation by word of mouth. It is transmitted even more dramatically through the Passover meal.

The Orthodox and Catholic communities claim that their creed is *apostolic.* That is to say, they claim that it goes back through an unbroken succession of teachers to the apostles, who received it from Jesus of Nazareth. The Second Epistle to Timothy describes the transmission through the laying on of hands:

> For this reason I remind you to rekindle the gift of God that is within you through the laying on of my hands. (2 Tm 1:6)

The gift of God is an inner fire kindled in the heart of the disciple. It is nothing other than the Holy Spirit who cries out: "Jesus is Lord."

And Timothy must pass this gift on to others:

> And what you have heard from me through many witnesses entrust to faithful people who will be able to teach others as well. (2 Tm 2:2)

In this way the living message that Jesus is Lord has been passed on and on through the centuries until today. Christians believe that the gift of God will continue to be transmitted through future ages until their Lord comes in glory.

But what is transmitted in a special way is the memory of the death of Jesus. For the church, following the gospel, has always taught that the most important event in the life of Jesus was his death. "The Son of Man came . . . to give his life a ransom for many" (Mt 20:28). The death of Jesus on the cross is a historical event that no serious historian questions. As for the resurrection, that Jesus rose from the dead is not history but an article of faith. Nevertheless, the historian can assert (and in fact does assert) that *the disciples claimed that Jesus rose from the dead.*

Now the memory of the death and resurrection of Jesus is transmitted through the eucharist, which is the Lord's Supper. Here the death of Jesus is made present and the people cry out,

> When we eat this bread
> And drink this cup
> We proclaim your death, Lord Jesus,
> Until you come in glory.

The council speaks of the inner fire that is transmitted in the eucharist. "The renewal in the Eucharist of the covenant between the Lord and humanity draws the faithful into the compelling love of Christ and sets them afire."[17] Through the fire of love and the light of wisdom the people come to know and to be united with Jesus, who died and rose and will come in glory.

THE WAY FORWARD

From what has been said it will be clear that there are two approaches to the search for Jesus of Nazareth. One is the search of prayer in faith.

This is the approach of those who read the gospels again and again, savoring the words and relishing the message of love, penetrating more and more deeply into the mystery. It has been the approach of saints and sinners, of meditators and mystics through the centuries. It has brought wisdom and enlightenment to millions who, feeling closely united with the crucified Jesus, have cried out with Paul: "Far be it from me to glory except in the cross of our Lord Jesus Christ!" (Gal 6:14).

The second approach is that of the scholar who works with historical documents, studies the original languages and engages in all forms of biblical criticism. He or she investigates the literary genre of each book and acquires extensive academic knowledge.

Now these two approaches need one another. Without scientific research the prayerful people, taking the text literally and ignorant of what the author really wanted to say, can fall into narrow fundamentalism or crude fanaticism. Without prayer in faith the scholar can be appallingly superficial and unenlightened, swayed by personal and cultural prejudices.

And so the challenge of today is the marriage between these two approaches: between science and faith, between prayer and scholarship, all leading to the historical Jesus of Nazareth.

But what of the future?

The marriage, like most marriages, will not be blissfully happy; but it will be successful. I believe that coming centuries will give birth to scholars and mystics with an ever-deepening knowledge of the gospels, and they will carry the search forward. This accords with the Second Vatican Council, which writes that "there is a growth in the understanding of the realities and the words that have been handed down."[18] The council goes on to say that this growth takes place through the prayer and study of the people together with the preaching of the episcopate. Already in our day is not this prayer and study going on? Are not devout scholars moving toward a happy consummation of the sacred marriage between wisdom and knowledge? Are not innumerable prayer groups studying and talking about the gospels? Our knowledge of Jesus of Nazareth is growing day by day.

I have stressed the subjective dimension of our knowledge, speaking of what scholars now call precomprehensions. John Meier puts it well, telling us that "Catholics worship a Catholic Chalcedonian Jesus, Protestants find their hearts strangely warmed by a Protestant Jesus, while Jews, quite naturally, seek to reclaim the Jewishness of Jesus."[19] He goes on to say that there is no neutral Switzerland of the mind in the world of Jesus research, that everyone who writes on the historical Jesus writes from some point of view.

Now it becomes increasingly clear that the next step in the evolution of theology and scriptural studies will come from Asia. And the mystical tradition of Asia will have quite different comprehensions from those of the West.

The Asian tradition can easily accept that a human being would claim to be sent by God, that a human being would be aware of his or her preexistence, that a human being would claim to be the Savior, that a human being would claim to be divine. Such human beings have existed in Asia in the past. Again, the Asian mystical tradition will easily accept that a human being could be in touch with cosmic energies so as to work miracles, walk on the waters and calm storms. Furthermore, the Asian tradition may be open to the possibility of physical resurrection. Already some Asian scholars speak tentatively of the *gross body* that Jesus had in his lifetime, *the subtle body* that he had after the resurrection and the *spiritual body* after his ascent into heaven.

Let me stress that I am speaking here about comprehension that might be useful in the creation of a new Asian theology. It will be necessary to consider these precomprehensions in the light of revelation and even in the light of modern psychology and science. What the future holds we do not know. But one thing is clear: Asian Christians, while respecting the metaphysics and the dogmas of the Greek and Latin churches, will express the mystery of Christ in their own way and from within their own culture. And their experience will make a great contribution to Christianity throughout the world.

FOURTEEN

Jesus the Mystic (I)

JESUS AND ASIA

In the mid 1990s I took part in an interfaith convention held in Tokyo to commemorate the birthday of Swami Vivekananda. Representatives of the various religions, we sat on the podium listening to lectures about dialogue, unity and the future of humanity. Beside me sat an ageing swami clothed in saffron robes. While a Japanese professor delivered a learned lecture on Buddhism, the old swami leaned over to me and said with a smile: "We love Jesus Christ as much as you do."

In saying this, the swami was faithful to Hindu tradition. From the middle of the nineteenth century a galaxy of Hindu holy people have spoken movingly about Jesus. For Ramakrishna, Jesus was the *jivanmukti*; that is to say, the one who has attained perfect liberation in this life. For Rabindranath Tagore, Jesus was the Son of Man seeking the poor of the earth. For Mahatma Gandhi, Jesus was the supreme *satyagrahi*, that is, the one who loves truth and fights for truth. For Sarvepalli Radhakrishna, Jesus was a mystic who believed in the inner light. It can safely be said that in the eyes of Hindus, Jesus was a mystic and a saint.

As for Buddhism, the Dalai Lama speaking at a seminar in London in 1994 and commenting insightfully on the gospels said: "For me, as a Buddhist, my attitude toward Jesus Christ is that he was either a fully enlightened human being or a Bodhisattva of a very high spiritual realization."[1] In the same line Zen Master Yamada, the enlightened teacher of Enomiya-Lassalle and other Christian searchers, spoke frequently of Jesus as a guide for all who seek enlightenment. Many Zen teachers speak in the same way.

Muslims, too, see Jesus as a great prophet and worker of miracles. In the Middle East and Central Asia millions know about Jesus and Mary through the Qur'an, which tells us of the annunciation and extols the virginity of Mary. It further describes the birth of Jesus, who was raised up to heaven and will come again. Like the old Hindu swami, many Muslims have a great love for Jesus.

It is surely one of the ironies of history that while the declining post-Christian West, embarrassed by the miracles and wonders of this Galilean carpenter, tries to demythologize the gospels, Asian religions see Jesus as one of the greatest mystics of all time.

CHRISTIAN ASIA

Asia today boasts of millions of committed Christians who live the gospel and pray to Jesus as their Savior. Many of these Christians, descended from martyrs who laid down their lives for Christ in Japan, China, Korea and Vietnam, would willingly die for Christ today. They accept the teaching they received from the West, but now they feel that the time has come to build their own Christology based on their own culture and their own social and political needs.

It is not a question of constructing a new Asian Jesus. Rather, it is a question of seeing more and more deeply into the New Testament and the Christian tradition, finding therein aspects of Jesus that the West has failed to see. Something analogous can be found in literature. The poet T. S. Eliot says that there is more in the poetry than the poet himself realizes. There are more treasures in *Hamlet* than Shakespeare himself realized, treasures that come to the fore in a new culture. In the same way there is more in the gospels than the evangelists realized. This "more" will come to the surface as the gospels are prayerfully read and contemplated in an Asian culture. Then the words of Jesus will be fulfilled: "But the Advocate, the Holy Spirit, whom the Father will send in my name, will teach you everything and remind you of all that I have said to you" (Jn 14:26).

Of some significance in this challenging enterprise is an internationally recognized Japanese novelist. Shūsaku Endō, fascinated by the Jesus of the gospels, began his adult life searching for a Jesus who would speak to Japan and ended his life searching for a Jesus who would speak to Asia. Such a Jesus he finds in India. *Deep River*, his last novel, is the story of a Japanese Catholic priest, a Christ figure, who leaves his own affluent country to live in dire poverty near the Ganges. A misfit in the institutional church, dissatisfied with the rationalistic theology he learned in France, and gifted with a mystical sense that is labeled pantheistic, he dies carrying bodies of the dead for burial in the holy river. For Endō, the Jesus who speaks to Asia is the Jesus of the *kenosis*, the Jesus who was despised and rejected, a man of suffering and acquainted with infirmity. The mysticism of Asia cannot be separated from the cross and a life of total poverty.

Surprisingly similar to Endō is Sri Lankan Jesuit Aloysius Pieris, who is deeply conscious of the intense poverty and the intense religiosity of Asia. For him, the Asian Jesus is "the poor monk." Always the *kenosis* is central.[2]

The Vietnamese-American theologian Peter Phan, in an article entitled "Jesus the Christ with an Asian Face," reacts against "the colonial Christ" imported to some Asian countries from the West.[3] He studies four Asian theologians who have attempted to answer the question "Who do you say that I am?" in terms that are both understandable to their people and faithful to the New Testament. All four have elaborated "liberation Christologies" centered on the poor and rejected Jesus.

The Korean feminist theologian Chung Hyun Kyung, quoting from the Asian Women's Conference in Singapore, maintains that Asian women reject images of Jesus as "triumphal king" and "authoritative high priest." Such images "have served to support a patriarchal religious consciousness in the Church and in theology." She claims that "the most prevailing image of Jesus among Asian women's theological expressions is the image of the suffering servant."[4]

Most important of all was the Asian Synod held in Rome in 1998. The bishops, aware of the dire poverty of their people, spoke of the poor Jesus whose self-emptying led to mysticism. Jesus is "the guru, the liberator and the wisdom of God." He manifests "the feminine or maternal, all-embracing love of God." He is "the enlightened one," the one who shares the *kenosis* of the Asian people.[5]

Asia, then, is searching for Jesus the mystic under the guidance of the Spirit. "When the Spirit of truth comes, he will guide you into all the truth" (Jn 16:13). And Asia is finding its mysticism in the *kenosis* of Jesus, who emptied himself taking the form of a servant and was raised up, seeing that the great mystical experience of Jesus was his death and resurrection.

Without denying the tradition that has gone before, Asia is already seeing more and more deeply into the mystery of Christ, formulating its mystical insights in its own way and making an enormous contribution to Christian wisdom throughout the world.

In the meantime, however, we must continue to study and to pray with the New Testament, asking what it teaches us about Jesus the mystic.

JESUS AT PRAYER

The synoptic gospels speak frequently of Jesus at prayer. Luke describes Jesus praying in the Jordan at the time of his baptism. The evangelist vividly describes the crowds milling around the great healer, and then he comments—"but he withdrew to the wilderness and prayed" (Lk 5:16). This is the Jesus who spent the night in prayer before choosing his apostles, who prayed on the mountain before walking on the water to greet his distressed disciples. This is the Jesus who prayed to his Father in Gethsemane and who died praying on the cross.

But what was the nature of this prayer?

Luke emphasizes the role of the Spirit. "Jesus, full of the Spirit, returned from the Jordan and was led by the Spirit in the wilderness" (Lk 4:1). "Then Jesus, filled with the power of the Spirit, returned to Galilee" (Lk 4:14). In the synagogue he read Isaiah, "The Spirit of the Lord is upon me" (Lk 4:18).

A key word in the prayer of Jesus is the Aramaic *Abba*. That this word came from the lips of Jesus himself is now commonly accepted. The Aramaic word is found only once in the gospel, in the prayer of Jesus in Gethsemane: "Abba, Father, for you all things are possible; remove this cup from me" (Mk 14:36). But scholars assure us that in other parts of the gospel the Greek *Pater* translates the Aramaic *Abba*, as in the prayer of the dying Jesus: "Father, into your hands I commend my spirit" (Lk 23:46).[6]

This is a word of great intimacy between father and son. Never before was God addressed in this way. Its use by Jesus shows us that his prayer was centered on a great love for his Father, a great intimacy with his Father and even a certain equality with his Father.

Jesus probably used the word *Abba* in yet another important text when he prayed: "I thank you, Father, Lord of heaven and earth, because you have hidden these things from the wise and the intelligent and revealed them to infants" (Mt 11:25). He then went on to utter words that show remarkable intimacy with the Father:

> All things have been handed over to me by my Father, and no one knows the Son except the Father, and no one knows the

Father except the Son and anyone to whom the Son chooses
to reveal him. (Mt 11:27)

This text implies that there is a mystery in Jesus known by God alone. It
also implies that Jesus had a knowledge of the Father that no other human being has had. God spoke to Moses face to face, as one might speak
to a friend. "Yet Jesus is worthy of more glory than Moses . . . for Moses
was faithful in all God's house as a servant . . . but Christ was faithful in
all God's house as a son" (Heb 3:6). As a son, Jesus has this exceptional
intimacy with God.

But the all-consuming love of Jesus for his Father shines out with
special splendor in the fourth gospel, where Jesus does what the Father
commands "so that the world may know that I love the Father" (Jn
14:31). Here there is an extraordinary communion and a loving indwelling—"Believe me that I am in the Father and the Father is in me" (Jn
14:11)—which reaches a climax with the mystical words, "The Father
and I are one" (Jn 10:30).

Furthermore, this intimate communion with the Father overflows on
the human relationships of Jesus—with Mary Magdalene and Mary of
Bethany, with the beloved disciple who laid his head on the Lord's breast
and with Peter, to whom he said, "Simon, son of John, do you love me?"
(Jn 21:16). Jesus loves them, and they love him. Jesus is united with
them and they with him. At the end, they are no longer disciples but
intimate friends who hear Jesus say, "As the Father has loved me, so I
have loved you; dwell in my love" (Jn 15:9). To dwell in Jesus as the
branches dwell in the vine (and, needless to say, this has eucharistic over-
tones) is the apex of Christian mysticism.

The mystical life of Jesus, then, consists in *communion and intimacy
with his Father, with his friends and with humanity.*

Jesus came to share this mystical life with us.

We are all called to mystical communion and to divine intimacy. The
Christian tradition expresses this through the Song of Songs, where Jesus
is the bridegroom and the human person is the bride: "You have ravished my heart, my sister, my bride, you have ravished my heart with
one glance of your eyes" (Sg 4:9). But union with Jesus is only the first
step. Through Jesus we are filled with the Spirit and are one with the
Father. As Jesus cried "Abba, Father," so also do we. "When we cry,
'Abba, Father!' it is that very Spirit bearing witness with our spirit that
we are children of God" (Rom 8:15). In this way the mystical life culminates in a Trinitarian experience.

Communion with God overflows in communion with other men and
women. "Just as I have loved you, you also should love one another" (Jn

13:34). Intimate human friendship leading to mutual indwelling is an integral part of the mystical life. All leads to the eschatological indwelling of the parousia: "On that day you will know that I am in my Father, and you in me, and I in you" (Jn 14:20).

JESUS THE PROPHET

"Yet today, tomorrow, and the next day I must be on my way, because it is impossible for a prophet to be killed outside of Jerusalem" (Lk 13:33).

Thomas Aquinas and the medieval theologians spoke of three levels of knowledge in the consciousness of Jesus. There was the "acquired knowledge" of one who spent his childhood in Nazareth and "increased in wisdom and in years, and in divine and human favor" (Lk 2:52). There was the "infused knowledge" of the prophet who wept over Jerusalem. And there was the beatific vision of the Word incarnate. Here let me speak about the infused or prophetic knowledge.[7]

Throughout the Bible we find prophets to whom came the word of God. This word, Aquinas held, was not acquired by human effort but was a gift of the Spirit. Like infused contemplation it was dark, obscure, formless wisdom in a cloud of unknowing. The prophets, knowing that ordinary words were inadequate to express this knowledge, spoke in paradox or through symbolic action. They were frequently misunderstood and persecuted.

The call to prophecy came in an inaugural vision that in Isaiah, Jeremiah and Ezekiel was a very powerful mystical experience. Here the prophet had a clear understanding of who he was and what his mission was. Jeremiah, for example, heard the interior words:

> Before I formed you in the womb
> I knew you. (Jer 1:5)

In this moment he found his true self, his unconditioned self, his original face (if I may quote Zen) "before his father and mother were born." He knew who he was and that he was chosen by God.

Jeremiah also understood his mission: "I appointed you a prophet to the nations" (Jer 1:5). He was appointed over nations and over kingdoms

> to pluck up and to pull down,
> to destroy and to overthrow,
> to build and to plant. (Jer 1:10)

He had no doubt about the mission entrusted to him by God.

Aquinas held that while the word came to the Hebrew prophets for a certain time and for a certain mission, Jesus enjoyed prophetic wisdom throughout his life. Jesus, the prophet, knew very well who he was and what his mission was. He knew that he was the Savior of the world and that his blood would be shed for the remission of sins. Yet there was a process through which he came to this realization.

I stress this point because some theologians of stature insist that Jesus had no more than acquired knowledge, that he did not know who he was and that he was uncertain about his mission. Yet to say this not only contradicts the Christian tradition of almost two thousand years, Orthodox, Protestant and Catholic, but it also contradicts the prophetic tradition of the Bible. It is equivalent to saying that Jesus was neither a mystic nor a prophet.[8]

The inaugural vision of Jesus took place at his baptism in the Jordan. Luke tells us that Jesus was praying. Matthew and Mark tell us that Jesus *saw* the descent of the Holy Spirit: "And just as he was coming up out of the water, he saw the heavens torn apart and the Spirit descending like a dove upon him" (Mk 1:10). And then Jesus heard the voice from heaven: "You are my Son, the Beloved, with you I am well pleased" (Mk 1:11).

What a cosmic experience! The heavens are torn apart and the voice of God pierces the stratosphere to the mind and heart of Jesus and to the very center of his soul. In a moment of shattering enlightenment he realizes that he is the Beloved Son. He is the Son of whom Isaiah said, "Here is my servant, whom I uphold, my chosen in whom my soul delights" (Is 42:1). And subsequent writers of the New Testament see Jesus as this Beloved Son who was wounded for our transgressions and crushed for our iniquities. Jesus sees clearly his vocation to the cross.

After his baptism Jesus, acutely aware of his great mission, proclaims the good news: "The time is fulfilled, and the kingdom of God has come near, repent and believe in the good news" (Mk 1:15). There is a progression in his prophetic knowledge and even a struggle. As he journeys to Jerusalem to suffer and to die, he is tempted by his best friend, whom he reprimands severely: "Get behind me, Satan! You are a stumbling block to me" (Mt 16:23). How vulnerable Jesus was! Yet nothing must deflect him from his cross.

Realization of who he is reaches a great climax with his resurrection when, in the words of Paul, "he was declared to be Son of God with power according to the Spirit of holiness by resurrection from the dead" (Rom 1:4).

TABORIC LIGHT

Yet another cosmic and earth-shaking mystical experience is the Trans-figuration. Together with his intimate disciples Peter, James and John, Jesus climbs the mountain by night in order to pray. As he prays, and before their very eyes, he is transfigured. His face and clothing radiate a blinding light. It is as though he is *a being of light*. Moses and Elijah, also surrounded by light, appear and talk to him about his "departure," which he is to accomplish at Jerusalem.

The mystical experience of Jesus overflows on his disciples who, sleepy though they are, stay awake. Peter, torn out of himself in the joy of ecstasy and not knowing what he is saying, cries out: "Master, it is good for us to be here; let us make three dwellings . . . " (Lk 9:33). Then comes the cloud, the sign of God's presence, and the voice: "This is my Son, my Beloved, listen to him!" (Lk 9:35).

This story has baffled many Western commentators who have thought out ingenious theories to explain it away. But the Eastern Orthodox tradition, preeminently mystical, has always accepted it just as it is. The Transfiguration appears in exquisite icons where the glorified Jesus, the light of the world, is raised up with Moses and Elijah, while the terrified apostles fall to the ground. Orthodox mystics see the transfigured Jesus as the model of all mysticism. They claim to see the light of Mount Tabor in their hearts and in the surrounding world. They experience the inner fire of love, and they believe that with Jesus they are divinized through divine grace. Eastern Christianity has elaborated a theology of uncreated light that is of great significance in the dialogue with Indian and Tibetan mysticism.

And this mystical event has a prophetic message.

First, it tells us who Jesus is: "This is my Son, my Beloved. Listen to him" (Lk 9:35). Jesus had no doubts about his identity; now the disciples have no doubts. But the message is not yet for the world: "Tell no one about the vision until after the Son of Man has been raised from the dead" (Mt 17:9).

Most significantly, it speaks not only of the cross and resurrection of Jesus but also of his glorification and second coming. On the mountain the apostles saw the radiant Jesus who has entered into his glory, and with him they saw the glorified Moses and Elijah. They had a glimpse of the message that *Christ has died, Christ is risen, Christ will come again.* "Was it not necessary that the Christ should suffer these things and then enter into his glory?" (Lk 24:26).

The message of the Transfiguration, then, is one of hope and opti-mism. Through his suffering Jesus entered into his glory. With him Moses and Elijah enter into glory. And the Transfiguration gives us hope that we, too, will enter one day into that glory.

THE DARK NIGHT

> He was despised and rejected by others;
>   a man of sorrows and acquainted with infirmity.
>
>   (Is 53:3)

The primitive church saw Jesus as the man of sorrows, the servant of Yahweh, who was wounded for our transgressions and crushed for our iniquities. Gethsemane was a central event in his life.

Together with those intimate friends who had been with him on the mountain, Jesus goes to the Garden of Gethsemane. He begins to be grieved and agitated. Throwing himself on the ground he prays: "My Father, if it is possible, let this chalice pass from me; yet not my will but thine be done" (Mt 26:39). Jesus experiences an intense loneliness. He wants the support of his disciples: "Remain here, and stay awake with me" (Mt 26:38). But they fall asleep, and he must go through the dark-ness alone, without human support. "And being in an agony he prayed more earnestly" (Lk 22:44). Strengthened by the angel, Jesus comes to deep peace. He who previously prayed that the chalice might pass can now say with confidence, "The cup my Father has given me, shall I not drink it?" (Jn 18:11). Through Gethsemane and the cross he enters into glory.

Luke in particular emphasizes that Gethsemane was a time of prayer. Jesus prays, and he insists that his disciples, however sleepy they may be, must pray. They must pray not only to accompany him in his agony but also to attain their own salvation. There is an acute sense of urgency in his words, "Why are you sleeping? Get up and pray that you may not come into the time of trial" (Lk 22: 46).

But why was Jesus so agitated? What was the root cause of his agony?

He was faced with crucifixion and, in the words of the inspired au-thor, "Jesus offered up prayers and supplications, with loud cries and tears, to the one who was able to save him from death" (Heb 5:7). But even more terrible than death was the darkness with which he was faced: "But this is your hour and the power of darkness!" (Lk 22:53).

Jung has written powerfully about the darkness in the human uncon-scious and the necessity of passing through this darkness on the way to the light of individuation. There is the darkness of neuroses and anxieties and fears in the personal unconscious, but even more terrible is the archetypal darkness that lurks in the collective unconscious. Passing through this darkness is a process of purification.

The darkness in Jesus did not come from personal sin or from original sin that he inherited from the past. The darkness came from the sin of the world, which he, the sinless one, had taken on himself. "All we like sheep have gone astray . . . and the Lord has laid on him the iniquity of us all" (Is 53:6). He was the Lamb of God who takes away the sins of the world. In the terrible words of Paul: "For our sake he made him to be sin who knew no sin" (2 Cor 5:21). Jesus had to pass through the frightening darkness of universal sin in order to save the world.

Yet Gethsemane is part of human life. All must pass through the darkness. Some pass through it in life; some pass through it at the time of death; some pass through it after death before coming to the light of God. For some saints and mystics the dark night is particularly painful because they suffer together with Jesus for the salvation of the world. But always the night is transitional. It is the path to resurrection and glorification.

St. John of the Cross reminds us that the dark night is a time of prayer. It is a time of purification. He calls it "dark contemplation." When it is over, he can sing with rapturous joy:

> O guiding night!
> O night more lovely than the dawn!
> O night that has united
> the Lover with the beloved,
> transforming the beloved in her Lover.[9]

Only through the agony of the dark night does one come to joyful and ecstatic union with the Beloved.

THE VISION OF GOD

Following the scriptures, traditional theology has always taught that human life culminates in the vision of God in eternity. The First Epistle of St. John, telling us that what we will be has not yet been revealed, goes on: "What we do know is this: when he is revealed, we will be like him, for we will see him as he is" (1 Jn 3:2). To see God as he is! What a mystical experience! St. Paul has a similar message: "For now we see in a mirror, dimly, but then we will see face to face. Now I know only in part; then I will know fully, even as I have been fully known" (1 Cor 13:12). The old theologians also quoted the Sermon on the Mount: "Blessed are the pure of heart, for they will see God" (Mt 5:8). And they quoted the eschatological text that tells us the elect "will see his face; and his name will be on their foreheads" (Rv 22:4).

With these and other texts the church taught that the human race is called to divinization through a face-to-face vision of God. This Christian teaching can profitably enter into dialogue with a Buddhist eschatology, which speaks of nirvana and the dawning of the Ground Luminosity.

While the vision of God was reserved for the elect in heaven, some mystical theologians held that this gift was granted in a fleeting way to privileged saints and mystics in this life. Chief among such privileged mystics was Moses. To prophets God makes himself known in visions and dreams. Not so to Moses—"With him I speak face to face—clearly, not in riddles; and he beholds the form of the Lord" (Nm 12:8). To Paul also, it was said, this privilege was granted when he was caught up into Paradise and heard things that are not to be told, that no mortal is permitted to repeat. And St. John of the Cross held that this privilege was granted to Elijah, once regarded as the founder of the Carmelite Order. In all these cases to receive the beatific vision was not to become less human but to experience momentarily the end for which human nature was created.

Aquinas and Thomists until the mid-twentieth century maintained that Jesus enjoyed the beatific vision all through his life. In support of this thesis Thomists appealed principally to the fourth gospel, where the historical Jesus fully enjoys the knowledge of the Father that the Word possessed before the Incarnation. Some of the texts they used were: "Not that anyone has seen the Father, except the one who comes from God; he has seen the Father" (Jn 6:46); "No one has ever seen God; it is the only Son who is nearest to the Father's bosom who has made him known" (1:18); "I am telling what I have seen and heard from my Father" (8:38). These and other Johannine texts show us a Jesus who has seen the Father and knows the Father. The Jesus of the fourth gospel is the mystic of mystics.

Yet few theologians today accept this teaching of Aquinas.

For one thing, some scholars hold that the fourth gospel is not a historical document. They maintain that it is overlaid with first-century theology and does not reflect the mind of the earthly Jesus. About this thesis (with which I do not agree) I will speak in the next chapter. Here it is enough to consider other objections made by modern scholars.

Jesus suffered. He was tempted, and he struggled. He had free will. There were things he did not know. He was completely human. He was "one who in every respect has been tested as we are, yet without sin" (Heb 4:15). How reconcile this with the beatifying vision of God?

This is a valid question. It is important to remember, however, that Aquinas and the medieval theologians were aware of the problems. They were not naive. Already in the second century church fathers were discussing *the ignorance of Christ* with special reference to the celebrated text of Mark 13:32, where Jesus says that no one knows the day and hour of the last judgment, neither the angels, nor the Son, only the Father. The medieval theologians, moreover, reflected on Gethsemane and the *Lama Sabbacthani*. They saw that the human psyche is multi-layered: at one level the person can be plunged in darkness while at another level be enjoying the vision of God. In his darkest hour in Gethsemane, Jesus still had the most intimate relationship with his Father and cried out, "Abba, Father" (Mk 14:36). One modern Thomist, François Dreyfus, puts it well, saying that Jesus "had agreed that the light of the presence of his Father burn only in the innermost, the most inaccessible abyss of his Being without shining upon his intelligence, his will, his sensibilities plunged, as they were, in the most impenetrable darkness."[10] Dreyfus continues:

> Jesus really wanted, on Golgotha as in Gethsemane, to undergo the consequences of the sin which distanced and separated from God—this God whom he continued to contemplate but with a contemplation which does not bring him any joy or comfort, since he was experiencing in all of its dire force, the opposition between the thrice holy God and the sin of humanity which he wished to assume.[11]

It was precisely because he enjoyed the vision of the thrice-holy God together with the dire force of evil and darkness that Jesus suffered in Gethsemane. And the vision of God, far from making Jesus less human, made him the most human of humans.

Yet only the mystics understand Gethsemane. Only the mystics understand the dark contemplation that brings no joy or comfort. The vast majority of scripture scholars of the twentieth century were not mystics. Influenced by the Enlightenment, they knew little about mystical experience. That this Galilean carpenter had really seen God was no less than preposterous. Jesus was human, they said; to be human means to be ordinary, like the proverbial man in the street.

But theology makes progress, and its future will be in Asia. In the third millennium, as Christian theologians enter into dialogue with India and Tibet, they will go beyond the Enlightenment. They will find mystics who claim to have experienced nirvana and the dawning of the Ground Luminosity. Then they will be open to the possibility that Jesus was a highly enlightened mystic. And they may take a second look at the teaching of Aquinas that the man Jesus saw God.

FIFTEEN

Jesus the Mystic (II)

JESUS AND *ADVAITA*

Christianity, I have said, is locked in dialogue with Asia, locked in a dialogue that will have incalculable repercussions on the world of the third millennium. We know that dialogue is a two-way process. Both parties share and learn. Christians share the good news of the gospel of Jesus Christ while opening their minds and hearts to the wealth and the wisdom of the mystical cultures and religions of Asia. And through this openness they find more and more treasures in the gospel that they love.

In sharing the gospel Christians are steering a perilous journey between Scylla and Charybdis. One extreme is that of preaching a Jesus who is so divine, so ethereal, so unworldly, so sinless, so different from us that he no longer seems human. To this Jesus we cannot pray with the intimacy that is distinctive of the Christian tradition. Moreover, such an attitude contradicts the gospel message that the Word was made flesh and dwelt among us.

The other extreme is that of seeing a Jesus so human that he is no longer divine. He becomes one mystic among many mystics, one prophet among many prophets, one *avatāra* among many *avatāras*. This Jesus is not the Savior of the world. And such an attitude overlooks the singularity of the great event whereby in the fullness of time God sent his only Son, born of a woman, born under the Law.

Only men and women who have met Jesus at the very core of their being can successfully trace this course between Scylla and Charybdis.

Here I would like to return to two saintly Christians of the twentieth century who, through their lived mystical experience in India, came to a new understanding of Jesus the mystic.

The first is Abhishiktananda.

I have already spoken of this holy man's spiritual practice under the saintly Ramana Maharshi and his claim to have experienced the Hindu *advaita* or non-dualism. Saying that the experience of the Absolute to which India's mysticism points is included in the words of Jesus, "My Father and I are one," he continues:

> All that the Maharshi, and countless others before him, knew and handed on of the inexorable experience of non-duality, Jesus also knew himself, and that in a pre-eminent manner.[1]

Yes, Jesus experienced non-dualism but in a preeminent manner. He was one with the Father and yet he loved the Father. In the words of Abhishiktananda: "At the very heart of all this, there remains 'the face-to-face' of the Son and the Father." After experiencing *advaita*, Abhishiktananda returns to the Christian revelation:

> That mystery which had first been glimpsed by the rishis is now revealed by St. John in all its splendor . . . It was as though we had returned from the *Upanishads* to the Bible with eyes miraculously unsealed . . . capable of a wholly new penetration into the mystery of the Lord.[2]

A new penetration into the mystery of the Lord! Will India see aspects of the mystery that the Greeks and even the Hebrews could not see?

The second saintly Christian was an admirer of Abhishiktananda. Bede Griffiths, quoting St. John on the union and intimacy of Jesus with his Father, gives the words of the gospel a similar interpretation:

> Here we have expressed in the clearest terms the "non-duality" of Jesus and God. He is one with the Father and yet he is not the Father. This is neither monism, a simple identity, nor dualism, a real separation. It is "non-dualism," the mystery revealed in the Hindu and Buddhist and Taoist scriptures and discovered in Judaism and Islam.[3]

Griffiths, furthermore, makes the important point that Jesus is not separate from us. He came to reveal the destiny of all humanity, as is clear from his prayer for his disciples "that they may be one, as thou, Father, art in me and I in thee, that they may also be one in us" (Jn 17:21). Griffiths goes on, "This is the destiny of all humanity, to realize its essential unity in the Godhead." Yet he sees that this cannot come about without the pain of self-sacrifice and the loss of all things.

Abhishiktananda and Bede Griffiths, then, sow the seeds of a new and exciting Christology for India. Yet both are aware that important aspects of the mystery of Jesus are peculiar to the Christian tradition as it has developed in the West, and they refer constantly to the fourth gospel.

About this gospel it is now necessary to speak.

THE EAGLE IN FLIGHT

"Around the throne, and on each side of the throne, are four living creatures . . . and the fourth living creature like a flying eagle" (Rv 4:6, 7).

From the time of Irenaeus in the second century the eagle in flight is the author of the fourth gospel, a profound mystic who points to Jesus the mystic and soars like an eagle into the dazzling noonday sun. This eagle-like mystic tells us of Jesus who said: "No one has seen the Father, except the one who comes from God. He alone has seen the Father"; "Before Abraham was, I am"; "I and the Father are one"; "Father, glorify me with the glory that I had with you before the world existed" (Jn 6:46; 8:58; 10:30; 17:5). Did any other mystic speak like this? What other human being has used this language? Small wonder if this gospel has nourished the mystical life of millions for two millennia and will continue to nourish millions in the millennia that lie ahead.

For almost seventeen centuries Orthodox, Catholic and Protestant believers saw the fourth gospel as the work of the apostle John, the Beloved Disciple, who laid his head on the Lord's breast at the Last Supper and stood at the foot of the Cross. Meditation on this gospel brought them close to Jesus of Nazareth, the Good Shepherd who laid down his life for his flock.

In the nineteenth century, however, at the time of the Enlightenment, some scholars began to have doubts. This gospel, they said, written in the second century by an anonymous Christian, tells us nothing about the historical Jesus of Nazareth. It belongs to the literary genre of Midrash. That is to say, it is a fictitious story like Jonas, Tobias, Esther, Judith and Job.

This theory lost credibility in the twentieth century when it became clear that the fourth gospel was written toward the end of the first century. Anglican Bishop Robinson even proposed the year A.D. 65 as a possible date of composition. This changed the picture. Nevertheless, many scholars still hold that the Jesus of the fourth gospel is different from the Jesus of the synoptics, and they continue to question its historicity.

Raymond Brown, who spent a lifetime studying the fourth gospel, has an interesting viewpoint. "The present writer believes strongly that there is a core of historical material in the fourth gospel," he writes. He continues:

> The Gospel was written to prove that Jesus is the Son of God (20:31), and the evangelist accomplishes this by letting Jesus speak as He is now in glory. The words may often be the words of Jesus of the ministry, but they are suffused with the glory of the risen Jesus.[4]

There is a core of historical material, but the words are those of the risen Jesus! Or the words are those of the historical Jesus, but suffused with the glory of the Resurrection! How explain this?

To scholars these words of Brown may sound enigmatic. But to contemplatives they make eminent sense. For contemplatives who read this gospel with faith feel that they are in contact at the same time with the Jesus of history and the risen Jesus. When they read the words "I am the bread of life" (Jn 6:48), they know intuitively that they are in touch with the Jesus who was teaching at Capernaum and the Jesus who is now in glory. They make no distinction between the Jesus of history and the Jesus of faith.

The same holds true for the author of the gospel. Tradition tells us that he was a mystic who, after witnessing the death and resurrection of Jesus, spent many years in prayerful reflection and profound mystical contemplation. Under the guidance of the Spirit he saw more and more deeply the significance of the words and the works of Jesus. In his life of prayer he made no distinction between the Jesus who taught in the synagogue at Capernaum and the Jesus who is now in glory. It is the same Jesus.

And something similar can be said about St. Paul. The crucified Jesus and the glorified Jesus are one and the same, so that the apostle can write of "always carrying in the body the death of Jesus, so that the life of Jesus may also be visible in our bodies" (2 Cor 4:10). Death and life are present at the same time.

Yet some questions remain.

What can be said about authorship?

The author of the fourth gospel claims to be an eyewitness to the events he describes. After describing the piercing of the side of the crucified Jesus he goes on:

> He who saw this has testified so that you also may believe.
> His testimony is true, and he knows that he tells the truth. (Jn
> 19:35)

If one works with a hermeneutic of suspicion one may explain this away.
If one trusts the writer, one will believe that the gospel was written by an
eyewitness.

And was this eyewitness John the Apostle?

Here tradition is clear. Irenaeus in the second century affirms that the
author of the fourth gospel is indeed John the Apostle, the Beloved Disciple who laid his head on the Lord's breast at the Last Supper, and that
he wrote this gospel in Ephesus toward the end of his life. Irenaeus,
moreover, knew Polycarp, bishop of Smyrna in Asia Minor, who was a
disciple of St. John and had listened to his teaching. We know this from
the historian Eusebius, who in his *Ecclesiastical History* quotes a letter
of Irenaeus telling us about Polycarp and his reverence for the apostle
John. This is basically accepted by modern historians, even when they
make minor qualifications in view of the literary genre of the history of
that time.

Nor does this mean that the actual writing was done by the apostle
John. There was a vibrant Johannine community in Ephesus; and the
gospel, as we have it, may be the work of a loving disciple. We know
that many biblical authors made use of an amanuensis. John may have
done this.

The eagle soars into the azure blue sky, carrying on its pinions those
who would see Jesus the mystic.

MORE THAN A MYSTIC

At a seminar held in London in 1994 the Dalai Lama put his finger on
the central problem facing Christianity in its dialogue with other religions. Speaking of the stages of evolution wherein the bodhisattva starts
from the state of an ordinary being and moves toward full enlightenment, the Dalai Lama went on to say that Jesus was different: "Whereas
in the case of Jesus we are referring to someone who is unique, who is
the Son of God. So the process of stages does not apply. Jesus Christ
does not progress through a series of spiritual stages, isn't that the case?"[5]

Theologians might nuance the Dalai Lama's statement, pointing out
that Jesus, being fully human, grew in wisdom and in the realization of
who he was. Nevertheless, the Dalai Lama did see to the core of things.
Nor was he introducing a new problem.

The early Christians saw Jesus as more than a prophet and more than a mystic. They saw him as the Son of God, who existed before he was born of the Virgin Mary. The exegete Martin Hengel shows that the doctrine of the divinity and the preexistence of Christ spread rapidly in the Mediterranean world and was well established fifteen years after the Resurrection. This doctrine, clearly affirmed in the fourth gospel, appears with equal clarity, Hengel affirms, in the famous *kenosis* hymn in the Epistle to the Philippians:

> though he was in the form of God
> [he] did not regard equality with God
> as something to be exploited,
> but emptied himself,
> taking the form of a slave. (Phil 2:6)

Paul, Hengel tells us, founded the church at Philippi not later than A.D. 49, and he is here quoting a hymn that was composed much earlier.[6]

Elsewhere Paul speaks of the preexisting Jesus. Take, for example, the text: "For you know the generous act of our Lord Jesus Christ, that though he was rich, yet for your sakes he became poor, so that by his poverty you might become rich" (2 Cor 8:9). This is an echo of the *kenosis* text, speaking of the richness of the preexistent Jesus whose state was divine. And to this richness he did not cling.

Other texts could be cited. Here it is enough to conclude with Rudolf Bultmann:

> The doctrine according to which Jesus Christ is the preexist-
> ing Son of God become man . . . is considered by Paul as cer-
> tain, and the Philippians Hymn 2:6-11 which is prior to Paul
> proves that he is not the first to have introduced it into Chris-
> tian thought.[7]

The Philippians text also refers to the adoration accorded to the risen Jesus:

> Therefore God also highly exalted him
> and gave him the name
> that is above every name,
> so that at the name of Jesus
> every knee should bend,
> in heaven and on earth and under the earth,
> and every tongue should confess

> that Jesus Christ is Lord,
> to the glory of God the Father. (2:9-11)

Here the risen Christ is adored as God. The name above every name is the name of Yahweh. Heavenly creatures genuflect before God alone. This hymn manifests the faith of the very early Christians.

Now some theologians, including Martin Hengel, say that the principal problem in Christology is to explain how knowledge of the historical Jesus was transformed so rapidly into faith in the heavenly Son of God. In the terminology of Bultmann, how did the "historical Jesus" become the "Jesus of faith"?

If one adopts a hermeneutic of suspicion one may say that the early Christians invented stories to prove a point. If, however, one approaches the scriptural texts with trust in the authors and faith in "the praying church," one will say that the writers were guided by the Holy Spirit. "But the Advocate, the Holy Spirit, whom the Father will send in my name, will teach you everything, and remind you of all that I have said to you" (Jn 14:26). In prayer the Spirit was teaching the people of God, reminding them of the things Jesus had said and done, helping them to see more and more deeply into his life and ministry. The historical Jesus and the Jesus of faith were one and the same person.

STORY OF LOVE

From what has been said it will be clear that there are two approaches to the mystery of Jesus. One is a "low Christology" based on a scientific or historical critical approach to the scriptures. The other is a "high Christology" based on faith in revelation and the word of God. The challenge confronting Christianity in our time is to recognize and unite these two approaches.

To some extent this work has already been accomplished by the fourth gospel. The author makes no distinction between the historical Jesus who walked by the Lake of Galilee and the risen Jesus who has entered into glory. The Word was with God in the beginning, and now the Word is incarnate. The teaching of the fourth gospel is at one and the same time that of the historical Jesus and the glorified Jesus. This is important when we speak about Jesus the mystic.

The Christian story begins with a great statement of the divine plan: "God so loved the world that he gave his only Son, so that everyone who believes in him may not perish but may have eternal life" (Jn 3:16). Jesus is very conscious that he has been sent by the Father and is loved by the

Father. "The Father loves the Son and shows him all that he himself is doing" (Jn 5:20). Jesus, too, loves the Father. And from their mutual love proceeds the Holy Spirit, of whom John the Baptist said: "I saw the Spirit descending from heaven like a dove, and it remained on him" (Jn 1:32).

Here we are at the heart of the mystical experience of Jesus. Filled with the Spirit of Love he cries out, "Abba, Father." This is a mysticism that future generations were to call Trinitarian.

Two aspects of this love are worthy of note.

One is that it brings total unity so that Jesus can say, "The Father and I are one" (Jn 10:30). This aspect attracted Abhishiktananda and Bede Griffiths, who saw Jesus as the supreme example of *advaita* or non-dualism. Yet it is important to remember that a Christian *advaita* (if we wish to use this terminology) is an *advaita* of love and communion.

The second aspect is that of intimacy or familiarity. Jesus speaks to the Father with great confidence, as when he said, "Father, the hour has come; glorify your Son" (Jn 17:1). Here is an interpersonal love leading to a mutual indwelling that is one of the chief characteristics of Christian mysticism. This aspect does not appear in the *rishis* of the Upanishads.

Again, Jesus has the conviction that he is sent by the Father to lay down his life for humanity. "I am the good shepherd. The good shepherd lays down his life for the sheep" (Jn 10:11). The eyes of Jesus are constantly fixed on the time when he will be handed over to the Gentiles to be mocked and flogged and crucified, and on the third day to be raised. The cross is the very center of his life; it is the supreme expression of love. "But God proves his love for us in that while we were sinners Christ died for us" (Rom 5:8). And how unforgettable are the words of Jesus, "Greater love than this no one has than to lay down one's life for one's friends" (Jn 15:13)!

The evangelists write graphically of Jesus' baptism in the Jordan and his transfiguration on the mountain. Great mystical experiences indeed! Yet they were pointing to the supreme mystical experience, which was his death and resurrection. On the cross Jesus emptied himself, taking the form of a slave, and was subsequently raised in glory.

THE ARCHETYPAL MYSTIC

If Jesus was a mystic and more than a mystic, he becomes a model for mystics of the third millennium and for all the millennia that will follow. That Jesus is a model for Christians is obvious. But Hindus and Buddhists and Muslims also may be inspired by the mysticism of Jesus, even when they do not accept the christological dogmas of the churches. Already I have spoken of Buddhists who resonate with the *kenosis* or emptiness of the crucified Jesus. I have also spoken of Abhishiktananda and Bede Griffiths, who saw Jesus as a model of Hindu *advaita*. Perhaps we can speak of Jesus as the archetypal mystic.

Here I would like to explain briefly how Christian mysticism moves through following Jesus to identification with Jesus and union with the Father.

The starting point is not my love for God but God's love for me. Just as Jesus had the deep conviction of being loved by his Father, so the Christian mystic has the deep conviction of being loved by Jesus. "As the Father has loved me, so I have loved you; dwell in my love" (Jn 15:9). While reading the fourth gospel he or she in a moment of enlightenment may come to the realization, "I am the disciple whom Jesus loved!" He or she may cry out with Paul, "He loved me and gave himself for me" (Gal 2:20).

The response is love. In most mystics it is love for the crucified like that of Paul, who writes, "I decided to know nothing among you except Jesus Christ, and him crucified" (1 Cor 2:2). Or it is like the love of Francis, in whose body the wounds of Christ appeared. Or it is like the love of Edith Stein, who went to her death in the gas chamber of Auschwitz. It is love not only for the historical Jesus but for Jesus in the poor, the sick, in persons with handicaps, the underprivileged, the persecuted and the dying. It is a love that leads to wisdom.

The distinctive feature of mysticism is that this love-and-wisdom is gift or, in traditional Catholic terminology, "infused." People who meditate may become aware of an all-pervading presence that is within and around and gives them deep peace. "I did not cause this," they say. "It is gift." Yet this sense of presence is no more than the first stage. After some time the consoling sense of presence gives way to a painful sense of absence and abandonment. Now one cries, "Lama Sabacthani." But the dark night does not last forever. The mature mystic experiences fire and light.

The fire is love and the light is wisdom. *The Cloud of Unknowing* speaks of "the blind stirring of love." Orthodox mystics speak of "the burning of the spirit." St. John of the Cross unites the light and the fire in his cry, "O Lamps of fire" *(Oh Lamparas de fuego)* and he tells us that the lamps of fire are the Holy Spirit.

What, then, is happening in the mystical experience?

Traditional theology teaches that the human person is purified and divinized through the fiery love of the Holy Spirit. The old theologians liked to quote the prayer of the Second Epistle of Peter: "that you may . . . become participants of the divine nature" (1:4). In a daring phrase they spoke of "becoming God by participation." One is divinized by union with Jesus, the Son, in whom one cries out, "Abba, Father!" Christian mysticism reaches a climax when through him, with him and in him, one enters into that communion of love that tradition calls the Blessed Trinity.

St. John of the Cross uses the Song of Songs. Consumed by the fire of love, the bride goes forth into the night to meet the bridegroom and to be united with him. But (and this is important for an understanding of Christian mysticism) the bride is not just the individual person. The bride is the church. In a modern context can we not say that the bride is the people of God—that the bride is the human family? Can we not say with Bede Griffiths that Jesus came to reveal the destiny of all humanity?

The Spirit is at work in the hearts of all men and women and in the scriptures and traditions of all authentic religions. In 1986 at Assisi Pope John Paul prayed with Hindus and Buddhists and Muslims and Jews, reminding us that the Spirit, who is at work throughout the world, is particularly active in the hearts of those who pray. The same Spirit is at work in all religions. The fire and the light will always be given to the human family.

One important corollary remains.

I said that Jesus is the archetypal mystic. This, I believe is true. His self-emptying to be raised is a model for all.

But there is one important difference between Jesus and other mystics. While others are the bride, Jesus is the bridegroom. Just as Yahweh is the bridegroom and the people of Israel are the bride, so Jesus is the bridegroom and the wedding guests are the bride. "The wedding guests cannot mourn as long as the bridegroom is with them, can they? The days will come when the bridegroom is taken away from them, and then they will fast" (Mt 9:15). Other mystics can humbly say with John the Baptist that they are no more than friends of the bridegroom: "He who has the bride is the bridegroom. The friend of the bridegroom, who stands and hears him, rejoices greatly at the bridegroom's voice" (Jn 3:29).

The mystical marriage, then, is not between the human person and the Father but between the human person and Jesus who is the incarnate Word. Such is the theology of St. John of the Cross, who tells us that his great *Spiritual Canticles* contains "stanzas which deal with the exchange of love between the soul and Christ, its Bridegroom." This is the bridegroom who calls to the bride, "Arise, my love, my dove, my beautiful one and come away."

When this marriage is consummated, the bride, one with Jesus in love, is divinized. Participating in the Blessed Trinity, she cries out, "Abba, Father!"

PART III

The Great Conversion

SIXTEEN

"One Lord, One Faith"

THE CALL OF THE SPIRIT

As the twentieth century progressed, Christians became more and more conscious of the call to unity and to mutual love. The prayer of Jesus "that they may be one" kept ringing in the ears of Christians everywhere; adherents of the various Christian denominations began to realize, as if for the first time, that there is "one Lord, one faith, one baptism, one God and Father of all, who is above all and through all and in all" (Eph 4:5). This message became all the more imperative as we saw ourselves in a world searching desperately for unity and peace. How could we Christians talk about world peace and the unity of religions if we were fighting and bickering among ourselves? Yet it was clear, and it remains clear, that union will not come about by human effort alone. We need prayer. We need God's grace. We need a great conversion of heart.

From the Catholic side the great step forward was made by the Second Vatican Council, which brought the Counter Reformation to a dramatic close. The enlightened Pope John called for a thoroughgoing conversion of heart. He asked for forgiveness. The heretics became "our separated brethren" who could teach us many things. We could speak of "sister churches." We could pray together, looking forward to the day when all Christians with joyful hearts would celebrate the eucharist in common. In short, as their enlightenment deepened, the council fathers came to see that church unity is primarily a spiritual problem. If only the Catholic church could undergo a radical conversion, and if only the separated brethren could undergo a similar conversion, the theological problems would quickly be solved.

THE POWER OF POWERLESSNESS

While the Second Vatican Council recognized the weaknesses of the institutional Catholic church, confessing that the people of God had sometimes gone astray, it did not plumb the depth of Catholic sinfulness. Only in the last decades of the twentieth century did the corruption and hypocrisy of the institution appear vividly and painfully before the eyes of the world.

Earlier in this book I wrote about the decline of the West, saying that the Catholic church shares in this decline. In the twentieth century we saw the collapse of structures that had upheld the institutional church for almost two millennia. Scholarly and unscholarly books told us about the dark and sordid side of the papacy. The media bombarded us with lurid stories about sexual scandals among priests and bishops and about financial scandals in the Vatican. As the institutional church lost credibility, vocations to the priesthood declined; whole congregations were left without the eucharist. Once flourishing religious orders showed signs of disappearing. Millions of disillusioned women left the institutional church. Clerical domination came to an end. Was the old institution falling to pieces?

To many, even today, the situation seems desperate. But discerning men and women are less anxious. They know that we live in an apocalyptic age when secular and religious institutions are everywhere collapsing. Like Mark Antony, they know that the evil that men do lives after them; the good is oft interred with their bones. The sexual aberrations and the cruelty in schools and orphanages live on, but the humble service and the heroic sanctity are forgotten. So let it be with Caesar.

This is a time of opportunity. Beneath the confusion the Spirit is at work. Wise old Ignatius of Loyola saw humiliation as the very basis of conversion of heart. One who would follow the Ignatian path must *choose* humiliation with Jesus humiliated, just as one who follows the gospel is glad to be treated and accounted as a fool for the love of Jesus. "Rejoice and be glad for your reward is great in heaven" (Mt 5:12). This is a time when the humiliated institutional church is called to experience *the power of powerlessness*. It is a time of purification. It is a dark night of the soul. It is a time of death and resurrection. "Unless the grain of wheat falling into the ground dies, itself alone remains; but if it dies, it bears much fruit" (Jn 12:24).

The signs of the times point to a second spring. We are witnessing the death of the old and the birth of the new. We are experiencing the painful death of one church and the painful birth of another. Through this suffering we are moving toward a Christianity that is richer and more beautiful than anything the world has known. "Arise, my love, my fair one, and come away; for now winter is past, the rain is over and gone" (Sg 2:10).

TOWARD DECENTRALIZATION

In its search for Christian unity the Second Vatican Council took an honest and courageous look at history:

> For many centuries, the Churches of the East and of the West went their own ways, though a fraternal communion of faith and sacramental life bound them together. If disagreements in belief and discipline arose among them, the Roman See acted by common consent as moderator.[1]

These words of the council have a solid historical basis. For many centuries the churches of East and West went their own way. Rome was a court of appeal, not a seat of power. *By mutual consent* conflicts were brought to the Roman See.

The Catholic acknowledgment of this simple historical fact could have vast repercussions. If for many centuries East and West went their own ways, could they continue to do so today? Could they have their own theology and their own liturgy? Could they appoint their own bishops? And if East and West could go their own ways, could Asia and Africa and Latin America and the United States also go their own ways? In other words, could there be an end to Roman juridical centralization? Could Rome once more become a court of appeal, always remembering that Christians are united by "a fraternal communion of faith and sacramental life?"

When it came to the concrete realization of this decentralization, the council spoke of *patriarchates*, many of which glory in taking their origins from the apostles themselves. "By the name Eastern Patriarch," said the council, "is meant the bishop who has jurisdiction over all bishops (including metropolitans), clergy, and people of his own territory or rite, in accordance with the norms of law and without prejudice to the primacy of the Roman Pontiff."[2] The council went on to say that the patriarch has the right to establish new dioceses and to nominate bishops "without prejudice to the inalienable right of the Roman Pontiff to intervene in individual cases."

In responding to this council document, however, the distinguished Orthodox Professor Alexander Schmemann objected to its "juridical ecclesiology." He makes his point clearly:

> To a great degree it remains thus a *Latin* text about the Eastern tradition. The institution of Patriarchates . . . is defined as a personal jurisdiction of the Patriarch over other bishops, which is alien to the Eastern canonical tradition, where the Patriarch or any other Primate is always a *primus inter pares*.[3]

Alexander Schmemann here highlights the issue that has always separated Rome from Constantinople. Rome, he claims, wants juridical power whereas Constantinople is content with spiritual power. Any bishop, including the bishop of Rome, can be no more than a first among equals *(primus inter pares)*. To satisfy the Greek tradition, he claims, Rome must be willing to give up its claim to juridical control.

Nevertheless, the question of patriarchates has arisen and will not go away. Could Anglicanism become a patriarchate in union with the Roman patriarch? Likewise Lutheranism and other Christian denominations? At the Asian bishops' synod in Rome in 1998, Bishop Francis Hadisumarta, speaking in the name of the Indonesian bishops' conference, brought up the question of new patriarchates in South Asia, South-East Asia and East Asia, and he asked for "a radical decentralization of the Latin rite."[4] Others have claimed that if China were a patriarchate, appointing its own bishops, many vexing problems between church and state could be resolved.

In an important article published in March 1999, Cardinal Franz König of Austria speaks of a Catholic church that has moved out of its European phase and is evolving impressively into a world church that, no longer Europe centered, is in process of discarding its European mold. This leads to the question: How are we to govern a Church of such diversity? And he answers his own question simply by saying: "We must decentralize."[5]

The cardinal is critical of "the present style of leadership" practiced by the authorities in the Roman Curia, who have appropriated to themselves the tasks of the episcopal college. He writes:

> A gradual decentralization is needed, so as to strengthen the concern and responsibility of the college of bishops for the whole Church, under and with the Petrine office.

The cardinal goes on to speak of the principle of subsidiarity whereby "higher-ranking organizations should not take over what lower-ranking ones can and should do on their own."

THE DAUNTING TASK

With honesty and courage the council urged all "but especially those who plan to devote themselves to the work of restoring the full communion that is desired between the Eastern churches and the Catholic church" to reflect on the situation of Christianity prior to the Great Schism:

> This sacred Synod urges all . . . to give due consideration to these special aspects of the origin and growth of the Churches of the East, and to the character of the relations which obtained between them and the Roman See before the separation, and to form for themselves a correct evaluation of these facts.[6]

The first challenge to the conscientious historian and theologian was, and still is, the papacy. Orthodox, Anglican and Protestant bishops, historians and theologians argue that Rome assumed a power and a control far beyond anything warranted by the New Testament and the early Christian tradition. While some Orthodox bishops would accept the successor of Peter as a spiritual leader within Christianity, they see no scriptural or historical basis for the Catholic teaching about the primacy and personal infallibility of the pope. Some even argue that the pope's claim to jurisdiction over the universal church is nothing less than heretical. The council courageously asked Catholic theologians and historians to examine this thorny problem.

Most of the difficulties stem from the teaching of the First Vatican Council (1869-70) concerning the primacy and teaching authority of the pope. As for the Second Vatican Council, it was ambivalent. On the one hand, it confirmed the teaching of the First Vatican Council: "And all this teaching about the institution, the perpetuity, the force and reason for the sacred primacy of the Roman Pontiff and of his infallible teaching authority, this sacred synod again proposes to be firmly believed by all the faithful."[7] On the other hand, it strengthened the power of the bishops with its doctrine of collegiality: "Just as, by the Lord's will, St. Peter and the other apostles constituted one apostolic college, so in a similar way the Roman Pontiff as successor of Peter, and the bishops as successors of the apostles are joined together."[8] This opened the Catholic church to dialogue with the Orthodox teaching on "first among equals."

And so, in obedience to the Second Vatican Council's decree on ecumenism, some Catholic historians and theologians began to ask if they could reinterpret the First Vatican Council. Could there be an interpretation of this council that would be acceptable to the separated brethren? Here it is not possible to describe in detail their research. Enough to say that some had difficulties with the word *infallible*, preferring to speak of an *indefectible* church. Even the much respected Hans Urs von Balthasar found the word *infallible* as applied to the pope unacceptable "because men are always fallible."[9] Others questioned the very validity of the First Vatican Council, which, they said, was too much influenced by petty church politics. Others said that the First Vatican Council was no more than a general council and could not be called an ecumenical council. The theological climate, however, became extremely tense when theologians challenged papal teaching on contraception and divorce, when they asked for a change in the legislation about priestly celibacy and when they questioned the papal ban on women priests.

The theologian, said John Henry Newman, should be a prophet. Many of these theologians regarded their work as truly prophetic. They hoped for exhilarating theological discussions as in the Middle Ages when theologians challenged one another, even fighting pitched battles in the streets. But if the theologians of the late twentieth century were prophets, they suffered the fate of all prophets.

For the Vatican saw things differently. It spoke not of prophecy but of dissent. It strengthened the authority of the pope and its own authority. Never in history was a bishop of Rome so famous and influential; never in history was a Curia so powerful; never in history was the church so centralized. So-called recalcitrant or disobedient theologians were systematically punished. They were investigated, silenced, removed from office, obliged to sign professions of orthodox faith. A climax was reached when in 1998 Pope John Paul issued a chilling apostolic letter bringing back the words *excommunication* and *heresy*. The letter, aimed at protecting the faithful from the errors of theologians, gave "new norms which expressly impose the obligation of upholding truths proposed in a definitive way by the magisterium of the church, and which also establish related canonical sanctions." Anyone who denies a truth that must be believed with divine and catholic faith and does not retract after being legitimately warned "is to be punished as a heretic or an apostate with a major excommunication," while others could be punished "with an appropriate penalty."[10]

So the Catholic church, rocked with financial, political and sexual scandals, now found itself engulfed in a theological scandal of draconian proportions. The distinguished Jesuit theologian Ladislas Orsy lamented that times had changed since the Second Vatican Council: "The Fathers of the Council wanted no threats or punishments; they trusted that truth will attract by its own beauty and strength. As it happens now, the first reform of the present Code of Canon Law includes precisely that, threat and punishment."[11] He further laments that theologians are distrusted: "Such a distrust (whatever its causes may be) is a wound within the body of the church; we all have a duty to work for the healing of it."

A wound within the body of the church! A self-inflicted wound! How can it be healed?

The answer of Bernard Lonergan is simple yet demanding. The great Canadian pleads for conversion. Shepherds and sheep alike need conversion. The pope and the Vatican congregations no less than the theologians and the people need conversion. All need intellectual, ethical and religious conversion. Without conversion we will betray the gospel and the world in which we live: with conversion we can look forward to a second spring.

LONERGANIAN CONVERSION

Lonergan's threefold conversion—intellectual, ethical and religious—is relevant not only for individuals but also for communities and institutions. Today more than ever we need institutional reform and institutional conversion. But let us not forget that Lonerganian conversion is a powerful philosophical experience. "The threefold conversion," writes Lonergan, "is not a set of propositions that a theologian utters, but a fundamental and momentous change in the human reality that a theologian is."[12]

First comes *intellectual conversion*.

I have written some pages in chapter 4 about this intellectual conversion, where I speak of "the tyranny of dogma" and of "the two theologies." I now ask my reader to peruse chapter 4 carefully before proceeding. There I follow Lonergan in speaking of two conflicting approaches to religion and theology.

One approach, which Lonergan names "classicist," is static. It sees religion as a series of unchanging propositions or dogmas to which the believer must give assent. He or she must use the correct words, for the classicist insists on verbal orthodoxy, and any departure from the traditional way of speaking is suspect. Fundamentalists are extreme classicists. The inquisitors were dyed-in-the-wool classicists who tortured and burned the so-called heretics—frequently because they used the wrong words.

Now Lonergan does not deny the validity of the propositions. Far from it. But he does insist that in order to find truth the theologian (or anyone who searches for wisdom) must go beyond the words to the reality in an experience he calls intellectual conversion. This intellectual conversion he describes in remarkable words that remind us of the Zen *satori*:

> It is not just a matter of finding out and assenting to a number of true propositions. More basically, it is a matter of conversion, of a personal philosophic experience, of moving out of a world of sense and of arriving, dazed and disorientated for a while, into a universe of being.[13]

Persons who are intellectually converted will not be *attached* to words and letters, realizing that these are always inadequate to express the mystery of life. They move toward the reality to which the words and letters point in accordance with the words of Aquinas much quoted by the schoolmen: "Faith does not terminate at the expression but at the object" *(Fides non terminat ad enuntiabile sed ad rem)*. Nor do they necessarily oppose all investigation. They demand only that so-called investigators be free from *obsessive clinging* to established formulations, realizing that the same truth can be expressed in another way. Thus they resonate with the prudent words of Ignatius of Loyola, who, faced with a cruel and vindictive Inquisition, made an appeal that is still relevant:

> It is necessary to suppose that every good Christian is more ready to put a good interpretation on another's statement than to condemn it as false. If an orthodox construction cannot be put on a proposition, the one who made it should be asked how he understands it. If he is in error, he should be corrected with all kindness. If this does not suffice, all appropriate means should be used to bring him to correct interpretation, and so defend the proposition from error.[14]

Here Ignatius asks the investigator to put a good interpretation on what people say. If they cannot do so, he asks them to talk to the person, entering into what we now call dialogue. He ends by saying that with all kindness the orthodox proposition must be preserved.

How sad that the methodology of Ignatius was neglected! Such horrendous mistakes were made by the Catholic church, so terrible was the persecution of the so-called heretics, that Pope John Paul II has invited historians and theologians to reflect on Catholic excesses so that he, in the name of the Catholic church, may apologize. Needless to say, this apology must be accompanied by conversion of heart and a determination that the enormities of the Inquisition will never be repeated.

But could they be repeated?

We live in a different world. Western Christianity now finds itself faced with theologians of a different cultural background, theologians who will express themselves in terms of Asian, African or Latin American culture. This is a time to distinguish with Pope John XXIII between "the substance of the ancient doctrine of the deposit of faith" and "the way in which it is presented." If Western theologians (particularly those who find themselves called to "investigate") insist that Asian and African theologians remain exclusively with the Western propositions, if they insist on the wording of Western theology and no other, if they threaten and condemn and punish the Asians and Africans who carry Christianity into a new world—they could make mistakes no less terrible than those of the inquisitors, and they could jeopardize the very existence of Roman Catholicism in Asia of the third millennium. On the other hand, if with intellectual conversion they can be open to development and to the new language of other cultures, Roman Catholicism, united with other Christian denominations, will be enriched beyond our wildest expectations.[15]

Next is Lonergan's *ethical or moral conversion*, which is closely associated with intellectual conversion.

For Lonergan, the morally converted person is motivated by value, not by the desire for satisfaction or the need to control or the craving to build up the ego. The consequences of this for the individual and for the community are enormous. Here it is enough to say that in the practical order moral conversion leads to respect for the dignity of the human person and recognition of his or her human rights. It is clear to everyone that in this area the Roman Catholic Church is in dire need of conversion. The church must be careful lest, after preaching to others, she herself go astray. Let me give an example of one lesson that must be learned from the very Roman law the church claims to follow.

In the Acts of the Apostles we read that Paul was accused by his enemies, who also asked that he be sentenced. When King Agrippa and Queen Bernice came to Caesarea, Roman Governor Porcius Festus put the case before them, explaining how he had spoken to Paul's accusers:

> I told them that it was not the custom of the Romans to hand
> over anyone before the accused had met the accuser face to
> face and had been given an opportunity to make a defense
> against the charge. (Acts 25:16)

And so Paul came face to face with his accusers and publicly defended himself.

This right to meet one's accusers and to defend oneself has passed into the legislation of all civilized countries. Only in police states can the accusers remain anonymous and legal proceedings be kept secret. Yet in 1998 when the Belgian Jesuit Jacques Dupuis was investigated by the Congregation for the Doctrine of the Faith, *The Tablet* could comment:

> Fr. Dupuis does not know who his accusers were, nor who
> was chosen to present his case; he cannot therefore tell whether
> these were persons of sufficient weight to be able to under-
> stand his very complex work, let alone judge it. Such proce-
> dures, in which the congregation is assessor, jury and judge,
> fall short of the minimum that would be regarded as just in
> the secular world.[16]

According to the rules of the Congregation, Fr. Dupuis must remain silent about the content of the accusations. The process must be shrouded in secrecy. Fr. Dupuis obeyed. How would Paul have reacted? "I appeal to Caesar." It would indeed be ironical if the Vatican, which has devoted so much energy to the defense of human rights, were to find itself censured by the United Nations Commission for Human Rights or investigated by Amnesty International.

Lastly comes *religious conversion*.

Lonergan's religious conversion is a conversion to love. It is clear that this is the answer to all our problems, whether in the church or in the world. He speaks eloquently of an unrestricted, unconditional love, telling us that "religious conversion transforms the existential subject into a subject in love, a subject held, grasped, possessed, owned through a total and so other-worldly love."[17] In a Christian context this is love for the Word incarnate, a love that goes through Jesus to all humanity but especially to one's enemies and to the poor and the suffering. Again, it is a love that goes through Jesus to the Father; my being becomes being-in-love as the Father is Being-in-Love.

Lonergan's religious conversion, however, is not for Christians alone. It is for all human beings. All are called to be loved and to love. Only through love can we transcend the little ego, thus becoming fully human and fully authentic. And this radical love leads to the sublime wisdom that we call mysticism. How extraordinary! Lonergan, probably unconsciously, calls not only for a mystical Christianity but also for a mystical world.

While conversion to love is the climax of Lonergan's threefold conversion, it may not come first in time. More often it is the basic experience, leading to the other two conversions. It is the indispensable condition not only for world peace but also for good theology.

I have said that all need conversion. Pope John Paul II was aware that he himself was no exception, and he asked for prayers.

PAPAL CONVERSION

After the Second World War there arose a movement, fostered by the United Nations and world opinion, whereby nations reflected on their past, admitted their guilt, apologized and sought reconciliation. This movement gathered momentum, and Pope John Paul II became part of it. Again and again he confessed to the sins of the institutional church, asking pardon, seeking reconciliation and praying for a great conversion of heart.

In an interesting book that deals with the "*mea culpas*" of John Paul II the Italian journalist Luigi Accattoli claims that the Pope was greatly influenced by a theologian for whom he had the greatest respect. Hans Urs von Balthasar, calling for a confession of the sins committed by the church throughout the centuries, did not hesitate to name the crimes quite bluntly:

> Forcible baptisms, inquisitions and *auto-da-fé*'s, the St. Bartholomew's Day Massacre, the conquest of new worlds with fire and sword as if the release of brutal exploitation were also the way of the religion of the cross and of love; unasked for and utterly absurd meddling in problems of developing natural science; proscriptions and excommunications by a spiritual authority which behaves as if it were political, and even demands recognition as such.[18]

And Pope John Paul apologized. He apologized for the crusades, for the condemnation of Galileo, for Catholic responsibility in religious wars, for Catholic responsibility in the Holocaust. In the course of his travels he apologized to various groups who had suffered at the hands of Catholic Christians. Accattoli claims that Pope John Paul publicly admitted church culpability no less than ninety-four times, on topics ranging from the Inquisition to the treatment of women. And more remains to be done. What a task it will be to become reconciled with those good Scots and Irish who see the pope as anti-Christ and splatter walls with the slogan, "No pope here!"

Hans Urs von Balthasar did not limit himself to the past. To avoid "unnecessary scandal," he said, the pope should "turn the Vatican into a museum and move to the gates of Rome." He also maintained that priests, bishops and popes should give up their titles, which are "antiquated and meaningless in a Christian sense." The titles "father, abbot *(abba)*, pope *(papa)* contradict the gospel's teaching: 'Do not call anyone on earth your father' (Mt 23:9)." Moreover, the word *infallible,* as I have already said, was unacceptable to von Balthasar.[19]

With this in mind we can better appreciate Pope John Paul's encyclical letter of 1995, entitled *Ut Unum Sint (That They May Be One)* in which he made an impassioned appeal for Christian unity. He apologized for the sins of the past, insisting that "Christian unity is possible provided we are humbly conscious of having sinned against unity and are convinced of our need for conversion."[20] He further said that "the commitment to Christian unity must be based upon conversion of heart and upon prayer." Indeed the themes of prayer and conversion run all through the letter.

John Paul II recognizes his own human frailty and his own need of conversion: "Indeed, if Christ himself gave Peter this special mission, he also made clear to him his human weakness and his special need of conversion." And so he asks for prayers:

> The Bishop of Rome himself must fervently make his own Christ's prayer for that conversion which is indispensable for "Peter" to be able to serve his brethren. I earnestly invite the faithful of the Catholic Church and all Christians to share in this prayer. May all join me in prayer for conversion.[21]

The main obstacle to unity, John Paul II saw clearly, is the papal claim to primacy. The Second Vatican Council follows the First Vatican Council with words that will always be ecumenically controversial: "In virtue of his office, that is, as Vicar of Christ and pastor of the whole Church, the Roman Pontiff has full, supreme, and universal power over the Church. And he can always exercise this power freely."[22] In his encyclical letter the pope honestly confronts this statement. The question of the primacy, he says, is to be studied; he writes that he himself is trying "to find a way of exercising the primacy which, while in no way renouncing what is essential to its mission, is nonetheless open to a new situation."[23] This immense task, however, he cannot undertake alone. And so he makes an appeal that will go down in history:

> Could not the real but imperfect communion existing between us persuade Church leaders and their theologians to engage with me in a patient and fraternal dialogue on this subject, a dialogue in which, leaving useless controversies behind, we could listen to one another, keeping before us only the will of Christ for his Church and allowing ourselves to be deeply moved by his plea "that they may all be one . . . so that the world may believe that you have sent me" (Jn 17:21)?[24]

This call for open dialogue about the primacy of the pope will surely make a great impact on Christian ecumenism of the future. Immediately, however, it was not received with enthusiasm. Some Orthodox leaders complained that under John Paul II ecumenical progress had been reversed because the Vatican made allegiance to Rome a criterion of true Christianity. The conciliatory and friendly Patriarch Bartholomew may well have spoken for many Christians when he said:

> The Pope's encyclical, *Ut Unum Sint*, would undoubtedly have been accepted with gratitude if the Church and its theologians were prepared to see the Pope as a co-ordinator and senior leader, without extreme and theologically mistaken demands for a world primacy in the jurisdictional sense or even worse, for personal infallibility.[25]

As can be seen, the patriarch was less than enthusiastic. He could not accept papal primacy and infallibility, and he felt that the pope and his theologians were not willing to compromise.

Nevertheless, John Paul II has opened a new chapter in the history of Christianity. He has set an example that will not die. In the third and fourth millennia his successors and their colleagues will surely beg pardon for their own sins and the sins of the past, thus opening minds and hearts to an ongoing conversion in the church. As John Paul asked pardon for the unjust treatment of Galileo, so they may ask pardon for the ruthless murder of Savonarola, the vindictive misinterpretation of Meister Eckhart and the shoddy treatment meted out to Teilhard de Chardin. They may ask pardon for injustices committed during the very pontificate of John Paul—injustices to women, to theologians and to Asians. The examination of conscience will go on. The cleansing process will continue. We can hope that the church, abandoning the triumphalism of Constantine, will follow in the footsteps of its Lord, who emptied himself, taking the form of a slave.

PROPHETIC VOICES

Within the Catholic church there was a powerful response to John Paul II from bishops and theologians who continued to demand deep conversion and radical reform in the institutional church. Here I will select three responses that show that the Spirit continues to bestow the gift of prophecy on the church.[26]

The first is from a saintly and prophetic Redemptorist priest. Bernard Häring (1912-98) expressed his hope "that John Paul II will go down in history for his courageous encyclical *Ut Unum Sint*, a prophetic sign, an invitation to all Christians to join in the search for a universally acceptable Petrine ministry." Yet he confessed that "an increasingly uncompromising Vatican centralism, together with punitive control mechanisms" had disillusioned him. He speaks frankly of the need of conversion and structural change in the papal office:

> Since Constantine . . . the church has gradually taken on monarchical—even at times absolutistic—structures, worldly trappings, triumphalistic pomp and ridiculous titles of honor . . . The church that so convincingly calls for conversion of the individual must recognize that she herself needs an in-depth renovation of structures, forms of address and mindsets, in a word, an authentic conversion.[27]

Häring laments that in church government and teaching of this pontificate everything comes "from the top down"; there is little collegiality and little consultation. He gives one striking example. The synod of bishops for 1980, he tells us, decided almost unanimously that the Roman Catholic Church could, in its pastoral care of the divorced and remarried, follow the example of the Orthodox church and permit remarriage. Yet in his ensuing encyclical the pope decided—without explanation or advice—that the divorced and remarried could not under any circumstances receive the sacraments without a declaration of nullity.[28]

Häring appeals for *the principle of subsidiarity,* whereby decisions could be made at the grassroots level. Asking for an end to "the sophisticated system of rewards and punishments in the papal service" he calls on the pope to renounce all temporal power:

The future pope must renounce his role as a political leader among world rulers, an action that will eliminate the entire system of nunciatures. The witness of the gospel will be stronger when pope and bishops refrain explicitly from political involvements.[29]

He concludes by asking for "a radically renewed Petrine ministry."

A second prophetic figure is an Austrian bishop. Just before his retirement Reinhold Stecher wrote a highly critical and controversial letter in which he deplored the church's emphasis on law and its lack of pastoral concern. He charged that the institutional church exists to preach the gospel and to administer the sacraments, but millions of people are deprived of the sacraments because there are not enough priests. By continuing to demand priestly celibacy the institutional church "is refusing to recognize the theological importance of the Eucharist for the Christian community and for the Church."[30] Bishop Stecher laments that "for some time now we have been offering people . . . a non-sacramental way of salvation." All this comes from a tendency to treat human regulations as though they were absolutes and to subordinate the teaching of Jesus to human authority. Insisting that priests are impossibly overworked, the bishop calls for reform in the priesthood and greater involvement of the laity.

Most disturbing of all, he says, is "our treatment of priests who have married." When these men look for reconciliation with God and the church, "all we hear is a merciless 'no.'"[31] What did Jesus say? Did he not make forgiveness and reconciliation the highest duty, and is not this particularly important at the time of death? Bishop Stecher, in words no less disturbing than those of Jeremiah or Ezekiel, speaks of loyal Catholics who love the pope:

> Should they not tremble before the judge of all the world when a Pope dies with thousands of petitions and requests unanswered? What do we do when someone who is dying refuses reconciliation? Don't we do everything in our power to soften the person's attitude, since a soul's eternal salvation is at stake? . . . Doesn't our theology tell us clearly that the refusal of forgiveness and reconciliation is a far worse sin than the violation of celibacy?[32]

The bishop asks for a fundamental change in the church's preaching of the gospel and in its treatment of sinners. People are longing for a pope for our times, a pope who will embody kindness before all else, and he sharply challenges the institution:

As things now stand, Rome has lost the image of mercy and assumed the image of harsh authority. Such an image will win the Church no tricks in the third millennium—despite all the pompous celebrations and many beautiful words devoted to the millennium celebrations.[33]

He concludes by speaking of his undiminished hope in the power of the Spirit and the future of the gospel of Jesus Christ, if only we can be sensitive to its demands.

The third prophetic voice comes from the bishops of New Zealand during a visit to Rome. The bishops express great respect for John Paul II and for his courageous encyclical letter *Ut Unum Sint*. However, they feel called to speak out lest they be like those false prophets who said that all was well when all was not well.

The bishops are critical of Roman congregations or "dicasteries" that make regulations with little or no consultation of the episcopate as such. Even more, they are critical of Roman mechanisms of "control" and "dominance" in liturgy and theology as well as in the complex but urgent area of inculturation. They are critical of a church that threatens with penalties those of her children who have difficulty in accepting certain nonessential teachings. They ask the church to be open to "honest dissent" and to each person's right and duty to search for the truth and to obey conscience. Finally, they ask the Holy See to exercise leadership in sharing with women all those roles that do not require ordination.[34]

It should be noted that the three prophetic voices I have quoted do not question any dogma of faith. They do not question infallibility or primacy. They simply ask for a conversion of heart through a return to the gospel. The same holds true for the Asian bishops about whom I will now speak.

THE PROPHETIC VOICE OF ASIA

In 1998 bishops from all over Asia assembled in Rome for a synod aimed at helping the Catholic church prepare for the millennium. The theme of the synod was *Jesus Christ the Savior and His Mission of Love and Service in Asia: That They May Have Life, and Have It More Abundantly (Jn 10:10)*. Journalists who visited Rome for the occasion tell us that the atmosphere was upbeat and good-humored. Nor is this surprising. Everyone knows that the gospel has a big future in Asia, that Jesus is loved by millions and that Asian spirituality and theology may well lead the Christian world of the third millennium. More problematic is the future of Roman Catholicism in Asia. Does Roman Catholicism have a big future? And if so, in what form?

The Japanese bishops, speaking no doubt for all Asia, said that Catholic Christianity *in its present form* is incorrigibly foreign and does not appeal to the Japanese soul. On the first day of the synod Bishop Toshio Oshikawa made this point:

> Notwithstanding the frequent exhortations for inculturation, it seems to me that the *norm* for Christian life, for Church discipline, for liturgical expression and theological orthodoxy continues to be that of the Western Church . . . the ingrained Westernization of the language of our theology, the rhythm of our liturgies, the programs of our catechesis fail to touch the hearts of those who are searching.[35]

Bishop Oshikawa then asks the Holy See to move away "from a single and uniform abstract norm that stifles genuine spirituality, Asian liturgical expression, earnest Asian theological search and real growth in maturity."

The Asian bishops were characteristically practical and pastoral. They made no attempt to reinterpret the First Vatican Council. They did not question primacy or infallibility. They simply said that if they are to preach the gospel in Asia they need autonomy. They need freedom to create their own liturgy. "Why do we have to send vernacular translations of the liturgy to Rome for approval?" asked Bishop Claver of the Philippines. Did that mean that the local people were not trusted to speak the language of orthodoxy? There was need for "internal dialogue" in the church if the inculturation process was to be successful.[36]

Then there was the question of an indigenous theology. "Western, and especially scholastic theology is not adapted to the religions of Asia because it is too rational," explained the Vietnamese bishops. "For Asians, one cannot analyze the truth nor explain the mystery. And there is a preference for silence over words and not getting entangled in quarrels over words."[37] Asian theology will be mystical theology, developed through profound dialogue with Asian religions.

Most important was the question of community. The Federation of Asian Bishops' Conferences (F.A.B.C.) had spoken of the church as "a communion of communities." It spoke of "a new way of being church" and of "a participatory church." Some of the Asian bishops were disappointed by the lack of warmth in the Vatican bureaucracy. The Japanese bishops, not without humor, said the holding of the synod was like an opportunity for the central office to evaluate the performance of the branch offices. They asked for a relationship based not on centralization but on collegiality and on trust.

Of great significance was the intervention of Bishop Francis Hadisu-marta of Indonesia, who insisted that local episcopal conferences should take over decisions from the Roman Curia and that the selection and appointment of bishops should be in the hands of the local church.

It should be noted that before the synod the suggestion that the local church appoint its own bishops was made in China. The official church prays for the pope, recognizing his spiritual authority and leadership; but the government will not permit an outside power to appoint the bishops. In 1989 the Jesuit canonist Geoffrey King wrote that the nomination of bishops by the Roman pontiff is "an ideal that will not be realized in China in any foreseeable future." He continued:

> In the early centuries of the Church, election by clergy and people of the diocese was the usual practice. Intervention by the Pope did not become common until the fourteenth century and did not become the legal norm until the code of 1917.[38]

Could the Chinese church elect its own bishops today? Geoffrey King is aware of the problems. He sees the danger of secular control. Nevertheless, he envisages a *modus vivendi* whereby bishops appointed by a bishops' conference in China would faithfully serve the church without being "mere puppets of the government." He concludes with a challenging question: "Would not some compromise (*not* capitulation) be a fair price to pay for greater freedom for Chinese Catholics at present part of the underground, and for removing one obstacle to the healing of divisions among Chinese Catholics?"

If some compromise is reached in China, the repercussions on the universal church will be immense.

IGNATIAN CONVERSION

We must distinguish between reform and conversion. In the sixteenth century Ignatius of Loyola saw that the Catholic church was in desperate need of reform, but he preferred to concentrate on the interior process of conversion that underlies all true reform. Through his Spiritual Exercises he directed bishops, priests and clerics of all kinds, knowing that if conversion took place reform would follow.

Today we face a somewhat similar situation. The church is in need of reform from top to bottom. But more important than exterior reform is the underlying conversion of heart.

For Ignatius, conversion of heart is a process, just as the path to evil is a process. The latter begins with love of money, leads to love of honor and glory and culminates in pride and all evil. This is the path of Satan. But the path to conversion is the following of Jesus. With God's grace one embraces the poverty of Jesus who was born in a stable, had no place to lay his head and died on the cross. One imitates Jesus, who loved sinners, who chose to be despised and rejected, who through his humility and emptiness redeemed the human race.

As Ignatius proposed this path to clerics, his eagle eye penetrated to the heart of those who secretly held ambition for the bishop's ring or the cardinal's hat or a position of power in the church. Before them he firmly placed the picture of Jesus despised and rejected, telling them to seek nothing but imitation of the one who was "a man of suffering and acquainted with infirmity" (Is 53:3).

Today, as we view massive poverty and starvation throughout the world, we realize that the whole church is called to be the church of the poor. Priests and bishops, cardinals and popes, clerics and lay—all are called to follow Jesus poor, despised and rejected. This is the message of Ignatius for the church of the third millennium. And what a revolutionary conversion Ignatius asks for!

For one thing is clear. The Spiritual Exercises of Ignatius teach a path of total renunciation in imitation of one who emptied himself taking the form of a servant. It is a very radical path. Yet it is the path to true wisdom. And there is no other. If the institutional church can walk this path it will preach the gospel not only by word but also by deed, it will offer true wisdom to a world that thirsts for truth.

I have spoken of the great conversion that is asked of Christians if they are to be united in accordance with the prayer of Jesus. In the next chapter I would like to speak of yet another conversion that is asked of all Christians if they are to be united in love with Buddhists, Hindus, Jews and Muslims in the third millennium.

SEVENTEEN

Toward Harmony

UNITED IN PRAYER

It has become a truism to say that there can only be world peace when there is peace among the religions. Today, as never before, believers of all religions are called to love one another, to talk and listen to one another, to collaborate with one another and in this way to preserve the environment, eliminate grinding poverty, fight injustice, build a new world and lead humanity to salvation. Buddhist and Jew, Muslim and Christian, Hindu and Taoist, all must ask, "Can we work together or must we perish in a gigantic conflagration? Can we bring salvation to the world or do we die in despair?"

The key to union and harmony between the religions is prayer. John Paul II saw this clearly when, in October 1986, he invited leaders of the great religions to pray for peace at Assisi. That was a turning point in the history of humanity. Religious leaders, many of whom had long lived in haughty isolation, now greeted one another warmly, joined in humble prayer, and opened their minds and hearts to a great enlightenment and a great conversion of heart. What drama was there! The astonished world saw that human beings of different religious traditions could pray together. A harmonious relationship among the religions is possible.

Assisi was a great symbolic event. Later John Paul explained it theologically, saying that the Holy Spirit is mysteriously present in the hearts of all human beings, inspiring them to pray:

> In every authentic religious experience, the most characteristic expression is prayer. Because of the human spirit's constitutive openness to God's action urging it to self-transcendence,

224

we can hold that every authentic prayer is called forth by the holy Spirit, who is mysteriously present in the heart of every person.[1]

In 1998, the year dedicated to the Holy Spirit in preparation for the millennium, John Paul went on to ask *how* the Holy Spirit is at work in the various religious traditions: "Even now, during this pneumatological year, it is fitting to pause and consider in what sense and in what ways the Holy Spirit is present in humanity's religious quest and in the various experiences and traditions that express it."[2] He speaks of the founders who, under the guidance of the Spirit, achieved a particularly deep religious experience, which they passed on to others. This religious experience took shape in doctrines and rites and precepts. With unprecedented openness the pope urged people to be faithful to their own religious traditions and thus find salvation:

> Normally, it will be in the sincere practice of what is good in their own religious traditions and by following the dictates of their own conscience that the members of other religions respond positively to God's invitation and receive salvation in Jesus Christ, even while they do not recognize or acknowledge him as their Savior.[3]

Note that he speaks of "salvation in Jesus Christ"; he goes on to say that, while all religious founders have their role, Jesus is "the one Mediator and Savior of the human race." About this paradox I will speak later. Here a word is necessary about prayer and dialogue. Again I will quote John Paul II:

> Dialogue is not simply an exchange of ideas. In some way it is always an "exchange of gifts" . . . There is a close relationship between prayer and dialogue. Deeper and more conscious prayer makes dialogue more fruitful. If on the one hand, dialogue depends on prayer, prayer also becomes the ever more mature fruit of dialogue.[4]

Those of us who have engaged in dialogue can resonate with John Paul's words. How easily the dialogical process can deteriorate into an intellectually stimulating but spiritually stultifying "exchange of ideas." We need to be reminded that authentic dialogue comes from prayer and leads to prayer. Elsewhere I have suggested that for every hour of talk we should have two hours of silence. Only then will dialogue bear fruit.

Equally fascinating is John Paul's description of dialogue as "an exchange of gifts." Every religion has its message. Every religion has its gifts. What, then, is Asia's gift to the world? John Paul hints at an answer when he speaks of an Indian mystical experience that liberates us from the shackles of time and space.

TIME AND SPACE

Earlier in this book I spoke about the thousands of young Westerners who wandered through the plains and the mountains of India in search of "something." I also spoke of the scholars, the intellectuals, the scientists and the psychologists who were fascinated by the religious experience of India. Novelists, too, like Shūsaku Endō and E. M. Forster were drawn to India. The theologians—spiritual giants like Abhishiktananda and Bede Griffiths—cast nostalgic looks at Indian mystical wisdom. This was a time when teachers of meditation came from East to West with a message of liberation and enlightenment. All in all, the mysticism of India was in the air.

The religious establishment became alarmed. In 1989 the Vatican issued a document on "certain aspects of Christian meditation" warning the faithful about the dangers of Asian spirituality. In 1994 Pope John Paul's best-selling book *Crossing the Threshold of Hope* criticized the "negative soteriology" of Buddhism, cautioning Christians that the enlightenment of the Buddha comes down to the conviction that the world is bad. This had the effect of making the Christian world wary of Hindu and Buddhist meditation. Even committed Christians like Abhishiktananda and Bede Griffiths fell under a cloud. People began to wonder when the Roman axe would fall and heads would roll.

And then everything changed. In 1998 John Paul II issued his powerful encyclical letter *Faith and Reason,* which speaks of *inculturation.* "In preaching the Gospel," he writes, "Christianity first encountered Greek philosophy; but this does not mean at all that other approaches are precluded."[5] Christianity meets new cultures; it faces problems not unlike those faced by the early church. John Paul writes beautifully: "My thoughts turn immediately to the lands of the East, so rich in religious and philosophical traditions of great antiquity."[6] Then, with words that future generations will see as a turning point in the history of Christian spirituality and theology, he puts his finger on the very core of Asian spiritual experience:

> Among these lands, India has a special place. A great spiritual
> impulse leads Indian thought to seek an experience which
> would liberate the spirit from the shackles of time and space
> and would therefore acquire absolute value. The dynamic of
> this quest for liberation provides the context for great meta-
> physical systems.[7]

An experience that would liberate the spirit from the shackles of time
and space! What is this experience?

Liberation from the shackles of time and space is the keynote to understanding the mysticism of India. It can refer to the *saccidananda* (be-
ing-conscious-bliss) of the *rishis* of the Upanishads about which I have
spoken earlier in this book. It can denote *moksa* or liberation from the
painful cycle of rebirth. It can denote the enlightenment of the Buddha
at Benares. It can be found in Sankara, Ramanuja, Nagarjuna and a host
of Indian mystics. Nor is it limited to India. We find the same experience
in the relentless quest of thousands upon thousands of monks throughout Asia. Liberation may be gradual or it may be found in an instanta-
neous mystical flash. In either case it leads to the wisdom and compassion that radiate from the tranquil features of the Buddha.

The young hippies, the psychologists, the philosophers, the scientists
and the theologians—were they unconsciously searching for an experience that would liberate them from the shackles of time and space? Were
they searching for the wisdom of Asia?

Needless to say, John Paul does not advocate total acceptance of Hindu
and Buddhist religious experience. But he does advocate dialogue through
which Christian faith will be enriched:

> In India particularly, it is the duty of Christians now to draw
> from this rich heritage the elements compatible with their faith,
> in order to enrich Christian thought.[8]

John Paul goes on to speak of "the universality of the human spirit," as
if to say that there is a universal dimension in Indian culture (as indeed
in all cultures) that Christianity needs if it is to fulfill its mission. At the
same time he does not hesitate to remind us that "the Church cannot
abandon what she has gained from her inculturation in the world of
Greco-Latin thought."[9] As Western Christianity can learn from India,
so Indian Christianity can learn from Greece and Rome.

In this way the pope canonizes the dialogue of Abhishiktananda, Bede
Griffiths and the rest. What a rich dialogue this is! Nor has it come to an

end. It will continue in the third and fourth millennia. John the Evangelist, Paul of Tarsus, the Greek fathers, Augustine, Eckhart, John of the Cross, Juliana and Teresa—all will encounter the mystics of India, and the result will be a flowering of wisdom such as the world has never known.

But now it is necessary to reflect on John Paul's interesting reflection that "the dynamic of this quest for liberation provides the context for great metaphysical systems." Of these metaphysical systems the most important is *advaita* or non-dualism.

THE ONE AND THE MANY

From the earliest times Greece and India faced the same philosophical problem. The Greeks called it the problem of the one and the many. Great philosophers, they intuited the unity of being. They saw that existence is one. At the same time they trusted their common sense, which told them that there are many things and that existence is *not* one. How reconcile the one and the many?

This problem flowed through Western philosophy. Aquinas, following Aristotle, said that all things are one by reason of their existence and many by reason of their essence. They are one in *that they are;* they are many by reason of *what they are.* This solution, however valid, is somewhat abstract. The unity of being made little impact on Western thought. Philosophers, scientists and even theologians were greatly preoccupied with "the many."

Western mystics, on the other hand, knew from experience that existence is one. Martha was anxious about *many things,* but Mary, the mystic, knew that *one thing* is necessary. "Martha, Martha, you are worried and distracted by many things, but only one thing is necessary" (Lk 10:41). The author of *The Cloud of Unknowing* urges his disciple to stop thinking about *what God is* and to concentrate on *that God is.* The person who follows this counsel may find that "the many" fall into the background, as he or she comes to a profound realization of oneness. Small wonder that the mystics were constantly accused of pantheism or monism.

The mystics of Asia had a different approach. They sat cross-legged on the ground, regulated their breathing, let go of all reasoning and thinking and anxiety, and sought silently for transcendental wisdom at the core of their being. After years or decades of assiduous practice, liberated from the shackles of time and space, they came to a profound realization of the unity of existence. Based on this experience they created a philosophical system called *advaita*, usually translated "non-dualism," which has spread throughout Asia and has become the warp and woof of Asian thinking.

Some scholars, East and West, interpret non-dualism in a monistic way. That is to say, they interpret Asian mystics as saying that existence is one and the experience of the many is illusory. I do not accept this interpretation. I prefer the interpretation of other scholars who claim that the conclusion of the Asian mystics is no different from that of their counterparts in the West. They have such a profound experience of the one that the many fall into the background. Some of their sayings may sound monistic or pantheistic, but careful study shows that they are not. The Asian mystics are like Mary, who sat at the feet of Jesus. "Martha, Martha, you are worried and distracted by many things but one thing is necessary. Mary has chosen the better part, which will not be taken away from her" (Lk 10:41-42). In focusing on the one thing necessary, Mary chooses the better part. But she does not belittle the chores of Martha. She does not deny the many. She is no monist.

THE ASIAN GIFT

The gift of Asia to the world, then, is meditation leading to mysticism. As for Asian Christianity, still in its infancy, it is rapidly entering into dialogue with its mystical neighbors. Soon it will come to maturity and will talk to a Western theology that has marginalized mysticism. It will remind the West, seduced by "the many" and the activity of Martha, that one thing is necessary. This is the message of Jun Ikenaga, archbishop of Osaka. At the Asian Synod of 1998 he did not hesitate to criticize a Christianity that, nurtured in the West, insists on distinguishing, dividing and separating, ending up with two opposing worlds:

> Nurtured in the West, Christianity makes a clear division between God and the universe, between heaven and hell, the reward of virtue and the judgment that awaits the sinner. Its image of God as a father figure is predominant and with its fondness for distinguishing, dividing and separating it ends up by having two worlds, one set over against the other.[10]

Ikenaga goes on to say that in contrast to this dualistic tendency of the West, Asia sees unity or oneness:

In Asia, however, vast numbers of people hold to a pantheistic world view, believe in reincarnation, and do not feel that it is possible to make judgments in terms of black and white, whether it be a question of the human heart or human actions. Neither are they given to distinguishing: it is the all-embracing maternal instinct that is uppermost.[11]

Other Asian bishops in the synod spoke in the same way, criticizing the endless distinctions of the Western theology in which they were trained. Ikenaga, it should be noted, speaks for a long line of Japanese intellectuals who could not accept Christianity because of its seemingly dualistic tendencies. After the synod he said he had been influenced by Shūsaku Endō.

Obviously the archbishop is not advocating pantheism, nor is he saying that Christianity should accept reincarnation. He does, however, advocate contemplation, reminding us that God is closely united with the universe, that life and death are a single process, that the just are sinful and the sinful are just. He hints at an experience that liberates mortals from the shackles of time and space. Perhaps he even hints that Western Christianity could modify its horrific teaching about hell.

Ikenaga's reference to "the all-embracing maternal instinct" is also very Japanese, influenced by the Japanese saying that the four most dreadful things are the earthquake, the fire, the lightning and the father. It is significant that the first Japanese catechism of the seventeenth century teaches the people to pray not "Our Father who art in heaven" but "Our parent who art in heaven." The translators did not use the character for father, read *chichi*,

父

but rather the character for parent, which includes father and mother, and is read *oya*.

Ikenaga observes that "the Christian God . . . is by definition endowed with both a paternal and a maternal character."

Ikenaga's aim is pastoral. In spite of the great number of missionaries who have labored in Asia down through the centuries, the faith has not taken root, baptisms are few and Christian thinking has not entered into the mainstream of Asian society. He has grave misgivings about the value of the "intellectual approach, with emphasis on kerygma, dogma and catechesis, its ultimate aim being baptism." Jesus was an Asian who spoke a language that Asians understand. He healed the sick, loved the poor and censured the misuse of authority. Ikenaga concludes with hope and optimism:

> If we begin to use, in our theology and in our art, in our catechesis and evangelization, a more Asian, a more maternal mode of expression, it is my belief that Christianity will be more acceptable to Asian people.[12]

In this way the bishop makes a powerful appeal for an Asian contemplative approach to the gospel. His words are significant not just for Asia but for a disillusioned Western world that hungers for mysticism and looks to Asia for inspiration.

THE CHRISTIAN GIFT

The gift of Christianity is Jesus.

I have already said that Jesus is much loved in Asia by Hindus, Buddhists, Muslims and people of no religion. Asia, moreover, can boast of thousands of martyrs who laid down their lives for Jesus Christ. About some of these little is known; only when history is written will we learn in detail about the martyrs of China. It is true that the gospel has not yet taken root in Asian culture. But this need not discourage us. It takes a millennium for a religion to penetrate the unconscious and activate the archetypes of a people. Yes, the gospel has a great future in Asia. It will penetrate more and more deeply into the hearts of the people and renew their society.

But what form will an Asian Christianity take? This we do not yet know. As Asian Christians get in touch with their traditional wisdom and their traditional religions, as they study their literary and philosophical classics they will create their own theology, their own liturgy, their own monasticism, their own spirituality, and their own institutional structures. In this way the universal church will be enormously enriched. But the challenge of the third millennium (let me be frank!) will be church unity. The challenge confronting East and West is that of creating a world Christianity that, rooted and grounded in the love of Christ, will proclaim "one Lord, one faith, one baptism, one God and Father of all, who is above all and through all and in all" (Eph 4:5).

In this context I would like to speak briefly about a prophetic Japanese Christian who, in spite of his deep love for Jesus Christ, could not be united with Christians throughout the world. His life and teaching are both an inspiration and a warning.

Kanzō Uchimura (1861-1930) at the age of seventeen met some fervent Protestant missionaries in Hokkaido. Together with a number of Japanese companions he signed his name to the "Covenant of Believers in Jesus," received baptism and conceived a deep love for Jesus that lasted throughout his life. Together with this love for Jesus he had a deep love for Japan and a conviction that his country, no less than Israel, had a vocation in the world. In the English language magazine he later edited, he wrote movingly: "I love two J's and no third; one is Jesus and the other is Japan . . . I am hated by my countrymen for Jesus' sake as *yaso*, and I am disliked by foreign missionaries for Japan's sake as national and narrow. No matter; I may lose all my friends, but I cannot lose Jesus and Japan."[13] This twofold loyalty is the key to understanding Uchimura's life.

In his twenties he traveled to America, thinking naively that he was visiting a great Christian country. Here disillusionment set in. He was shocked by the fighting among the Christian churches, and later he was to insist that *a divided Christianity could have no place in Japan.* He was dissatisfied with the theology he studied at the seminary. It was spiritless and superficial, he said. He sensed a distressing racism that disturbed him. Yet he never lost his personal love for Jesus. While in America he wrote in his English Bible words that were later inscribed on his tombstone:

> I for Japan
> Japan for the world
> The world for Christ
> And all for God

He was exhausted in America, and suffering from chronic insomnia he returned home.

Back in Japan, Uchimura was increasingly frustrated by institutional Christianity. In the churches he found no joy but only formalism, competition and jealousy. The missionaries he had formerly respected he could no longer admire. "Believe in Christianity, but don't eat the bread of the missionaries," he told his disciples; he refused to accept money from abroad.

So he founded his own church, which was a "non-church" known as *Mukyōkai.* Insisting that Christianity is Christ, he wrote:

> Christianity is not an institution, a church, or churches; neither is it creed, nor dogma, nor theology; neither is it a book, the Bible, nor even the words of Christ. Christianity is a person, a living person, Lord Jesus Christ "the same yesterday, today and forever." If Christianity is not this, the ever-present living HE, it is nothing. I go directly to Him, and not through churches and popes and bishops and other useful and useless officers.[14]

For Uchimura, Christianity was not a body of truth but an experience. It was a living relationship with Jesus. Truly he was a mystic.

My professor of theology in Tokyo used to say that in his rejection of church Uchimura was the most logical disciple of Martin Luther, and that through him Protestantism achieved in Japan what it was unable to achieve in Europe. This is only partly true. Uchimura rejected the *institutional* church and wanted the minimum of organization, but he was a great teacher with many disciples, he was a prolific writer, and he founded a community. *Mukyōkai* is alive today.

Uchimura's influence in Japan is very great. He is particularly loved and respected by intellectuals and professors who find institutional Christianity obnoxious and incorrigibly foreign. His disciples, many of whom are distinguished writers and lecturers, gather to read the Bible and to pray. Regarding their number we have no statistics, since Uchimura wanted no successor and no organization to perpetuate his ideas. Probably they exceed one hundred thousand.

What, then, is Uchimura's message for today?

Uchimura reminds us that a deep love for the risen Jesus is the essence of Christianity and that Asians no less than Europeans and Americans are called to this love. At the same time, we who claim to inherit the faith that comes from the apostles believe that he would have come to an even deeper union with Jesus had he grasped the full implications of the words "I am the bread of life" (Jn 6:35) and "Those who eat my flesh and drink my blood dwell in me and I in them" (Jn 6:56). Likewise, we believe, his followers would come to an even richer experience if, together with their Bible reading and prayer, they could unite with Christians throughout the world reciting the words, "When we eat this bread and drink this cup, we proclaim your death, Lord Jesus, until you come in glory."[15]

Uchimura's sad disillusionment with the fighting and quarrelling Christian churches reminds us Christians that we must take seriously the Lord's injunction to love one another as he has loved us. We must pray and strive for unity. We must pray and strive for the time when all Christians will celebrate the Lord's Supper and share his body and blood with the world. Furthermore, Uchimura reminds us that a highly centralized, institutionalized, legalistic, political church that tries to control Asia from outside will surely fail. Only a church that respects the working of the Holy Spirit in the indigenous culture will bring the good news to Asia.

At this point in history, then, we must open our minds and hearts to a Christology that will speak to Asia. Such a Christology, based on scripture and tradition, will come from the prayer and life style of Christians like Uchimura whose lives may well point to a new era within Christianity.

AN ASIAN CHRISTOLOGY

John Paul II, following the Second Vatican Council, showed the greatest respect for religions other than Christianity. He spoke appreciatively about the deep religious experience of the founders. He affirmed that normally it will be in the sincere practice of their own religion that human beings find salvation in Jesus Christ, even while they do not recognize or acknowledge him as their Savior. This respect for other religions he balanced with an unequivocal statement about Jesus Christ:

> This does not mean forgetting that Jesus Christ is the one Mediator and Savior of the human race. Nor does it mean lessening our missionary efforts, to which we are bound in obedience to the risen Lord's command: "Go therefore and make disciples of all nations, baptizing them in the name of the Father and of the Son and of the Holy Spirit" (Mt 28:19).[16]

In this way the pope formulates what may well become the most challenging theological question of the third millennium: Jesus Christ is the one Mediator and Savior of the human race, yet other religious founders have their role to play, and the religions they founded are ways of salvation for those who believe in them. This gives rise to the practical question: How reconcile proclamation and dialogue? How reconcile our preaching of the gospel with our belief that human beings are saved through fidelity to their own traditions? John Paul briefly gives an answer, explaining why Christians must respect other religions:

> The attitude of respect and dialogue is . . . the proper recognition of "the seeds of the Word" and "the groanings of the

Spirit." In this sense, far from opposing the proclamation of the Gospel, our attitude prepares it, as we await the times appointed by the Lord's mercy.[17]

Quite simply, John Paul formulates a doctrine that is patristic and traditional, even if it was forgotten for centuries: the seeds of the Word *(semina verbi)* and the groaning of the Spirit are at work in all authentic religions. In respecting other religions and their founders Christians are recognizing the action of the same Spirit who is at work in Christianity and the same Word who became flesh in Jesus of Nazareth.

Yet this problem continues to cause considerable controversy among theologians, as they ask about the role of Jesus in other religions. Karl Rahner's "anonymous Christianity" was not well accepted. After his death, as the "theology of religions" developed, theologians began to speak a new language. They asked about *pluralism.* They asked whether Christianity is *ecclesiocentric* or *Christocentric* or *theocentric.* They asked whether the life and death of Jesus is *normative* or *constitutive* of salvation. They spoke of a Christology that is *inclusive* and one that is *exclusive.* They talked about *new paradigms* and *models,* and they discussed the various meanings of the word *unique.* A new theological literature came into existence. What is its value?

It seems to me that while this jargon may appeal to the West, it will cut no ice in Asia. I am reminded of Archbishop Ikenaga's comment about the Western penchant for distinguishing, dividing and separating, and of other bishops who rejected a plethora of words, saying that Asia prefers "silence before the mystery." I am reminded of the scholastics speculating about how many angels could stand on the head of a pin. How much more impressive is the poetic simplicity of the great Asian Christian Kanzō Uchimura who writes, "Buddha is the Moon; Christ is the Sun . . . I love and admire Buddha; but I worship Christ." He continues:

> I love the moon and I love the night; but as the night is far spent and the day is at hand, I now love the Sun more than I love the Moon; and I know that the love of the Moon is included in the love of the Sun, and that he who loves the Sun loves the Moon also.[18]

These moving words come from the lived religious experience of a mystic. They are profoundly theological.

ASIA AND HARMONY

The theme of the Asian Synod of 1998 was:

> Jesus Christ the Savior and His Mission of Love and Service
> in Asia: That they may have life, and have it abundantly (Jn
> 10:10)

Such was the title given by Pope John Paul. However, in the preparatory documents another formulation crept in: "Jesus Christ, the one and only Savior."

Invited to respond to the initial guidelines, known as *lineamenta*, the Japanese bishops caused something like consternation by questioning the wisdom of this second formula. They wrote, "If we stress too much that 'Jesus Christ is the One and Only Savior' we can have no dialogue, common living or solidarity with other religions."[19] To some Western theologians these words sounded like a betrayal. Were the Japanese bishops putting dialogue before commitment to Jesus?

Yet surely this is one more instance of misunderstanding between Asia and the West.

A key to the understanding of all Asian culture is the word *harmony*, in Japanese *wa*, represented by the important character

Early in the seventh century the devout Buddhist Prince-Regent Shōtoku opened his famous Constitution with the words:

> Harmony is to be valued, and discord is to be deprecated.

From that time harmony has been basic to all Japanese society. That is why the Japanese bishops, criticizing the "distinctions" and "differences" of traditional scholastic theology, could say that "in the tradition of the Far East, it is characteristic to search for creative harmony rather than distinctions."[20] Nor is Japan alone. In 1995 the Asian Bishops' Conference, in a document entitled "Asian Christian Perspectives on Harmony," wrote of harmony in Hinduism, Buddhism, Islam and Chinese Tradition, and called for a Christian theology and spirituality of harmony in Asia.[21]

The bishops, then, are very sensitive to any mode of speech that would disrupt the harmony of their society. They are struggling to express the mystery of Christ in a way that harmonizes with Asian culture and will not be offensive to believers in other religions. They want to avoid triumphalism. They want to present Jesus as a lover not as a threat. They want to avoid any evangelization that says: "Believe in Jesus, or else!"

How to present Jesus as the universal Savior who loves all and died for all? How can Christians present Christ in such a way that they can have dialogue, common living and solidarity with other religions? This is the leading question; and the answer of the Japanese bishops is brief yet profound:

> The church, learning from the *kenosis* of Jesus Christ, should
> be humble and open its heart to other religions to deepen its
> understanding of the Mystery of Christ.[22]

This simple sentence could be revolutionary. For it cannot be denied that the earlier missionary effort (which influenced me when first I came to Japan) was based on the notion of conquest. Constantine saw the cross in the heavens and heard the voice: "In this sign shalt thou conquer!" The missionaries were conquering the world for Christ—all the more so since they worked hand in glove with the colonial powers, first with the Spaniards and the Portuguese, and then with the French, the British and the Dutch. And now the Japanese bishops propose humility! They want to preach the humble Jesus who emptied himself, taking the form of a servant. What a revolutionary idea!

"He humbled himself and became obedient to the point of death—even death on a cross. Therefore God highly exalted him" (Phil 2:9). Paul was probably quoting an ancient Christian hymn that was influenced by the story of the Suffering Servant in Isaiah. Be that as it may, the *kenosis* theme is central to the whole New Testament, telling us of the humble Jesus who came not to be served but to serve and to give his life as a ransom for many. It is also a key to understanding Jesus the mystic, who surrendered everything to be glorified, the Jesus who inspired the *todo y nada* of St. John of the Cross.[23]

The Jesus who emptied himself has also inspired many Zen Buddhists, who write movingly about this text. They may not accept the incarnation in its fullness, but they accept Jesus, and often they have original insights into the mystery of his death and resurrection. The Japanese bishops' comment that the church should open its heart to other religions *to*

deepen its understanding of the Mystery of Christ is profoundly theological; it accords with the traditional doctrine that "the seeds of the
Word" and the "groaning of the Spirit" can be found in all authentic
religions. It reminds us that we can learn about the mystery of Christ
from Zen Buddhists. Indeed, some committed Christians have already
done so.

We can conclude that the way to harmony among the religions is
humility and poverty of spirit. This was the spirit of the Assisi meeting
that honored Francis, *the poverello* who renounced everything and died
on the bare ground.

Iranian President Mohammed Khatami, meeting John Paul II in Rome
in March 1999, asked for prayers and expressed the hope that "the spirit
of Assisi" would be the model for future relations between religions and
peoples.

The Second Spring

In the mid-nineteenth century John Henry Newman (1801-90) composed a famous sermon known as "The Second Spring." Looking back on history, Newman saw the death of the old English church with its galaxy of saints and scholars, its glorious martyrs—"its religious orders, its monastic establishments, its universities, its wide relations all over Europe, its high prerogatives in the temporal state, its wealth, its dependencies, its popular honors—where was there in Christendom a more glorious hierarchy?" And that flourishing church died and became a corpse. In his elegant, poetic, Ciceronian prose Newman says sorrowfully: "That old Church in its day became a corpse (a marvelous, an awful change!); and then it did but corrupt the air which once it refreshed, and cumber the ground which once it beautified. So all seemed to be lost." But all was not lost. Thrones are overturned and are never restored. States live and die, and then are matter only for history. But the church dies and rises again. Newman makes his point in the classical style that has made him famous: "Babylon was great, and Tyre, and Egypt, and Nineve, and shall never be great again. The English church, was, and was not, and the English church is once again. This is the portent, worthy of a cry. It is the coming in of a Second Spring."

This Second Spring is the child of martyrdom. With characteristic exuberance Newman cries out: "The long imprisonment, the fetid dungeon, the weary suspense, the tyrannous trial, the barbarous sentence, the savage execution, the rack, the gibbet, the knife, the cauldron, the numberless tortures of those holy victims, O my God, are they to have no reward?"

There will be a reward. The martyrs will gain a better life for the children of those who persecuted them. Newman's sermon reaches a climax with resurrection and new life. Enthusiastically he quotes Isaiah: "Arise, Jerusalem, for thy light is come, and the glory of the Lord is risen upon thee. Behold, darkness shall cover the earth and a mist the people; but the Lord shall rise upon thee, and His glory shall be seen upon thee." The coming years would give birth to even greater saints and scholars, and the church would have its martyrs. Truly a Second Spring was at hand.

Nor does Newman speak in abstractions. He pinpoints time and place: the Second Spring of the English church begins with the first synod of the new hierarchy held in Oscott in July 1852. As Newman preached his moving sermon at St. Mary's College, members of the congregation dissolved in tears.

And now, as we enter the third millennium, can we again see the advent of a Second Spring?

Undoubtedly we have witnessed a great death. We have witnessed a death such as the great Newman could never have imagined. Even now we are engulfed in what John Paul II sorrowfully calls "a culture of death." For the twentieth century saw violence, bloodshed, torture, oppression, terrorism and injustice such as the world never saw before; it saw death camps, attempted genocide, degradation of women, destruction of whole cities, slaughter of the unborn and ruthless massacre of the innocent. With this we witnessed, and still witness, the death of a civilization that produced music and art and poetry of unparalleled beauty. And at the heart of this civilization was a Christianity that inspired the culture, giving birth to saints and scholars, a Christianity graced with all the glories that Newman describes so eloquently. Is this Christianity also dying?

The superstructure is collapsing. The cathedrals, the churches, the chanceries, the schools, the universities, the hospitals, the orphanages, the monasteries, the convents, the publishing houses are crumbling. Seminaries and noviceships no longer attract the idealistic young. Clerical domination has come to an end. Will future generations say with Newman: "That old Church in its day became a corpse (a marvelous, an awful change!); and then it did but corrupt the air which once it refreshed, and cumber the ground which once it beautified"? Future generations may well quote Newman, but with Newman they will also speak of new life, of resurrection and of a Second Spring.

The superstructure may collapse, but the human spirit does not collapse. Beneath all the confusion a greater power is at work, and something new is coming to birth. How well and how poetically did John Paul II say of the twentieth century—"The tears of this century have prepared the ground for a new springtime of the human spirit!" Already this springtime appears in the hunger for spiritual experience, the long-ing for meditation, the search for mysticism, the martyrdom for social justice, the solicitude for the underprivileged, the compassion for the suffering. Even if buildings collapse, the spiritual thirst of humanity will never die.

Newman, I have said, situated the Second Spring at a specific time and in a specific place. Can we of the third millennium do likewise?

I believe we can. I would point to October 27, 1986, when religious leaders of the world prayed together at Assisi. This was the beginning of a new era of peace in the world and of love and collaboration among religions. Above all, it was the beginning of a new era of interreligious prayer. As that prayer moves more and more deeply into mysticism and the cloud of unknowing, union among men and women of all religions will grow and they will dedicate themselves to peace and to the salvation of the world.

The Beloved speaks and says to humanity,

> Arise, my love, my dove, my beautiful one,
>   and come away;
> for now the winter is past,
>   the rain is over and gone.
> The flowers appear on the earth;
>   the time of singing has come,
> and the voice of the turtledove
>   is heard in our land. (Sg 2:10-12)

Acknowledgments

Many people helped me in writing this book, and I thank all of them. First I would like to express my gratitude to Amy Lim and Takashi Kitahara, who read each chapter carefully as the book was written. Then I thank Frank Mathy, Dan Collins, and Rich Curé who read the completed manuscript and made valuable suggestions for improvement. Others with whom I discussed the ideas both by conversation and by letter are Caroline Carney, Jill Black and Ikiko Horiguchi. I thank Francis Britto who taught me all I know about computers, and Iván Doszpoly who with great patience corrected and edited my manuscript, preparing it for publication. None of these people is responsible for any errors that may appear in the book.

Notes

INTRODUCTION

1. For an eyewitness account of Assisi, see Pierre-François de Béthune, "After Assisi—Dialogue Is New," *Aide Inter-Monastères* (Oklahoma), Bulletin 28 (February 1987).

2. I have written at some length about the *Heart Sutra* in *Mystical Theology* (Maryknoll, N.Y.: Orbis Books, 1995), chap. 10. There is more about *saccidananda* in the later chapters of this book.

3. See Bede Griffiths, *A New Vision of Reality* (Springfield, Ill.: Templegate Publishers, 1990), 253.

PART I: THE NEW CONSCIOUSNESS

1. NEW ERA

1. Griffiths, *A New Vision of Reality*, 295.

2. John XXIII, "Opening Speech to the Council." On October 11, 1962, the first day of the council, Pope John delivered this address in St. Peter's Basilica. An English translation may be found in *The Documents of Vatican II*, ed. Walter Abbott (New York: America Press, 1966), 710-19.

3. "Humanae Salutis." This apostolic constitution is dated December 25, 1961. By it Pope John convoked the Second Vatican Council for some time in 1962. See Abbott, *The Documents of Vatican II*, 703-9.

4. John XXIII, "Opening Speech to the Council."

5. Ibid.

6. "Prayer of the Council Fathers," in Abbott, *The Documents of Vatican II*, xxii.

7. "Humanae Salutis."

8. John XXIII, "Opening Speech to the Council."

9. *Gaudium et Spes* ("joy and hope"), also known as *The Pastoral Constitution on the Church in the Modern World,* was promulgated on December 7, 1965. The council came to an end on the following day.

10. *Nostra Aetate*, or the *Declaration of the Relationship of the Church to Non-Christian Religions,* was promulgated on October 28, 1965.

11. *Gaudium et Spes*, no. 10.

12. "Humanae Salutis."

2. AGE OF REVOLUTION (I)

1. Bernard Lonergan, *A Second Collection* (London, 1974), 103.

2. Ibid., 101.

3. Bernard Lonergan, *Method in Theology* (New York: Herder and Herder, 1972), 1.4.2.

4. Ibid., 1.4.3.

5. Ibid., 1.4.4

6. See Johnston, *Mystical Theology,* C. 17. Lonergan insists that the scientific method stays in this world and cannot lead to God. My point is that the scientific method *can* lead to God if it is married to love.

7. *Gaudium et Spes,* no. 36. Ken Wilber makes the interesting claim that scientists today are talking religion in an attempt to explain the hard data of science. The very facts of science, the actual data seem to make sense only if we assume some sort of implicit or unifying or transcendental ground underlying the explicit data. He writes of the scientists that "without the assumption of the transcendental, spaceless and timeless ground, the data themselves, the very results of their laboratory experiments, admitted of no cogent explanation" (*The Holographic Paradigm and Other Paradoxes,* ed. Ken Wilber [Boston and London: Shambhala, 1985], 1).

8. Ken Wilber, *The Marriage of Sense and Soul: Integrating Science and Religion* (New York: Random House, 1998), 3.

3. AGE OF REVOLUTION (II)

1. *Gaudium et Spes* no. 5.

2. Ibid., no. 4.

3. Ibid., no. 54.

4. Ibid., no. 9.

5. Ibid., no. 77.

6. Lonergan, *Second Collection,* 113.

7. *Lumen Gentium,* no. 90.

8. I am thinking here of Risshō Kōseikai, founded in 1938 with more than six million members in Japan and many thousands abroad. Whereas traditional Buddhism is monastic, Risshō Kōseikai is a religion of laity and has no clergy. It carries on a vibrant dialogue with Christianity. The late President Nikkyō Niwano was an observer at the Second Vatican Council.

9. Karl Rahner, "Theological Interpretation of Vatican II," in *Theological Investigations* (London and New York, 1981), 20:82ff.

10. Lonergan, *A Second Collection,* 94.

11. Ibid.

12. Melchior Cano (1509-60) was a Spanish Dominican known for his treatise *De Locis Theologicis,* which was the basis of the old dogmatic theology.

13. Lonergan, *A Second Collection,* 231.

14. Bernard Lonergan, *Collection* (New York, 1967), 266.

15. *Gaudium et Spes,* no. 10.

4. THE GREAT SEARCH

1. *Dei Verbum,* no. 8.

2. Ibid.

3. John of the Cross, *The Spiritual Canticle,* 37, 4.

4. Lonergan, *A Second Collection,* 57.

5. Ibid., 57.

6. Heinrich Denzinger (1819-83) was a Belgian Catholic theologian. His most famous work was *Enchiridion Symbolorum et Definitionum*. First published at Würzburg in 1854 it passed through thirty-two editions and was used by all Catholic theologians and seminarians until the Second Vatican Council.

7. Lonergan, *A Second Collection*, 71. Lonergan clearly affirms the objectivity of truth. One of his great achievements is that he answered Immanuel Kant. At the same time, he emphasizes the subjective process by which one comes to truth, saying that objectivity is the fruit of authentic subjectivity. That is to say, one comes to objectivity by being attentive, intelligent and reasonable.

8. Ibid., 71.

9. Ibid., 72.

10. John XXIII, "Opening Speech to the Council."

11. Ibid.

12. *Unitatis Redintegratio*, no. 4.

13. Lonergan, *A Second Collection*, 2.

14. *Gaudium et Spes*, no. 92.

15. In certainties unity
in doubts liberty
in everything
charity.

16. *Dei Verbum*, no. 25

17. "To People of Thought and Science," in "Closing Messages of the Council," in Abbott, *Documents of Vatican II*, 730-31.

18. Ibid.

19. Ibid.

20. *Dignitatis Humanae*, no. 2.

21. Ibid., 3.

22. Pope John devoted a whole section of his "Opening Speech to the Council" to the repression of errors. He said that "the truth of the Lord will remain for ever" and, in words that recall Gamaliel, he said that frequently "errors vanish as quickly as they arise, like fog before the sun." In the past the church condemned errors with great severity. "Nowadays, however, the Spouse of Christ prefers to make use of the medicine of mercy rather than that of severity. She considers that she meets the needs of the present day by demonstrating the validity of her teaching rather than by condemnation."

23. *Gaudium et Spes*, no. 80.

24. Lonergan, *A Second Collection*, 63.

25. Ibid., 67.

26. Ibid.

27. *Gaudium et Spes*, no. 16.

5. THE AWAKENING OF ASIA

1. Simone Weil, *Selected Essays, 1934-43*, ed. and trans. Richard Rees (New York: Oxford University Press, 1962), 205.

2. *The Gospel of Sri Ramakrishna*, trans. and intro. Swami Nikhilananda (New York: Ramakrishna-Vivekananda Center, 1980), 34.

3. Bede Griffiths, *Christ in India* (Springfield, Ill.: Templegate Publishers, 1966), 105.

4. *Gaudium et Spes*, no. 22.

5. John Paul II, *Crossing the Threshold of Hope* (New York: Alfred A. Knopf, 1994), 74.

6. *Nostra Aetate,* no. 3.

7. John Paul II, *Crossing the Threshold of Hope,* 77.

8. Ibid., 82.

9. *Nostra Aetate,* no. 1.

10. Ibid., no. 2.

11. Aldous Huxley, *The Perennial Philosophy* (New York, 1946), 12.

12. *Nostra Aetate,* no. 2.

13. Dalai Lama, *The Good Heart* (Boston: Wisdom Books, 1996), 80.

14. Ibid., 82.

15. "Parliament of World Religions' Global Ethic" (1993).

16. An English translation of this letter can be found in the English *L'Osservatore Romano,* January 2, 1990.

17. John Paul II, *Crossing the Threshold of Hope,* 87.

18. *Nostra Aetate,* no. 2.

19. In *For All the Peoples of Asia: Federation of Asian Bishops' Conferences Documents from 1970 to 1991,* ed. G. Rosales and C. G. Arevalo (Maryknoll, N.Y.: Orbis Books; Philippines: Claretian Publications, 1992), 22-23.

20. Ibid., 110.

21. See "Documentation," *The Tablet,* May 2, 1998.

22. *Unitatis Redintegratio,* no. 9.

23. *Ad Gentes,* no. 11.

24. The distinguished Jesuit professor of canon law, Ladislas Orsy, writes: "In regard to excommunication . . . I have consistently held (and do hold) as follows: (1) Automatic excommunication *(latae sententiae)* should have no place in modern canon law because it is an anachronism: it compels a person to be accused and the judge in his own case and it allows persons and communities to be condemned without the benefit of a hearing. Such a procedure is hardly in harmony with the Scriptures and it offends contemporary sensitivities concerning human rights. (2) In our age in doctrinal matters excommunication is not an effective policy to lead an errant soul back to the 'obedience of faith'" ("Infallibility Explored," in *Céide,* Ballina, Ireland [May/June 1999]; this article is published in German in *Stimmen der Zeit* [May 1999]).

6. ASIAN MEDITATION

1. Bede Griffiths, *The Marriage of East and West* (London: Collins, 1982), 8.

2. Ibid., 9.

3. Ichirō Okumura, *Awakening to Prayer* (Washington, D.C.: ICS Publications, 1994), 78, 87.

4. The founder of the Kyoto School was Nishida Kitarō (1870-1945). His most widely known book is *An Inquiry into the Good* (1911). Other distinguished philosophers were Hisamatsu Shin'ichi (1889-1980) and Nishitani Keiji (1900-1990).

5. For an appraisal of Sanbōkyōdan, see Robert H. Sharf, "Sanbōkyōdan, Zen and the Way of the New Religions," *Japanese Journal of Religious Studies* (Nagoya, Japan) 22, nos. 3-4 (1995), 417-58.

6. I have treated of emptiness in the *Heart Sutra* in relation to the *kenosis* of St. Paul in *Mystical Theology,* chap. 10.

7. Elain MacInnes, "Light Behind Bars," *The Tablet* (London), August 17, 1996.

7. SEARCHING FOR MYSTICISM

1. Griffiths, *The Marriage of East and West,* 11.
2. Ibid., 73.
3. *Gaudium et Spes,* no. 37.
4. Ibid., no. 13.
5. For a more detailed treatment of Jung on Oriental meditation, see William Johnston, *The Mirror Mind,* 2d ed. (New York: Fordham University Press, 1990), 145 ff.
6. I have written more about the New Age in *Letters to Contemplatives* (Maryknoll, N.Y. (USA): Orbis Books; HarperCollins London, 1991), 51 ff.
7. John Cornwell, *Powers of Darkness, Powers of Light* (London: Viking, 1991).
8. Quoted in Martin Repp, "Who's the First to Cast the Stone?" *Japan Mission Journal* (Winter 1995).
9. *Gaudium et Spes,* nos. 13, 37.
10. *Nostra Aetate,* no. 1.

PART II: THE NEW MYSTICISM

8. JOURNEY OF PRAYER

1. Okumura, *Awakening to Prayer* 1ff.
2. *Presbyterorum Ordinis,* no. 18.
3. *The Book of Privy Counselling,* chap. 1.
4. Bernard Lonergan, *Insight* (London, 1958), 699.
5. In earlier books I did not accept the distinction between acquired and infused contemplation. Now, however, I have come to see that it is useful to distinguish between contemplation that is the fruit of human effort aided by ordinary grace and contemplation experienced as undeserved and gratuitous gift.
6. *Katha Upanishad,* 2:23.
7. Traditional mystical theology gives us certain signs by which we may know that the time has come to enter into infused contemplation. I describe these signs in *Silent Music,* 2d ed. (New York: Fordham University Press, 1997), 94ff.
8. St. John of the Cross, *The Ascent of Mount Carmel,* 2.21.7.
9. Ibid., 2.19.1.
10. Ibid., 2.19.5.
11. Ibid.
12. Ibid.
13. Ibid., 2.31.1.
14. Ibid., 2.31.2.
15. Ibid., 2.26.11.
16. Ibid., 2.29.4.
17. Ibid., 2.29.12.
18. Ibid., 2.19.1.
19. Ibid., 2.19.5.
20. Cornwell, *Powers of Darkness, Powers of Light,* 4-5.

9. THE ROAD TO MYSTICISM

1. *Makyō,* literally "the world of the devil," is the hallucinatory phase that those who practice Zen sometimes pass through. The word itself is derived from the Sanskrit *maya,* meaning "illusion."

2. Sogyal Rinpoche, *The Tibetan Book of Living and Dying* (San Francisco: HarperSanFranciso, 1992), 106.

3. I have written about Buddhist transcendental wisdom in *Mystical Theology,* chap. 10. An English translation of the *Heart Sutra* is printed in the appendix of that volume.

4. St. John of the Cross, *The Living Flame of Love,* Prologue 4.

5. *The Cloud of Unknowing,* chap. 22.

6. Ibid., chap. 16.

7. Ibid., chap. 17.

8. *The Book of Privy Counselling,* chap. 13.

9. Aquinas, *In Joann.* 7.32.

10. Aquinas, *Summa Theologica,* 11a-11ae, q. 82, a 3, ad 9.

11. Quoted in William Johnston, *The Mysticism of "The Cloud of Unknowing"* (Trabuco Canyon, Calif.: Source Books, 1985), 72.

12. St. John of the Cross, *The Ascent of Mount Carmel,* 2.11.7.

13. *Gaudium et Spes,* no. 24.

14. Ibid., no. 12.

15. I have written about *kundalini* in *Mystical Theology,* chap. 9.

10. SANNYASIN, BODHISATTVA AND MYSTIC

1. Sten Rodhe, *Jules Monchanin: Pioneer in Christian-Hindu Dialogue* (Delhi: ISPCK, 1993), 34.

2. Ibid., 30.

3. Ibid., 47.

4. Ibid.

5. Ibid., 60.

6. Jacques Dupuis, *Jesus Christ at the Encounter of World Religions* (Maryknoll, N.Y.: Orbis Books, 1991), 73. See also *Ascent to the Depth of the Heart: The Spiritual Diary of Swami Abhishiktananda (Dom Henri Le Saux)* (Delhi: ISPCK, 1948 [reprinted 1973]).

7. Ibid., 74.

8. Abhishiktananda, *The Further Shore* (Delhi: ISPCK, 1984), 105.

9. Jesu Rajan, *Bede Griffiths and Sannyasa* (Bangalore: Asian Trading Corporation, 1988), 111.

10. Ibid., 226.

11. Ibid., 247.

12. Ibid.

13. Ibid., 237.

14. Ibid., 242. Aquinas saw that Aristotle's notion of God as First Cause was different from the notion of God in the Bible and yet not opposed to it. As Aquinas wrote commentaries on Aristotle, so Bede wrote a commentary on the Bhagavad Gita.

15. *Lumen Vitae,* no. 1.

16. Griffiths, *The Marriage of East and West,* 42.

17. Ibid., 43.

18. Jesu Rajan, *Bede Griffiths and Sannyasa,* 228.

19. Ibid. The scholastics said that "God is not bound by the sacraments" *(Deus non alligatur sacramentis).*

20. The bodhisattva (in Japanese, bosatsu) is the person destined for enlightenment—a future Buddha. The bodhisattva seeks enlightenment not only for self but

also for others. Compassion is the bodhisattva's chief virtue. He or she postpones entrance into nirvana in order to save others.

21. *Story of a Soul: The Autobiography of Saint Thérèse of Lisieux*, trans. John Clarke, O.C.D. (Washington, D.C.: ICS Publications, 1996), 14.

22. Alcoholics Anonymous was founded in Akron, Ohio, in 1935. The twelve steps were composed by the founders, Bob S., an Akron surgeon, and Bill W., a New York stockbroker.

23. For more about this subject, see Johnston, *The Mysticism of "The Cloud of Unknowing,"* 299 n.20.

24. St. John of the Cross, *The Dark Night,* 1.14.1.

25. Joseph Cardinal Bernardin, *The Gift of Peace* (Chicago: Loyola Press, 1997), 22.

26. Ibid., 89.

27. Ibid.

28. Ibid., 152.

11. "THAT ULTIMATE AND UNUTTERABLE MYSTERY"

1. *Nostra Aetate,* no. 1.

2. Ibid., no. 2.

3. *Gaudium et Spes,* no. 44.

4. *Nostra Aetate,* no. 2.

5. See Bede Griffiths, *The Cosmic Revelation* (Springfield, Ill.: Templegate Publishers, 1983), 72.

6. Griffiths, *A New Vision of Reality,* 253.

7. That philosophers like Nagarjuna are not pantheistic is stressed by Bede Griffiths. Telling us that Professor Zaehner refers to the teaching of the Upanishads as a "pantheistic monism," Bede Griffiths goes on: "I think that this is a complete misconception. I hope to make it clear that Hindu teaching is infinitely deeper. . . . These are Greek words, and they do not apply to the Hindu understanding of God" (*The Cosmic Revelation,* 50).

8. Yves Raguin, *Alpha Omega* (Paris: Vie Chretienne, 1986).

9. Rodger Kamenetz, *The Jew in the Lotus* (San Francisco: HarperSanFrancisco, 1994), 85.

10. Ibid., 86.

11. Ibid.

12. Ibid., 157.

13. Aquinas, *Summa Theologica,* 1 q.13, a.11.

14. Martin Heidegger, *Identity and Difference,* trans. Joan Stambaugh (New York: Harper & Row, 1969), 72.

15. Jean-Luc Marion, *God without Being,* trans. Thomas A. Carlson (Chicago: University of Chicago Press, 1991).

16. Walter Kasper, *The God of Jesus Christ,* trans. M. J. O'Connell (New York: Crossroad, 1984), 156.

17. John P. Keenan, *The Meaning of Christ: A Mahayana Theology* (Maryknoll, N.Y.: Orbis Books, 1989).

18. Quoted in Johnston, *The Mysticism of "The Cloud of Unknowing,"* 47.

19. The problem in the West was not metaphysics but *metaphysics divorced from mysticism.* Ken Wilber makes this point: "Since Kant we have been forced to acknowledge, not that metaphysics is meaningless but that metaphysics without direct experience is meaningless" (*The Eye of Spirit* [Boston: Shambhala, 1997], 270).

12. INCARNATION

1. The emperor of Japan is called *tennō*, literally "heavenly sovereign." According to ancient mythology the emperor is descended from the Sun Goddess, Amaterasu Ōmikami.

2. Bhagavad Gita, 4. 7-8.

3. The doctrine of the Eternal Buddha is elaborated in the *Lotus Sutra*. In esoteric Buddhism (the Shingon sect in Japan) the central place is occupied not by the historical Buddha but by the cosmic Buddha.

4. Aquinas, *Summa Theologica,* p.3, q.1, c.

5. Bede Griffiths, "The New Consciousness," *The Tablet* (London), January 16, 1993.

6. Ibid.

7. *John Ruusbroec: The Spiritual Espousals and Other Works,* trans. James A. Wiseman (Mahwah, N.J.: Paulist Press, 1985), 41.

8. St. John of the Cross, *Spiritual Canticle,* 22.3.

9. *Ad Gentes,* no. 3.

10. Vladimir Lossky, *The Mystical Theology of the Eastern Church* (New York: St. Vladimir's Seminary Press, 1976), 134. "Felix Culpa" (happy fault) is found in the Easter Week liturgy of both the Orthodox and the Catholic churches. The sin of Adam is called a happy fault because it merited such a savior. Lossky further claims that the doctrine that "God became man in order that man might become God" is found in St. Irenaeus, St. Athanasius, St. Gregory Nazianzen and St. Gregory of Nyssa.

11. *Gaudium et Spes,* no. 22.

12. Quoted in *Lumen Gentium,* no. 26.

13. *The Confessions of St. Augustine,* 7.10.

14. *Gaudium et Spes,* no. 38.

15. Lossky, *The Mystical Theology of the Eastern Church,* 155.

16. Leonid Ouspensky, *Theology of the Icon,* vol. 1, trans. Anthony Gythiel (New York: St. Vladimir's Seminary Press, 1992), 8.

17. Ibid., 36.

18. Ibid., 161.

19. Ibid., 46.

20. Ibid., 60.

21. *The Confessions of St. Augustine,* 9.10.

13. THE SEARCH FOR JESUS

1. The Jesus Seminar was founded in 1985 by R. Funk and J. D. Crossan. It consists of some fifty to seventy-five scholars who meet regularly, write papers and vote on decisions about what the historical Jesus did and said.

2. Heinz Pagels, *Perfect Symmetry: The Search for the Beginning of Time* (New York: Bantam, 1985), 362.

3. For Lonergan, authenticity consists in fidelity to the transcendental precepts: be attentive, be intelligent, be reasonable, be responsible and love. See especially his essay "The Subject," in *A Second Collection.*

4. Feminist theological method also emphasizes the subject. This is the thesis of Mary Aquin O'Neill. See "The Nature of Women and the Method of Theology," *Theological Studies* (December 1995).

5. Lonergan, *A Second Collection*, 57.

6. Ibid., 185. Lonergan puts great emphasis on belief in tradition: "Human knowledge results from a vast collaboration of many peoples over uncounted millennia. The necessary condition of that collaboration is belief. What any of us knows . . . for the most part results from believing" (ibid.).

7. *America*, September 9, 1995. For Raymond Brown's assessment of the Jesus Seminar, see *An Introduction to the New Testament* (New York: Doubleday, 1996), 82-23.

8. John Meier, *A Marginal Jew: Rethinking the Historical Jesus* (New York: Doubleday, 1991), 6.

9. Kenneth L. Woodward, "Rethinking the Resurrection," *Newsweek*, April 8, 1996.

10. Rinpoche, *The Tibetan Book of Living and Dying*, 260.

11. *Dei Verbum*, no. 12.

12. Ibid., nos. 9 and 10.

13. Ibid., no. 7.

14. Ibid., no. 19.

15. Ibid., no. 25. The council here quotes St. Ambrose, *On the Duties of Ministers*.

16. *Hara* in Japanese means "belly." It is the locus of cosmic religious experience.

17. *Sacrosanctum Concilium*, no. 10

18. *Dei Verbum*, no. 8.

19. Meier, *A Marginal Jew*, 57.

14. JESUS THE MYSTIC (I)

1. Dalai Lama, *The Good Heart* (Boston: Wisdom Publications, 1996), 83.

2. Pieris writes that the true local churches of Asia are those prophetic basic human communities (made up of Christians and others) that "have been baptized in the Jordan of Asian religion and the Calvary of Asian poverty" (*Asia's Struggle for Full Humanity* [Maryknoll, N.Y.: Orbis Books, 1983], 50).

3. Peter Phan, "Jesus the Christ with an Asian Face," *Theological Studies* 57, no. 3 (September 1996).

4. Chung Hyun Kyung, *Struggle to Be the Sun Again: Introducing Asian Women's Theology* (Maryknoll, N.Y.: Orbis Books, 1990), 53.

5. Reported in *The Tablet* (London), May 9, 1998.

6. See J. Jeremias, *The Prayers of Jesus* (Philadelphia: Fortress Press, 1978); idem, *The Central Message of the New Testament* (London: SCM Press, 1965).

7. For Aquinas on prophecy, see *Summa Theologica*, 111a.

8. James Mackey speaks of the "extraordinarily radical" faith of Jesus. He claims that this faith had its roots in the ordinary experience of life and did not give special knowledge. He writes: "The man Jesus—apart from his tradition, of course, which had already tried to verbalize this faith—had no more 'information' about God than could be gleaned from the birds of the air, the farmers in their fields, kings in their castles, and merchants in the market-place" (*Jesus the Man and the Myth* [London: SCM Press, 1979], 171).

9. St. John of the Cross, *The Dark Night*, stanza 5.

10. François Dreyfus, *Did Jesus Know He Was God?* (Chicago: Franciscan Herald Press, 1989), 98.

11. Ibid., 124.

15. JESUS THE MYSTIC (II)

1. Abhishiktananda, *Saccidananda*, 82.
2. Abhishiktananda, *Hindu-Christian Meeting Point* (Delhi: ISPCK, 1983), 77.
3. In Bede Griffiths, *Universal Wisdom* (London: HarperCollins, 1994), 39.
4. Raymond E. Brown, *Jesus, God and Man* (Milwaukee: Bruce Publishing Co., 1968), 92.
5. Dalai Lama, *The Good Heart*, 118.
6. M. Hengel, *The Son of God* (Philadelphia: Fortress Press, 1976), 1-20.
7. R. Bultmann, *Theology of the New Testament*, 4th ed. (New York: Scribners, 1965), 1:131.

PART III: THE GREAT CONVERSION

16. "ONE LORD, ONE FAITH"

1. *Unitatis Redintegratio*, no. 14.
2. *Orientalium Eccclesiarum*, no. 7.
3. Alexander Schmemann, "A Response" (to *Orientalium Ecclesiarum*), in Abbott, *The Documents of Vatican II*, 387-88.
4. Francis Hadisumarta, *The Tablet* (London), May 2, 1998, 565.
5. Cardinal Franz König, "My Vision for the Church of the Future," part of a commemorative volume for the 150th anniversary of the Austrian Catholic Bishops' Conference (March 1999). An English translation can be found in *The Tablet* (London), March 27, 1999.
6. *Unitatis Redintegratio*, no. 14.
7. *Lumen Gentium*, no. 18.
8. Ibid., no. 22.
9. Hans Urs von Balthasar, quoted in Luigi Accattoli, *When a Pope Asks Forgiveness* (New York: Alba House, 1998), 229.
10. John Paul II, "For the Defence of the Faith," *Ad Tuendam Fidem* (July 1998).
11. Ladislas Orsy, "Intelligent Fidelity: The Apostolic Letter *Ad Tuendam Fidem* and Its Roman Commentary Revisited," *Céide* (Ballina, Ireland) (November/December 1998); published simultaneously in German in *Stimmen der Zeit* (Munich).
12. Lonergan, *Method in Theology*, 270.
13. Lonergan, *A Second Collection*, 79.
14. "Presupposition," *The Spiritual Exercises of St. Ignatius*, 22.
15. Archbishop Henry D'Souza makes this point without using the terminology *intellectual conversion*. He is alarmed that "any thought which is not stated in the same words as in the past becomes suspect" (*The Tablet*, November 21, 1998, 1550).
16. *The Tablet* (London), November 21, 1998, 1531.
17. Lonergan, *Method in theology*, 242.
18. Hans Urs von Balthasar, quoted in Accattoli, *When a Pope Asks Forgiveness*, 4.
19. Ibid., 229.
20. *Ut Unum Sint*, no. 34. Throughout this encyclical Pope John Paul follows the Second Vatican Council, which spoke of *continual reformation* within the Church: "Christ summons the Church, as she goes on her pilgrim way, to that continual reformation of which she is always in need" (*Unitatis Redintegratio*, no. 6).
21. *Ut Unum Sint*, no. 4.

22. *Lumen Gentium,* no. 22.

23. *Ut Unum Sint,* no. 95.

24. Ibid., no. 96.

25. Patriarch Bartholomew, quoted by Jonathan Luxmore, "The Wound That Will Not Heal," *The Tablet,* December 6, 1997. However, when John Paul visited Romania in April 1999, Patriarch Teoctist greeted him warmly and explained to reporters that John Paul had made a great step forward by agreeing to rethink the primacy of Peter and that he is the first pope to have done so. Teoctist said: "The goal of dialogue is clear—we want to go back to the first millennium, when the pope was the first among equals" (*The Tablet,* May 15, 1999).

26. When I say that a person is a prophet, I do not mean that everything this person says is correct. I simply mean that he or she has a message.

27. Bernard Häring, "Church Needs Renewed Petrine Ministry," *National Catholic Reporter* (Kansas City, Missouri), October 17, 1997.

28. The Orthodox churches permit the innocent party to remarry; in pastoral practice, both parties may be considered innocent.

29. Häring, "Church Needs Renewed Petrine Ministry."

30. Reinhold Stecher, "Challenge to the Church," *The Tablet,* December 20, 1997.

31. Some people will think that the bishop exaggerates. However, he writes: "In my own experience, requests for laicization forwarded with the bishop's urgent endorsement, for pastoral and human reasons, lie unread for ten years and even more."

32. Stecher, "Challenge to the Church."

33. Ibid.

34. Peter James Cullinane (bishop of Palmerston North), "A Time to Speak Out," *The Tablet,* November 28, 1998, 1589.

35. Toshio Oshikawa, *Japan Catholic News,* May 1998, no. 1029.

36. *The Tablet,* May 2, 1998, 566.

37. Ibid., 571.

38. Geoffrey King, S.J., "The Catholic Church in China: A Canonical Evaluation," *Tripod* (Hong Kong) (May-June 1992), 24.

17. TOWARD HARMONY

1. See *L'Osservatore Romano* (English ed.), N. 37-16, weekly ed., September 7, 1998. Here John Paul II summarizes his teaching on Christianity's relationship with other religions.

2. Ibid.

3. Ibid.

4. *Ut Unum Sint,* no. 28.

5. *Fides et Ratio,* no. 72.

6. Ibid.

7. Ibid.

8. Ibid.

9. Ibid.

10. Jun Ikenaga, *Japan Catholic News* (Tokyo) (May 1998), no. 1029.

11. Ibid.

12. Ibid.

13. Kanzō Uchimura, quoted in Raymond P. Jennings, *Jesus, Japan, and Uchimura* (Tokyo: Kyō Bunkwan, 1958), 1.

14. Ibid., 49.

15. From the early Christian centuries the faithful chanted this "epiclesis" after the consecration in the eucharist.

16. John Paul II, *L'Osservatore Romano,* September 16, 1998.

17. Ibid.

18. Kanzō Uchimura, quoted in Jennings, *Jesus, Japan, and Uchimura,* 58.

19. "Responses to the *Lineamenta,*" *East Asian Pastoral Review* (Manila) 35, no. 1 (1998).

20. Ibid.

21. See *For All the Peoples of Asia: Federation of Asian Bishops' Conferences Documents from 1992 to 1996,* vol. 2, ed. Franz-Josef Eilers (Philippines, 1997).

22. "Responses to the *Lineamenta.*"

23. In speaking of Jesus as the one Savior we must not forget that believers, who are members of his mystical body, have their role in the work of salvation, in accordance with the words of St. Paul: "And in my flesh I am completing what is lacking in Christ's afflictions for the sake of his body, that is, the church" (Col 1:24).

Index